Kid's
Bible Story
Book

Kid's Bible Story Book

JESSE LYMAN HURLBUT

Edited by

TONI SORTOR

Illustrations by

MARVIN JARBO

A BARBOUR BOOK

Copright © 1994 by Barbour and Company, Inc.

ISBN 1-55748-550-X

Published by   Barbour and Company, Inc.
                  P.O. Box 719
                  Uhrichsville, Ohio 44683

Printed in the United States of America

CONTENTS

INTRODUCTION

page vii

PART 1

In the Beginning:
From a Beautiful Garden to a Promised Land

page 9

PART 2

God Is on Our Side!
The Fight for the Promised Land

page 83

PART 3

The Triple Threat of Israel:
Saul, David, and Solomon

page 125

PART 4

Elijah, Elisha, and Others:
Adventures in the Kingdom of Israel

page 163

PART 5

Tales of Crowns and Courage:
Adventures in the Kingdom of Judah

page 201

PART 6

A World Is Saved!
God Sends His Son to Earth

page 243

PART 7

Go, and Teach All Nations!
The Beginning of the Church

page 323

INTRODUCTION

To every family was once bestowed a storyteller, or so it seemed. Whether from memory or with story book in hand, this near or distant relative with voice and gestures could create settings in thin air and pull up a chair for real or imagined heroes and heroines.

Jesse Lyman Hurlbut was such a storyteller. The Bible stories you are about to read are based on his original stories once told to his own children. The power of the storyteller should not be underestimated. Since its initial publication in 1904, *Hurlbut's Story of the Bible* has been read in millions of homes and translated into several languages.

Kid's Bible Story Book, while a simplified version of the original text, remains faithful to Dr. Hurlbut's premise: If a child learns the story of the Bible early in life, he or she will never forget it. No Bible story has been omitted from the original edition; the stories form a continuous history of Bible times from the creation of the world and Adam and Eve to John's apocalyptic visions on the island of Patmos.

A first reading of the stories may be merely entertaining, much like the storyteller's yarns, a television program, or video or computer games. *But a second reading is all important.* According to Dr. Hurlbut, it is then that the divine message may touch the child's heart and conscience, and encourage a pattern of Bible reading that will last through adulthood.

This new edition has been especially written for children ages eight through twelve years old. No Bible story has been changed from the sacred text, and doctrinal issues while simplified should be acceptable to Christians of all denominations. Every effort has been made to define technical terms where they occur.

New part and chapter titles have been added to create a more modern sense of adventure. New also to this edition is the "Think About It" section that follows every chapter. The questions posed here may cover the facts of the story, challenge the child to examine his or her own heart or life, or seek to define the character of God and God's role in the child's life. Many of these questions might be best addressed during family devotions or while sharing a meal.

The dedication to the 1904 edition bears repeating here:

To the Young People of the World

This Book is Dedicated, in the hope
that it may interest them
in the reading of

The Best of All Books.

Indeed the best of all books, the Bible, is for kids of all ages.

THE PUBLISHER

PART 1

In the Beginning:

FROM A GARDEN TO A PROMISED LAND

The Most Beautiful Garden

✤ GENESIS 1:1-3:24 ✤

Once there was no earth at all. No sun, no moon, no stars, just darkness. But God was here. God has always been and will always be with us. There never was a time when God did not exist. One day God spoke, and His words made the earth. Day by day the earth began to take shape. God made light and dry land. He made all the plants and animals. When He was done, the earth was beautiful. It had hills and oceans and birds and bears. But there were no people to enjoy the earth.

So God picked up some dirt from the ground. He formed it into a shape, the way we do with clay. When He was done, He had made the figure of a man. God breathed on the figure and the man came to life. Then God gave this first man a name, Adam. Because God loved Adam very much, God put him in the most beautiful garden in the world, the Garden of Eden.

But God knew that Adam would be lonely by himself. He needed another person to talk to and love. So one night while Adam was asleep, God took a rib from his side and from that rib He created Eve, the first woman.

After having made the solar system and the earth in only six days, and all that is on the earth, God rested on the seventh day.

Adam and Eve were very happy in the garden. They had all the food they needed; they simply had to take care of the garden. God would often come and visit them there, much like a good friend.

But God was more than a friend. He was God, and Adam and Eve needed to obey Him too. One day God told Adam and Eve there was one tree they could not touch. Just one. All other trees were theirs to enjoy. God told Adam and Eve they would die if they ate the fruit from that one tree.

Among the animals in the garden there was a snake, and this snake had overheard God's warning to Adam and Eve. When Eve was alone, the snake slithered up to her and hissed, "You won't die. That fruit will make you as smart as God."

As smart as God? Eve knew God was *very* smart. Who wouldn't want to be that smart? So Eve picked one fruit from the tree and ate it. When she didn't die she gave Adam some of the fruit to eat too.

The next time God came to visit, Adam and Eve tried to hide from Him. They knew they had done something wrong. But no one can hide from God. God found them and said, "Did you eat the fruit I told you to leave alone?"

Adam looked at the ground. Then he nodded to Eve. "She gave it to me," he said.

"Well," Eve said, "the snake said I could!"

Because they had disobeyed God, Adam and Eve were sent out of the Garden of Eden. God put angels with flashing swords in front of the garden's gate to keep them out.

Life changed for Adam and Eve. Now they had to dig in the dirt and plant their own food. They had to work hard to keep alive. Pain and suffering came into their lives for the first time. And, as God had said, in time they both died.

THINK ABOUT IT

✛ *How did Adam and Eve try to keep God from punishing them? (Find two ways.)*

We speak of "The Fall of Man" as the time when Adam and Eve ate the forbidden fruit. List ten events or developments that have happened in the world that could be a result of The Fall of Man. ✛

STORY 2

The First Brothers

✛ GENESIS 4:1-18 ✛

After Adam and Eve were sent out of the Garden of Eden, they had a baby. Cain was the first baby ever born to a woman. After a while, Cain had a baby brother named Abel.

When the boys grew up, they had to work too. Cain was a farmer. He raised grain and fruit in the fields. Abel raised animals and took care of a flock of sheep.

Adam and Eve could no longer walk and talk with God but they could pray to Him. They built an altar of stones and put a gift, most likely an animal sacrifice, for God on this altar. Then they burned the gift to show it was not their own but was for God only. After that Adam and Eve asked God to forgive them for all they had done wrong.

Cain and Abel prayed the same way. Cain burned some of his best grain and fruit on the altar. Abel gave one of his best sheep to God. We don't know why, but God was happier with Abel's offering than He was with Cain's. Maybe Abel was a better person than Cain. Only God would know that.

This made Cain so angry and jealous of Abel that he killed his own brother! God said to him, "What have you done? I can see your brother's blood on the ground. Because of this, you will never have a home of your own."

Cain cried, "Don't do this to me! If I am all alone, someone will kill me."

So God put a mark of some kind on Cain. When people saw the mark, they knew he was under God's protection. Cain and his wife moved away from Adam and Eve. In time they had children of their own, and a city grew up where they were living.

————————

THINK ABOUT IT

✢ *Have you ever felt jealous of your brother or sister or a friend? How does it make you feel inside? How do you act when you feel this way?*

What might Cain have done instead of his terrible act? List three steps in order of their importance. ✢

————————

The Amazing Ark

✤ GENESIS 5:1-9:17 ✤

In Bible times people lived to be very old. Some lived for 800 or 900 years! They had many children and grandchildren and great-grandchildren. In those days people didn't travel far; they stayed near where they were born. Before long the land was full of people.

Most of these people had forgotten about God. They didn't pray to Him or listen to Him anymore. They lived sinful lives. God looked at all the people and only found one good man. His name was Noah. God said to Noah, "Everyone on earth must die. They are all evil. But you are trying to be good. I will save you and your family."

God told Noah to build a huge ship, or an ark. "I am going to flood the entire world," God said. God told Noah to make the ark big enough to hold two of every animal on earth. Then Noah was to put enough food on board the ark to feed every animal and every person for a year.

Noah and his sons worked 120 years to build this boat! Noah's neighbors and people he didn't know must have laughed and laughed. Who would build a boat in the middle of a desert?

When the ark was completed according to God's directions, God told Noah the time to board had come. He was to take his wife and three sons and their wives, and all the animals, birds, and amphibians. The rain was coming soon. When all were on the ark the door was shut tight. No one else could enter the ark.

In a few days the rain began to fall. Every stream was filled to overflowing; the rain even filled the dry desert. The water crept up the sides of the mountains where the

evil people had run. By the end of forty days, the tallest mountain was covered with water. Nothing was left alive on the earth except the people and animals bobbing around in Noah's ark.

The rain finally stopped. But because there was nowhere for the water to run off, the land stayed flooded for the next six months. Then God sent a wind to dry up the water a little at a time. Slowly the mountaintops peeked above the water, and the great boat landed on top of a mountain, Mount Ararat. (Find an atlas or globe and see if you can locate Mount Ararat. *Hint*: Find the country of Turkey.)

Finally God told Noah to open the door of the ark and let the animals go. The first thing Noah did on dry land was to thank God for saving him and his family. God was glad to see this. He promised Noah that He would never send another flood to destroy the world, no matter how bad the people were. As a sign of this promise, God put a rainbow in the sky. Whenever we see a rainbow, we remember God's promise to Noah.

THINK ABOUT IT

✛ *For over a hundred years Noah followed God's plans*

15

exactly when building the ark. Why do you think Noah never questioned God? What does it mean to have faith in God? ✝

The Tower of Babel

✝ GENESIS 10:1-11:9 ✝

After the flood Noah's family grew bigger and bigger. They moved south from Mount Ararat to a land between two great rivers, the Tigris and Euphrates. The soil in that land could easily be made into bricks. With bricks the people could build houses and walls to protect themselves.

The people of this region decided to build a great brick tower that would reach into the sky. They thought the tower would keep them all together and help them rule the world. Layer by layer, the people began to build a tower of bricks.

But God did not want everyone to live in one place or be ruled by one city. He wanted the whole earth to be used. God knew that if the people stayed together they would soon turn away from Him and the world would become as evil as it was before the flood.

God began changing the way the people in the area spoke. Over the hundreds of years needed to build the tower, the people began to speak different languages. After a time the people working on the tower couldn't understand each other. They began to move away and live with those who spoke their own language. The brick tower was never finished.

The city where this happened was named Babel. Afterward Babel became known as Babylon and for a time was one of the greatest cities in the world. The tower was not finished in Babylon either.

Some of the people who left Babylon went north and built a city called Nineveh. Others went west and settled in what is now Egypt. Still others moved northwest to the Mediterranean Sea and there they started the cities of Sidon and Tyre. Soon the earth was filled with people living in many lands and speaking many languages.

THINK ABOUT IT

✛ *Have you ever been around many people speaking a different language? How did you feel? Can you speak more than one language?*

What does this story tell you about God? ✛

STORY 5

Abram's Long Journey

✛ GENESIS 11:27-13:18 ✛

Close to the city of Babylon was another city called Ur. The people of Ur prayed to little stone or wooden statues called *idols*, and not to the one true God. They did not behave the way God

17

...nts people to behave.

But as in the days of Noah, there was one good man living in Ur. His name was Abram. God told Abram to pack up his family and move to a faraway land. Further, God promised Abram that in the new land Abram's family would become a great people. God would bless him, and so would all the families of the world!

Abram had no idea where God would take him or what God's blessing meant, but he did what God said. He took all his tents, his flocks of sheep and cattle, and everything he owned. His elderly father went with him. So did his wife, his brother, and his nephew whose name was Lot.

They traveled far up the Euphrates River and into the mountains. They stayed in a town called Haran for a while. When it was time for them to move on, Abram's brother, Nahor, decided to stay in Haran. The rest of the family traveled on to the land of Canaan (now called Israel). There were cities and towns there, but Abram and his family were shepherds. They lived outside the cities in their tents.

Shepherds have to travel with their flocks looking for food for the animals. Abram and Lot moved around, even going as far as Egypt one time. But they always came back

to Canaan when they could.

After a time both Abram and Lot had large flocks of animals to feed. The hilly land they were living on did not have enough grass to feed them all. Abram told Lot they had to split up so everyone would have enough food. He let Lot choose his land first.

Lot looked down from the mountain they were standing on. He saw the rich land in the valley below and decided to go down there. Abram would stay up in the mountains.

After Lot moved into the valley, God said to Abram, "Look around you. Everything you can see belongs to you and your children. Go anywhere you want to. It is all yours."

Abram moved south near the city of Hebron and put up his tent under an oak tree. Wherever Abram had camped he had built an altar and worshiped God. This time was no different.

THINK ABOUT IT

✛ *Why did God want Abram to move away from his first home? Why did Abram and Lot split up?*

God's blessing to Abram would soon happen. Abram's family grew after many years to be known as the Israelites and today live in the country of Israel, as well as other countries. Based on the story of Abram's journey, why do you think many wars have occurred in Israel in recent years and throughout history? ✛

God's Promise to Abram

✝ GENESIS 14:1-15:21 ✝

After leaving Abram Lot moved eventually to the city of Sodom down on the plain. There were five cities down there, each ruled by its own king. Another king ruled over them. Soon the five kings refused to obey the main king. He went to war with them and beat the kings of Sodom and Gomorrah.

In those days the winner of a war won everything the loser owned: money, flocks of sheep, and even people. The people were taken away by the winning king who made them his slaves.

Lot and his family were captured and taken away from Sodom by the winning king. As soon as Abram heard about this, he took his people and chased the army that had captured Lot. In a great battle Abram defeated the main king and freed Lot and his family. Now everything belonged to Abram!

A certain king from Jerusalem came to see Abram. Unlike most other kings in the land, King Melchizedek worshiped God. Because Abram loved God too he gave King Melchizedek all the riches he had captured. Abram refused to take anything for himself. All he wanted was for Lot to be free. Once that was done, Abram went back to his home. Lot, however, went back to the wicked city of Sodom.

Back home God visited Abram. Because Abram had been faithful, God promised him great riches. This made Abram sad, not happy. Abram and his wife Sarai were getting very old and they had never had a baby. "Who will I leave all my riches to when I die?" Abram asked the Lord.

God answered, "All you own will go to your son." Then God took Abram outside and showed him the sky filled with stars. "You will have more people related to you than those stars in the sky," He promised.

Abram didn't see how this was possible, but he believed what God said. Somehow he would have children of his own. Somehow he would live a happy and safe life. Abram left it all up to God.

THINK ABOUT IT

✝ *We call such a promise as God made with Abram a covenant.*

Can you remember someone else with whom God made a covenant?

What does this story tell you about Abram's personality or character? ✝

STORY 7

The Angel by the Well

✝ GENESIS 16:1-17:27 ✝

bram's wife, you remember, was named Sarai. Living in a shepherd's tent was hard for an old woman, so she had a servant named Hagar to help her. Hagar was a woman from Egypt.

Sarai and Hagar did not agree on many things and Sarai was often mean to Hagar. One day Hagar ran away. She hoped to reach her old home in Egypt. On the way she stopped by a spring for a drink. Suddenly, an angel of God appeared and asked what she was doing.

Hagar told the angel how mean Sarai had been to her and how she had nothing of her own. The angel said, "Go back to Sarai and be a good servant. Soon you will have a son of your own and you will call him Ishmael."

The name Ishmael means "God hears."

Then the angel told Hagar that Ishmael would be a mighty warrior. No one would ever be able to defeat him or any of his children. With the angel's promise, Hagar went back to Sarai.

One day after that, the Lord appeared to Abram again. "Abram," He said, "I am giving you a new name. From now on, you will be called Abraham."

The name Abraham means "Father of many people."

"And your wife is to be called Sarah."

The name Sarah means "princess."

"You and Sarah will have a son whom you will call Isaac. And when he grows up, he will have children. A great nation will come from Isaac."

From then on Abram was called Abraham and Sarai was called Sarah.

THINK ABOUT IT

✛*Names are important in the Bible. They often show what a child will become later in life. Do you know what your name means? If your parents don't know, see if you can find out at the library.* ✛

STORY 8

The Rain of Fire

✛ GENESIS 18:1-19:30 ✛

O ne day Abraham was sitting by his tent. Suddenly he saw three men coming toward him. Somehow he knew that two of the men were angels and the third was God Himself, in the form of a man. Bowing before them, Abraham offered them food and rest at his tent.

Again God told Abraham that he and his wife Sarah were going to have a son named Isaac and the whole world would be blessed through him. The name Isaac in the Hebrew language means "laughing," and that describes exactly Abraham and Sarah when they heard the happy news.

As the two men who were angels began walking down

the road that led to the city of Sodom, the Lord told Abraham their mission. They wanted to see if Sodom and the other cities there were as bad as they seemed.

Remember Abraham's nephew Lot? Lot and his family lived in Sodom! God's news frightened Abraham. Abraham was afraid God would destroy the city of Sodom. He begged the Lord not to destroy the city if He could find just ten good men there.

The Lord agreed. He sent his angels to see if there were ten good people in Sodom. But the only good person in the entire city of Sodom was Lot.

The angels warned Lot. They told him to take his family into the mountains so they would not be killed when the city was destroyed. Lot said he was too old to climb the mountains. Could he live in the little town called Zoar? Yes, they would save Zoar for Lot's sake. But Lot had to hurry up and get out of Sodom!

Lot and his wife and two of their daughters were ready. Some of his other daughters were married and they would not leave their husbands behind. Lot talked and talked to them. Finally the angels had to drag Lot away, leaving these women behind.

On the way out of the wicked city, the angels warned Lot not to look back at Sodom. Lot and his two daughters obeyed. But Lot's wife did not listen. As she looked back, she was turned into a pillar of salt!

What did Lot's wife see? She saw a fire falling like rain from the sky. Great clouds of yellow smoke covered the plain. And all the cities of the plain were destroyed, except for little Zoar, where Lot had asked to live.

Think About It

✛ *Sodom must have been a very bad place, filled with crime and violence. Still, Lot remained a good man and continued to live there. But he was the only one. Imagine you are Lot. Could you convince your entire family to leave Sodom*

STORY 9

Isaac and Ishmael

✦ GENESIS 21:1-21 ✦

A fter Sodom and the other wicked cities were burned to the ground, Abraham moved away. He went to Gerar, to the south and west.

When Abraham was 100 years old, he and Sarah had Isaac, the son God promised them. But before Isaac was born, Hagar the servant had Ishmael, the son promised to her by the angel. So now there were two boys in Abraham's tent.

As the boys grew, they began to fight, like boys do. But

Ishmael was older and stronger. Sarah did not want him around anymore because he was hurting her son. She told Abraham to send Hagar and Ishmael away.

Abraham loved both boys. He worried about what would happen to Ishmael. But the Lord told Abraham He would take care of Ishmael. In fact, God promised that Ishmael would someday be the father of a great tribe of people.

Abraham sent Hagar and Ishmael away with food and water for the trip. But Hagar got lost in the desert. They ran out of water, and Ishmael nearly died.

Then an angel came to Hagar and told her not to worry. When he was gone, Hagar found a spring of water nearby and saved her son.

Instead of going home to Egypt, Hagar stayed by the spring and raised Ishmael in the desert. God took care of them. Ishmael grew and learned to use a bow and arrow to hunt and fight. He and his children lived in the desert forever and became the people we call Arabs.

Isaac and his people became the Israelites, or the Jews.

THINK ABOUT IT

✛ *God promised to take care of both Ishmael and Isaac. Today we can read in the newspaper about Arabs and Israelis. Are they friendly toward each other or are they still fighting?* ✛

A Father's Test

✛ Genesis 22:1-23:20 ✛

In those days people worshiped God in a different way. First they built an altar of stone and dirt. Then they took an animal and placed it on the altar and offered it as a gift to God. To show the animal was really God's, the animal was killed and then burned on the altar.

Animals were all the money that people had then. When a person sacrificed one, he was giving away something very valuable.

One day God gave Abraham the most difficult order: "Take your only son Isaac and offer him to me," God told Abraham.

Sometimes people in the area did make human offerings, but these people did not worship God. God never wanted another human being to be killed for Him and He wished to show Abraham that. God also wanted to be sure that Abraham would trust Him. In a way, God was testing Abraham.

Abraham's heart must have broken. Still, God had given Isaac to him. But God had promised that Isaac would be the father of a whole tribe! How could that happen if Abraham sacrificed Isaac?

Abraham thought that maybe God would raise Isaac from the dead. In any case, Abraham would obey God.

He took Isaac to the top of a mountain God showed him. He built an altar there. He put wood on the altar for the fire.

Isaac looked around. "Where's the lamb for the offering, Father?" he asked.

"God will provide it, son," Abraham said sadly.

Just as Abraham was about to kill his only son, an angel of the Lord called out. "Don't hurt your son, Abraham! Now I know you love God more than your only son."

Abraham looked around in relief. There, caught in a bramble bush, was a sheep. Abraham sacrificed the sheep to God instead of his son.

From this story we are told that because Isaac had been offered to God, he and his tribe (the Israelites) belong to God even today. Since God was not pleased by human offerings, the Israelites would only offer such animals as oxen, sheep, and goats to God.

THINK ABOUT IT

✝ *Do you ever have to do things you don't understand? Do you think Abraham would have killed Isaac if God had not stopped him?* ✝

STORY 11

A Journey for a Wife

✝ GENESIS 24:1-25:18 ✝

braham's wife, Sarah, died when she was 120 years old. Abraham bought a cave near Hebron and buried her there.

By now their son Isaac was old enough to be married. In those days parents chose husbands and wives for their children. Abraham did not want Isaac to marry a

girl from Canaan because none of them worshiped the Lord. Abraham wanted his grandchildren to be brought up by two parents who loved God.

Nahor, Abraham's brother, had stayed in Haran when the family stopped there on their way to Canaan. Abraham hoped he could find a wife for Isaac from Nahor's family but he was too old to travel that far. Abraham's head servant, Eliezer, would go instead.

When Eliezer reached Haran he stopped by a well to rest. There he prayed that God would send him the right woman for Isaac. As he prayed, a beautiful young woman came to the well. She gave him water and even watered his camels.

Eliezer thanked the woman. He asked if he might spend the night with her family. In those days there were no hotels or inns. Then he gave her a gold ring and gold bracelets as presents.

The young woman was named Rebekah. She was Nahor's granddaughter. That meant she worshiped the Lord. When she went home to see if Eliezer could stay with them, she showed her family her gifts. Her brother Laban went out and welcomed Eliezer to their house.

Eliezer told Rebekah's family about Abraham and Isaac.

He said they were very rich. He also said he was sure Rebekah was meant to be Isaac's wife.

Rebekah's father agreed that it was God's will. Eliezer gave them all wonderful gifts and they had a great feast. The next day Rebekah's family asked Rebekah if she wanted to marry Isaac. She said yes, and Rebekah and her family along with Eliezer began the trip back to Canaan.

As soon as Isaac saw Rebekah, he fell in love with her. They were married and stayed together the rest of their lives.

When Abraham was nearly 180 years old he died. Isaac and Ishmael buried him in the cave with Sarah. Isaac became the owner of all that had belonged to Abraham: his tents, flocks of sheep, herds of cattle, camels, and servants. Although he was very wealthy, Isaac lived a quiet, peaceful life and lived in his tent in one place most of his years.

_____

THINK ABOUT IT

✛ *Was Abraham being a good father when he helped choose Isaac's wife? Do you think God wants you to marry a Christian?* ✛

_____

Jacob and Esau

✛ GENESIS 25:27-27:46 ✛

Isaac and Rebekah had two sons. The oldest was named Esau. He was a hunter who liked being out in the wild. Great manners weren't his thing. He was rough and tough and hairy. He was also his father's favorite son.

The younger son was named Jacob. He was quiet and smart. Staying at home and taking care of the flocks were his favorite things. Unlike Esau, Jacob had smooth skin. He was Rebekah's favorite son.

In those days the oldest son inherited twice as much as the younger ones. This was called the *birthright*. Furthermore, God had promised the family of Isaac should receive great blessings. The boy who was blessed by Isaac would be very lucky.

As they grew up Esau didn't care much about his birthright and blessing. They didn't seem important to him. All he cared about was *right now*. Jacob was the smart one. He knew how important these things could be.

One day Esau came home tired and hungry. He saw that Jacob was cooking something and he asked for a bowl of food.

"I'll give you some," Jacob said, "if you give me your birthright."

"Fine," Esau answered. "I'm starving *right now!*" For a bowl of food Esau had traded to Jacob his birthright.

It was wrong of Jacob to be so greedy. But it was stupid of Esau to give up so much for one bowl of food.

When Esau was forty years old he married two women from Canaan. In those days having more than one wife was not bad. What was wrong was that his wives worshiped idols. They didn't follow God. And they brought up Esau's children to worship little stone statues too.

Even then Isaac still loved Esau more than Jacob. By now Isaac was very old and nearly blind. One day he said to Esau, "Go hunting and cook me a good meal of meat. When I've eaten, I'll give you my blessing. I don't think I'll live much longer."

Rebekah overheard Isaac talking to Esau. Jacob was still her favorite. She wanted him to have the blessing. She told Jacob to bring her two young goats to cook. Then Jacob would take the food to Isaac and get Esau's blessing.

"But I'm not hairy like Esau," Jacob said.

"I'll take care of that," Rebekah answered.

When the food was ready she dressed Jacob in Esau's rough clothes. Then she put the skin from the goats over his neck and hands. Now he would feel hairy to his blind father.

Jacob took the food to his father.

"Who is it?" Isaac asked.

"Esau. I have your food," Jacob said.

"How did you get it so soon?"

"The Lord showed me where to go," Jacob said.

Isaac wasn't sure. "You sound more like Jacob," he said. "Come here. Let me feel you." He felt the goat's hair on Jacob's hands. "You feel like Esau. Are you *really* Esau?"

"Yes," Jacob lied.

Isaac gave Jacob his blessing. He promised Jacob would rule over his brother. He would have everything he needed. Many nations would bow down to him.

Soon after Jacob left, Esau came back with his food. Isaac was terribly upset when he found he had blessed the wrong son. So was Esau. "Is there no blessing left for me at all?" he asked.

"Jacob will have the best land," Isaac said. "And his family will rule yours. I can't take the blessing back."

Instead Isaac gave a second blessing to Esau. "You will

live by your sword," he said. "And your family must serve his. But someday you will all be free of him."

This wasn't a great blessing but it was better than nothing. And it would all come true in the future.

Because God knows everything it was God's plan that the blessing went to Jacob. Jacob followed the Lord. Esau's family later became wicked people. But the way Jacob stole his brother's birthright was still not right.

THINK ABOUT IT

✝ *Like many brothers, Esau and Jacob were very different. Can two people who like different things still be friends?* ✝

STORY 13

Jacob's Wonderful Dream

✝ GENESIS 27:46-30:24 ✝

Esau was furious when he saw Jacob had stolen his birthright and blessing. He told others that when their father died, he was going to kill Jacob.

Rebekah heard about Esau's threats. She called Jacob to her. "Run away from here," she said. "Maybe Esau will forget in a while. Then you can come home." She sent him to the city of Haran, where he could stay with her brother, Laban.

With only a walking stick in his hand, Jacob set out for Haran, a long distance to the north. One night, over sixty miles away from home, Jacob lay down on the ground to sleep. He was so tired he used a rock for a pillow.

That night Jacob had a wonderful dream. He saw stairs leading up to heaven. Angels were going up and down the stairs. At the top of the stairs was the Lord God.

God talked to Jacob in his dream. He said, "I am the God of Abraham and your father. I will be your God too. This land will belong to you and your children. Your family will cover the earth. And from them, the world will receive a great blessing." The Lord promised to stay with Jacob and protect him forever.

In the morning Jacob remembered his dream and smiled. He no longer felt lonely and afraid. He took the rock he had slept on and poured oil over it as a gift to God. Then he made a promise to God. "If God will protect me and bring me home again, I will give Him one-tenth of everything He gives to me."

Finally Jacob reached Haran. He sat by the well to rest. This was the same well where Eliezer had first met Jacob's

34

mother.

Soon a beautiful young woman arrived to water her sheep. Jacob pulled buckets of water up for her and helped with the animals. To Jacob's surprise and delight, he discovered that the young woman was Laban's daughter Rachel, his cousin!

Laban took Jacob into his house, and Jacob and Rachel fell in love. Jacob told Laban that if he could marry Rachel, he would work for Laban for seven years. Laban agreed to the offer.

At last the seven years were up. On the day of the wedding the bride was covered with a long veil. When Jacob lifted the veil, he found he had been tricked. He had been married to Leah, Rachel's older sister! Leah was not beautiful, and Jacob did not love her.

Laban tried to calm Jacob down. He explained that the oldest daughter had to marry first. If Jacob still wanted Rachel, he could work for Laban for seven more years.

Jacob loved Rachel so much that he stayed the extra seven years until he could marry her. Finally, Jacob and Rachel were married.

While Jacob was in Haran he had eleven sons. Ten of them were Leah's. The eleventh was named Joseph. He was Rachel's son, and Jacob loved him the most.

THINK ABOUT IT

✦ *How did Jacob pay for tricking his brother and father? What good things came from this?* ✦

STORY 14

A Midnight Wrestling Match

✛ GENESIS 30:25-33:20 ✛

Jacob stayed in Haran for twenty years. To pay Jacob, Laban always gave him a share of the sheep, oxen, and camels he cared for. Since Jacob was very smart and careful in his work, he was soon very rich.

One night when Laban was away, Jacob packed up his family and animals. He was going home.

Laban wanted Jacob to stay. He would miss his daughters and grandchildren. When he found them gone, Laban followed after them. But the Lord warned him not to hurt Jacob, so they met as friends. They agreed not to bother each other and to live apart.

Jacob was nearing Canaan when he heard that his brother Esau was coming to meet him. Esau had an army of 400 men with him!

That night Jacob divided his family and herds into two parts and sent them in different ways. That way maybe some would live if Esau attacked him. He also sent presents ahead to his brother: oxen, cows, sheep, goats, camels, and donkeys. When he had done all he could, he prayed for God to help him. He stayed alone that night so he could pray some more.

Suddenly, Jacob felt someone grab him! It was an angel of the Lord. They fought so hard that Jacob hurt one of his legs, but he would not give up. Finally the angel said, "Let me go. Dawn is coming."

"No," Jacob said. "Not unless you bless me."

"What is your name?" the angel asked.

"Jacob."

"You have a new name now. You are Israel." (Israel means "he who wrestles with God.") Then the angel blessed him and left. From then on, Jacob walked with a limp. He was called Israel, and his family were known as the Israelites.

When Jacob looked up, Esau was standing in front of him. Afraid for his life, Jacob quickly bowed to the ground in front of his brother. But all Esau did was hug and kiss Jacob. He had forgiven Jacob for stealing his birthright and blessing.

Jacob and his family lived in Shechem, in Canaan. He dug a deep well there for his flocks. If you go there today, you can still drink water from Jacob's well.

Soon Jacob and Esau's father, Isaac, died. The two brothers buried him in the cave of Abraham and Sarah. Then Esau moved his family south of Canaan, to a land called Edom. Israel (Jacob) stayed in Canaan with his family and herds.

THINK ABOUT IT

✝ *Esau could have remained angry at Jacob for the rest of his life. Instead, he chose to forgive him. Why is it important to forgive someone who has hurt you?* ✝

The Jealous Brothers of Joseph

✝ GENESIS 37:1-36 ✝

After Jacob and his family moved to Canaan, Rachel had a second son, Benjamin. Now Jacob had twelve sons. Ten of them were Leah's and two were Rachel's. Leah's sons were grown men by now. Joseph, Rachel's first son, was only seventeen years old. Soon after Benjamin was born, Rachel died.

Jacob still loved Joseph more than any of his children. He was a good boy, and smart like his father. When Jacob gave Joseph a beautiful coat of many colors, all the older boys were jealous. They also didn't like Joseph because he had dreams where his whole family was bowing down to him. The older brothers thought Joseph considered himself better than the rest of his family.

One day Jacob needed to send a message to his older sons. They were over fifty miles away with the flocks. He sent Joseph off with the message.

When his older brothers saw Joseph coming, one of them said, "Let's kill him. We'll say a wild animal ate him. We are so far from home that no one will know the truth."

One of the brothers—Reuben—didn't want to kill Joseph. But he was afraid of his brothers. "Let's just throw him in that hole over there. We'll leave him there to die," Reuben said. He planned to come back later and save Joseph.

The brothers grabbed Joseph and tossed him into the hole in the ground. Then they sat down and ate dinner

while Joseph called to them for help. Reuben was upset by this. He wandered off a little so he couldn't hear Joseph's cries.

While Reuben was gone some traders came by. They were on their way to Egypt. Judah, one of the brothers, had an idea. "Why don't we sell Joseph as a slave to these men? Then we won't be killing him, but he'll still be gone." So they pulled Joseph up and sold him for twenty pieces of silver.

There was nothing Reuben could do when he came back and saw Joseph was gone. Before they went home they killed a goat and put its blood all over Joseph's fine coat. Then they showed the coat to their father and said they had found it in the wilderness.

Jacob's heart was broken. As his sons had planned, he thought a wild animal had killed and eaten his favorite son. Nothing his other sons said made Jacob feel any better. They couldn't tell him that Joseph was now a slave in Egypt. Jacob cried and cried.

THINK ABOUT IT

✝ *Joseph's brothers were very jealous of Joseph, and for*

good reason. When you are jealous of someone, you can do and say things that are not kind. How can you stop feeling jealous? ✛

STORY 16

From the Prison to the Palace

✛ GENESIS 40:1-41:44 ✛

The men who bought Joseph were called Ishmaelites. They were from the family of Ishmael, Abraham and Hagar's son who grew up in the desert. In Egypt these Ishmaelites sold Joseph to a soldier named Potiphar. Joseph was made a house servant.

Joseph did not waste time crying about his fate. He worked hard for Potiphar. Everything he did worked out well. Soon Joseph was in charge of Potiphar's whole house and all his other servants.

But Potiphar's wife wanted Joseph to do something that was against the law. Joseph would not do it. So she told Potiphar that Joseph *had* broken the law, and he was thrown in jail.

Even in jail Joseph was cheerful and helpful. Soon the head guard put him in charge of all the other prisoners. Two of them were servants of the king of Egypt, or the

Pharaoh. When they had dreams they could not understand, Joseph told them what the dreams meant. He was
always right too: All of Joseph's predictions came true.
Soon one of the men was set free and went back to work for
Pharaoh.

Two years passed. Joseph was still in jail. One night the
king had a dream he could not understand. None of his
wise men understood it either. Then the servant remembered Joseph, and Pharaoh had him brought to the palace.

Right away Joseph understood what Pharaoh's dream
meant. God was giving the king a warning. The next
seven years would be times of plenty for Egypt. The seven
that followed would be filled with famine and death.

"You need to store up food during the seven good years,"
Joseph told the king. "Then there will be food for the seven
bad years to come. You must put someone in charge of all
the food in the country now, while you can."

The king was a wise man. He chose Joseph! No one in the
land had more power than Joseph, except the king himself. Joseph would save Egypt from the coming famine.

God had not forgotten Joseph.

_____

THINK ABOUT IT

✛ *Everything went wrong for Joseph for a while. How did
he act during those bad years? What does that tell you
about Joseph?* ✛

_____

Joseph's Dream Comes True

✝ GENESIS 41:46-42:38 ✝

As always, Joseph worked hard at his new job. He traveled all over Egypt and saw that the crops were good. People had more food than they needed. He warned them to save all their extra food for the bad times to come.

During the seven good years Joseph collected one bushel of grain out of every five bushels the people had left over. Soon he had so much food stored away that no one could count it all. Joseph also married and had two sons.

Soon the seven good years passed. The people of Egypt ate up all the food they had saved in their own homes. When that was gone, they bought from the supply Joseph had saved up. Thanks to Joseph, there was plenty of food for everyone.

The famine hit other countries besides Egypt. Even Canaan was running out of food. Joseph's father, Jacob (Israel), had plenty of flocks and cattle, gold and silver. But he was not a farmer. He had no grain to feed his large family. Hearing there was food in Egypt, Jacob sent his ten older sons there with money. He kept his youngest son, Benjamin, home with him.

Joseph was now almost forty years old. He had been in Egypt for nearly twenty-three years. When his brothers came to him to buy food, they did not know who he was. He was dressed like a prince and sitting on a throne.

His brothers bowed down to him, just as they had done

in his dream years ago. Joseph knew them at once. He wondered if they were as selfish as they had been when he was young.

Joseph pretended he did not know their language. He spoke to them in Egyptian and had others translate back and forth.

"Who are you?" Joseph asked. "Are you spies coming to see how weak we are so you can attack us?"

"No," one of his brothers said. "We are all the sons of one man. We have come to buy food."

"Tell me about this man."

They told Joseph about his father and brother Benjamin and about the other son who was lost years ago (Joseph). Joseph pretended not to believe them and sent them to prison for three days.

Then he sent for them again. One of the brothers said to the others, "We deserve this because of what we did to Joseph."

"Yes," said Reuben. "God is punishing us."

They didn't know Joseph understood what they were saying. But now he knew they were sorry for what they had done to him.

"I will give you food," Joseph said. "But one of you must

stay here until the rest bring this Benjamin back. Only then will I know you are not spies." He had his brother Simeon tied up and put into prison.

While his servants were putting grain in sacks for his brothers, Joseph gave them a strange order. "Put each man's money back in the sacks. Put it right on top, so they will see it."

When his brothers found the money later, they were frightened. Someone might say they had stolen the grain! They explained everything to Jacob when they got home. They had to take Benjamin back to Egypt with them.

"No," Jacob said. "Joseph is gone. Now Simeon is a prisoner. I will not lose Benjamin too."

THINK ABOUT IT

✛ *Why do you think Joseph sent for his younger brother Benjamin? Is Joseph being fair to his brothers?* ✛

STORY 18

A Lost Brother No More

✛ GENESIS 43:1-45:24 ✛

The food the brothers brought from Egypt soon ran out. Jacob now had sixty-six people in his family to feed. In addition he had to feel all the servants and the men who cared for his flocks.

He told his sons to go back to Egypt and buy more grain.

"He won't even see us," one of them said. "Not unless we bring Benjamin."

Jacob finally agreed that Benjamin could go. He sent gifts with them for the ruler: spices, perfumes, nuts, and almonds. He also sent back the money found in the sacks.

When Joseph saw Benjamin he told his servant to prepare a meal. The brothers were treated as honored guests. Joseph asked about his father. "Is he well?"

"Yes. He is healthy and alive," they answered.

"And this is your little brother? God bless you, son." Joseph was so happy to see Benjamin alive and well that he had to leave the room. Once in his own room Joseph cried freely.

When it was time to eat Joseph had them sit at the table in order of their ages, with the oldest brother closest to him. How did he know their ages? the brothers wondered. Joseph also saw that Benjamin, the youngest, got five times as much food as his brothers.

After dinner Joseph told his servants to fill the men's sacks with grain. Again he put their money in with the grain. He also had his own silver cup put in Benjamin's sack. When his brothers left, Joseph sent his servants after them. They found the cup and brought everyone back to Joseph.

"The rest of you may go," Joseph said. "But the thief must stay." Would his selfish brothers let Benjamin suffer for them?

Judah, the brother who sold Joseph years ago, spoke up. "It will kill our father if he loses Benjamin. Take me as a slave instead," he begged.

Now Joseph knew his brothers had really changed. He then sent his servants away. "Come here," he said to his brothers. "I am Joseph. Is my father really alive?"

His brothers stood terrified. Joseph, the second-most powerful man in Egypt, was the brother they had once sold as a slave! Now he spoke to them in their own language.

But Joseph was kind. "God sent me here for a reason," he said. "Because I am here, I can save my family. Go home and bring everyone back here. The famine will last for five more years. But you will be safe here with me."

THINK ABOUT IT

✝ *When you love someone, like Joseph loved his family, time away from them or the distance apart does not make you love them less. Why is it important for everyone to love someone this much? Do you know how God feels about you?* ✝

STORY 19

Joseph's Last Request

✝ GENESIS 45:25-50:26 ✝

J oseph's eleven brothers went back to Canaan. They told their father that Joseph was alive and wanted them all to go to Egypt. On their way there the family stopped at Beersheba. There the Lord came to Jacob. "I will go to Egypt with you," the Lord said. "Your people will be a great people. And I will bring them back here again."

Joseph rode out in his chariot to meet his family. He hugged his old father and cried with joy. Then Joseph took his father to meet the king of Egypt. Jacob gave his blessing to the king who had treated his son so well.

Joseph gave his family some of the best land in Egypt. But the famine was still in Egypt. Jacob and his family lived on the food Joseph had stored up, just like the Egyptians.

By now, Jacob (Israel) was almost 150 years old. He knew he would die in Egypt. "When I die," he said, "take me back to Canaan. Bury me in the cave of Abraham and Isaac."

Joseph brought his two sons to see their grandfather for the first time. Jacob couldn't see very well, but he was happy to meet his grandsons. He put his right hand on Ephraim's head and his left on Manasseh's. Since Manasseh was the older son, he should have had the better blessing. Joseph tried to put his father's right hand on Manasseh but Jacob told him to leave him alone. "I know what I am doing," the old man said. "God will bless both your sons. But the younger will be greater than the older."

Later this came true. Ephraim's family was more powerful than Manasseh's.

When Jacob died his sons buried him in Canaan, as he had asked.

Joseph lived to be 110 years old. Before he died he told all the children of Israel not to bury him in Egypt. "You will go back to Canaan someday. Take me with you and bury me there."

After Joseph died his body was preserved the way the Egyptians did, with certain drugs and spices. His body was then put him in a stone coffin. Every time the Israelites saw Joseph's coffin, they remembered God's promise to take them home again.

THINK ABOUT IT

✤ *A younger son is again given the better blessing. Why did Jacob say that he knew what he was doing?* ✤

STORY 20

The Little Boat of Reeds

✤ EXODUS 1:1-2:22 ✤

Israel's children would stay in Egypt for 400 years. They lived on the fertile land Joseph had given them, far away from where the Egyptians lived. By living far apart, the Israelites were less likely to worship the Egyptian gods and marry Egyptians. They stayed faithful to God.

Each of Israel's twelve sons became the father of a large tribe of people. Joseph was the father of two tribes: one named after each of his sons.

For a long time the Egyptians were good to Israel's people. They remembered how Joseph had saved them from starving. But many years later Egypt's kings forgot that. These rulers saw how strong the Israelites (they called them the Hebrews) were becoming. They were afraid of them.

So they made slaves of the Israelites. To keep them from growing stronger, the Egyptians killed all the boy babies that were born to the Israelites. Even then, the Israelites grew stronger.

One Hebrew mother found a way to save her baby boy. She knew that the king's daughter took baths at a certain place on the river. She built a little boat out of reeds and put the baby in it. Then she let it float down to the bathing place. Her daughter, Miriam, watched the boat carefully.

When the princess saved the baby, Miriam ran up to her. "Do you want me to find you a nurse for the baby?" she asked. The princess said yes. Then Miriam brought her mother—the baby boy's mother—to the princess. The princess paid the mother to take the baby back to her own house and raise him. This special baby would be called Moses.

When Moses was old enough to leave his mother, he went to live with the princess. He learned many things at the palace and lived a good life. But he always loved his own people better than the Egyptians. When he was a man he left the palace and went back to his own people.

The king (Pharaoh) hated Moses for leaving. It wasn't safe for him to stay in Egypt. He moved into the wilderness of Arabia, to a land called Midian. There he met a man named Jethro and married one of his daughters. For a long time Moses lived in Midian, helping Jethro with his flocks.

THINK ABOUT IT

✦ *The Egyptians saw that the Israelites had become a*

*strong and wealthy people. What is the secret of th[e]
Israelites' success? Give at least two reasons.* ✛

The Burning Bush

✛ EXODUS 3:1-4:31 ✛

Moses had spent forty years in the home of the king of Egypt. He spent forty more in the wilderness of Midian. There he lived alone most of the time, wandering with his father-in-law's sheep.

He no longer dressed like an Egyptian prince. Now he wore skins to keep warm and sandals on his feet. He carried a shepherd's staff to help protect his flock. His life was hard, but he was happy.

One day Moses saw a bush burning nearby. He walked closer to the bush and became very curious. No matter how much the bush burned, the bush was still there.

Suddenly a voice came out of the bush. "Moses!" it called.

"Yes?" Moses must have been surprised to hear a bush talking to him!

"I am the Lord your God. I am going to set your people in Egypt free. Go to Egypt and lead my people out of there."

"Me?" Moses said. "I'm just a shepherd. My people will ask who this God is." Moses had been away from Egypt for years. He didn't even know if the Israelites still worshiped God.

"My name is I AM. Tell them I AM has sent you. They will believe you. Go to the king and tell him the people need to worship Me in the wilderness. At first he will say no. Later I will show him My power and you will be set free."

Moses was willing to obey God, but he felt unworthy. He wanted something he could show the Israelites to prove he was their leader.

"What do you have in your hand?" God asked him.

"My staff. I use it to guide my sheep."

"Throw it on the ground," God said.

As soon as the staff hit the ground, it turned into a snake. Moses backed away.

"Pick it up by the tail," God commanded.

As soon as Moses did, the snake became his staff again.

"Now put your hand on your chest, under your clothes, and then take it out again."

When he did, Moses saw his hand was white with leprosy, a terrible disease everyone feared.

"Do it again," the Lord ordered.

This time, Moses' hand came out perfectly normal.

"Show these signs to your people. If you need another, scoop some water from the river. It will turn to blood."

Even then, Moses was afraid. He told God that he wasn't

a good speaker. God told him to take his brother Aaron with him to do the talking. Finally, Moses began the walk to Egypt. He was very happy when he met Aaron on the way.

In Egypt the two men went to the leaders of all the tribes. They told them what God had said and showed them God's signs. The people of Israel believed them. God had not forgotten them.

THINK ABOUT IT

✤ *Moses told God he wasn't a good speaker, which meant he had trouble speaking in front of others. Did God already know this? How do you know? What special skills do you have that God might want you to use someday?* ✤

STORY 22

The River of Blood

✤ EXODUS 6:28-10:29 ✤

Moses, Aaron, and the leaders of the Israelites went to see the king of Egypt, or Pharaoh. They told Pharaoh God wanted them to pray to Him in the wilderness for three days. They didn't say anything about leaving for good.

Pharaoh thought they were just looking for a vacation! "You people don't have enough work to do. I'll fix that," he said.

The Israelites made bricks for the Egyptians. To do that, you need clay and straw. The straw holds the clay together. Until this day the Egyptians had given the straw to the Israelites. Now Pharaoh said the Israelites had to find the straw themselves. This made the hard work even harder. The Israelites became angry at Moses and Aaron.

Moses called on God to help him. God said they should ask Pharaoh to let the Israelites go free. They should go back and show the signs God gave them to Pharaoh.

"Who is this God? Why should I listen to him?" Pharaoh said.

Aaron turned his staff into a snake. When some of Pharaoh's wise men did the same thing (probably by a trick), Aaron's snake ate their snakes. Still Pharaoh refused to free the Israelites.

Then Aaron waved his staff over the river, the canals, and the lakes. All the water turned to blood. All the fish died, and everything smelled awful. But the water where the Israelites lived was still clear and clean.

After a week Moses, with God's power, made the blood disappear. Pharaoh still refused their request. When Aaron waved his staff this time, God sent frogs, *millions* of frogs! They were in the food, in the beds, under everyone's feet. The frogs were everywhere.

Pharaoh promised the Israelites could go if their God killed the frogs. God did, and the Egyptians cleaned up the mess. Then Pharaoh changed his mind and said no again.

Time and again, Pharaoh lied to Moses. God sent lice and fleas and great swarms of flies. He killed all of the Egyptians' animals but saved those of the Israelites. He caused ugly sores to apear on the Egyptians' bodies. Hail destroyed all the crops. Then locusts ate everything that was still green. Still Pharaoh would not let the Israelites go.

God told Moses there would be one more punishment. This one would make Pharaoh *happy* to see the Israelites leave!

THINK ABOUT IT

✛ *Why do you think Pharaoh wanted the Israelites to stay in Egypt? What does this story tell you about slavery?* ✛

STORY 23

The Night a Nation Was Born

✛ EXODUS 11:1-13:22 ✛

While the Egyptians were suffering, nothing bad happened to the Israelites. God protected them. Many Egyptians wanted help from this powerful God. To make God love them, they brought gold and silver and jewels to the Israelites. We know God loves you as you are, but the Egyptians didn't know that. Soon the Israelites were all very rich people.

Moses told the people to get ready to leave. Then he told them about the next thing God was going to do.

At midnight an angel was coming. He would kill the oldest son in every house. Pharaoh's son would die. So would the first son of the poorest man in Egypt. "But if you do as I say, your children will be safe," Moses told the people.

Every family was to kill one lamb. They were to sprinkle some of the lamb's blood around the door of their houses.

54

Then they must cook the lamb and eat it. But they had to eat it all dressed and ready to leave, standing by their tables. Most important, no one could go outside. If they met the angel, they would die. If they obeyed Moses' instructions, the angel would pass over their houses.

All the Israelites did as they were told. Safe inside their houses, they heard the cries of the Egyptians. It must have been hard to hear all the mothers and fathers in Egypt crying at once.

Pharaoh sent a message to Moses. "Go! Get out of my

land. And pray to your God to leave us alone."

Early in the morning the tribes of Israel left Egypt. They left so suddenly that the morning bread did not have time to rise, so they ate flat bread on the way.

The Lord God went before them. In the day there was a great cloud leading them. At night a mighty pillar of fire protected them. When the cloud stopped they camped for the night. When it moved they followed it.

The tribes of Ephraim and Manasseh—Joseph's two sons—took Joseph's body with them out of Egypt, as he had asked years ago. He was going home again.

✛ *To remember this night when the angel of death "passed over" the houses marked by the blood of the lamb, the Jewish people still eat a special dinner each year. The feast is called the* Passover, *or the* seder. *Why did God lead the Israelites out of Egypt anyway? (Hint: Remember Abraham.)* ✛

STORY 24

A Sea to Cross and a Journey to Make

✛ EXODUS 14:1-16:36 ✛

The Israelites wanted to go to Canaan. But the Philistines, a strong people who liked fighting, lived between Egypt and there. The Israelites didn't want a war, so they decided to take a longer route through the desert instead. Moses had lived there for years. He knew the way.

Between Egypt and the desert was the Red Sea. Soon the Israelites were at its edge.

Not surprisingly, Pharaoh had changed his mind again. He sent a great army after the Israelites. They could bring them back or kill them. Pharaoh didn't care which they did. He just wanted the Israelites punished.

That night God's pillar of fire stayed between the Israelites and the Egyptian army. The Egyptians wouldn't go near it. The Israelites were safe for the night.

All night a strong wind blew over the Red Sea. It moved the water aside a little. In the morning there was a little strip of damp land with water on both sides of it. The great cloud moved over the land bridge. The Israelites followed it to the edge of the wilderness.

Then the Egyptian army tried to follow. But the path was still damp, and their horses and chariots all got stuck. Seeing them all piled up below, Moses lifted his hand. A great tide of water rushed in and drowned the entire Egyptian army.

The Israelites were safe now. But they had no food or water in the desert. Moses called to God for help. God promised to make bread rain down every night for the people.

In the morning, there were little white flakes covering the ground. These flakes looked like snow or frost. Everyone said, "What is it?" In their language the word they said was "Manhu?" So that's what they called the flakes, *manna*.

Moses told them that the manna was food from God. They could take all they needed for the day. But the manna wouldn't keep overnight. They would have to collect it every day. Whatever they left behind melted away during the day. On the sixth day of the week, they could take two days' supply of manna. The extra would not spoil on that day. This was because the seventh day was a day of rest. No one should work on that day.

The Israelites would live in the desert for the next forty years. Every single day, God would send them the food they needed.

THINK ABOUT IT

✛ *God has now rescued the Israelites from slavery and*

delivered them from the fierce Egyptian army. He is even providing all their food. How do you think the Israelites will act toward God? Make a prediction now and see if you are right. ✝

The Mountain of God

✝ Exodus 17:1-31:18 ✝

Soon the Israelites ran out of water. They could find no streams or springs in the desert. All their animals were thirsty. Their children cried for something to drink. The people began to hate Moses for taking them into the desert.

Moses asked God to help him, and God did. Moses brought everyone to a big rock. He hit the rock with his staff. Right away water began to flow out of the rock, more than enough for everyone.

There were other people living in the desert too. A wild, rough people didn't want the Israelites there. One day when the people were tired and sick, these wild people attacked them. Moses sent out every healthy man he had. Would it be enough?

Moses stood high on a rock above the fighting. Everyone could see him there. He raised his arms and asked God to help the people in the battle. As long as Moses kept his arms up in prayer, the Israelites fought well. But if his arms fell, the wild people began to win. Moses was an old

• I • II • III • IV • V • VI • VII • VIII • IX • X •

man by now. He wasn't strong enough to keep his arms up
in the air for hours. So two men, Aaron and Hur, stood
beside Moses and held his arms up for him. With God's
help, soon the Israelites drove the wild men away.

Three months after the Israelites left Egypt they came to
Mount Sinai. They camped at the foot of this mountain for
many days.

At Mount Sinai God gave Moses a warning. "Don't let
anyone come near the mountain. If an animal even touches
it, you must kill it. This is a holy place."

A few days later a great storm covered the mountain.
Lightning flashed and thunder rolled over the desert. The
huge mountain shook and smoked, as if it were going to
blow apart.

The people ran away from the mountain, shaking with
fear. Then they heard a great booming voice coming from
the mountain. "I am the Lord, your God. I am the one who
brought you out of slavery in Egypt," the voice said.

Then God spoke what we call the Ten Commandments:
1. You will have no other gods besides God.
2. You will not worship idols.
3. You will not use the name of God as a curse.
4. You will keep the Sabbath day holy.

5. You will honor your father and mother.
6. You will not kill.
7. You will remain faithful to your husband or wife.
8. You will not steal.
9. You will not tell lies about anyone.
10. You will not want other people's possessions.

Everyone could hear His voice, it was so loud. The Israelites were so frightened that they begged Moses, "Please tell God to stop talking to us! Have Him talk just to you. You can tell us what He says."

Moses tried to tell the people it was a good thing to hear the voice of God. He had talked with God many times and was not afraid. But the people were too frightened to listen anymore.

God heard the people crying and told Moses to come up the mountain. God took pity on the scared people. Joshua went part of the way to help Moses climb up. But Moses was to climb the rest of the way alone.

Moses stayed at the top of Mount Sinai with God for forty days. God gave him many laws the people were to obey. There were laws about food and family and work, about living the right way every day. Then God took two flat pieces of stone and wrote the Ten Commandments on them. These were the most important rules. They needed to be written down.

THINK ABOUT IT

✝ *Moses had heard God's voice many times before and was not afraid. How do you think Moses felt about God?* ✝

A Golden Calf

✝ EXODUS 32:1-34:35 ✝

Moses was on the mountain for so long the people thought he was dead. Who would lead them now? They went to Aaron, Moses' brother. "Can you make a god to lead us?" they asked. "One we can all see."

What they wanted was an idol, a statue. They wanted a quiet little piece of metal that they wouldn't be afraid of. Moses' God was scary! They knew other people worshiped idols. Why couldn't they?

They had all heard God's voice giving them the Ten Commandments. The very first commandment was this: "You will have no other gods but me." What they wanted went against God's law.

Aaron knew better. Maybe he thought Moses was dead too. Maybe he was afraid of the people. Anyway, he took all the people's gold jewelry and melted it together to make a golden calf. The people had a great feast in front of the calf and worshiped it as if it were God.

Up on the mountain God saw what was happening. "Get down to the camp," He told Moses. "Your people are worshiping an idol. I will kill them all for this!"

Moses begged God not to do that. He rushed down the mountain, carrying the two stones with the laws on them. Joshua was waiting for Moses on the way. Soon they could see the people below them.

Moses was so mad that he threw the stones on the ground and broke them. Then he raced into the crowd. He grabbed the statue and broke it and then he burned the pieces. He ground the burned pieces into a powder and mixed the powder with water. Then he made all the people drink some of this bad-tasting water as punishment.

Moses also yelled at his brother for making the golden calf. Then he called out, "Everyone who wants to follow God, come over here!"

Only one tribe of the twelve came over. Called the Levites, they came from Levi, one of Jacob's sons. That was the family Moses and Aaron belonged to.

Moses told them, "Go and kill anyone you find still worshiping the idol. No matter who it is, kill them." That day, the sons of Levi killed 3,000 people who were still going against God's first law.

Moses spoke to the people who were left. "You have done wrong. But I will ask God to forgive you." God listened to Moses' prayer and forgave the people. Then He told Moses to bring two new pieces of stone up the mountain. Moses stayed on the mountain for another forty days. This time, the people behaved.

When Moses came back with the laws, the people could not even look at his face. He had been so close to God that his face was shining like the sun. Moses had to wear a cloth over his face when he talked to the people.

THINK ABOUT IT

✛ *The golden calf was an idol the Israelites could worship instead of God. Do people still worship idols instead of the one true God?* ✛

The Tent Where God Lived

✦ EXODUS 35:1-40:30 ✦

God knew that the Israelites were not ready to worship a God they could not see. They were used to seeing people worship idols. They needed something they could see every day.

God told the Israelites to build a special tent. They called this tent a *tabernacle*. The tabernacle would go with them as long as they were in the desert. The people believed God lived in this tent. They couldn't see Him, but they could see His house. God put His cloud over this tent in the daytime and the pillar of fire at night.

The tent had everything the people needed to worship

God: an altar, candlesticks, and a special chest that held the stones with the laws on them. Everything about this tent was built exactly the way God told the Israelites to build it.

Every time the people moved, they packed up the tabernacle and took it with them. The tabernacle was always at the head of the line, leading them on. The tribe of Levi, which had stayed faithful to God, always carried the tabernacle. It was a special honor. Every time the people camped, they set the tabernacle up first. Their own tents went around it. Now they had no need of idols. They had the house of God to see every day.

THINK ABOUT IT

✛ *The tabernacle helped the people of Israel live the way God wanted them to live. What do you have that helps you live the way God wants you to live?* ✛

STORY 28

In the Tabernacle

✛ LEVITICUS 1:1-13; 8:1-13; EXODUS 27:20, 21 ✛

Every morning and afternoon there was a special service in the tabernacle. The priests of Levi would kill a young animal and burn it on the altar. When the people gave animals to God this

way, they were giving Him their best. They were saying
they belonged to God. And God would always forgive them
for what they had done wrong.

The fires and lights of the tabernacle were never allowed
to go out. They were holy. When the people were traveling,
they took the coals of the fire with them to build new fires
when they camped again.

There was a special table in the tent that always had
bread on it. There was one loaf of flat bread for each of the
twelve tribes. On the seventh day of the week fresh bread
would be put there. The priests would then eat the old
bread.

God chose Aaron and his sons to be His priests. A son of
Aaron would be a priest as long as the people worshiped
in the tabernacle. Later they would build a stone temple
in Canaan. Aaron's relatives would be the priests there
too. As a reward for being faithful, Aaron's family would
always serve God in a special way.

THINK ABOUT IT

✦ *We know God can't be seen. How did God give the
Israelites something they could see?* ✦

Aaron's Sons

✝ LEVITICUS 10:11 ✝

The priests had to do things just the way God said in the tabernacle. There were certain areas of the tabernacle that were especially important to God and God was very specific about how things were done in these places.

One of the jobs of the priests was to take fire from the altar and light another fire to burn the sweet-smelling incense God loved. This other fire of incense burned in an important area of the tabernacle known as the Holy Place.

Two of Aaron's sons did this every day. But one day they were not concentrating on their job. Instead of taking the holy fire from the altar, they took some other fire to light the incense. This fire was not holy fire. It was unclean.

They had offered God something that was not their best. God became so angry at the two men that he struck them both dead.

Poor Aaron was not allowed to bury his own sons. He was wearing his special priest's clothes and offering God a sacrifice. If he touched the bodies, he would be unclean. Then he couldn't serve God anymore.

Two of Aaron's cousins took the bodies out and buried them in the sand. Aaron's other two sons took over their brothers' jobs in the tabernacle. They were very careful to obey God's orders from then on!

THINK ABOUT IT

✛ *Why do you think God had very specific rules concerning the tabernacle? What did these rules teach the Israelites?* ✛

STORY 30

The Scapegoat

✛ LEVITICUS 16:1-34 ✛

Inside the tabernacle tent was a special room called the Holy of Holies. The Holy of Holies contained a large box or chest known as the Ark of the Covenant. Inside the Ark of the Covenant were the two stones on which God had written the Ten Commandments. God was supposed to live in the Holy of Holies and only the high priest could enter the room—one day in the year—on the Day of Atonement.

A special service was held on the Day of Atonement to make up for the sins of the people during the year. (When we talk about *sin*, we mean actions or thoughts that go against what God wants us to do. We don't have a special day of atonement, but every day when we pray we should ask God to forgive our sins, because only God can do that.)

From sunset the day before until three o'clock in the afternoon on the Day of Atonement, no one was allowed to eat anything. Only tiny babies could have their milk.

Early on the Day of Atonement the high priest gave a sacrifice, or a sin offering, for himself and his family. The high priest had to be pure, or forgiven, before he could help the people with their sins. Then he took the blood of the young ox he had sacrificed into the Holy of Holies and sprinkled the blood on the golden lid of the Ark of the Covenant as a gift to God.

When the priest came out, two goats were brought to him. One of them would be a sacrifice for all the people's sins. The high priest would sprinkle some of its blood on the special chest too. The other goat—the *scapegoat*—would be taken far away from camp, never to find its way back. This showed the people that God forgave their sins and sent them far away. Today we use the word scapegoat to mean a person that takes the blame for something.

After the service was over, the people would have a great feast to celebrate God's forgiveness of their sins.

———————

THINK ABOUT IT

✝ *Remember, the Israelites had no Bible to tell them about God. They couldn't even read. So God had to show them what He wanted. What did the Day of Atonement teach them about God and their sins? Why is the death on the cross and the Resurrection of God's Son, Jesus Christ, so important? Be sure to ask a parent or an older Christian to explain this to you.* ✢

Grapes from Canaan

✢ NUMBERS 13:1-14:45 ✢

The people stayed by Mount Sinai for almost a year, building the tabernacle and learning God's laws. At last the cloud over the tabernacle rose into the sky. The people packed up all they owned and got ready to move on.

Finally they came to the border of Canaan, the land that God had promised would be theirs. God told Moses to send some men into the land to check it out. They would need to know about the people who were living there. They also needed to know that the land was good land, and where they should live.

Moses chose one man from each of the twelve tribes to act as spies in the new land. The men wandered around the land of Canaan, looking at the cities and the fields. They stayed there for forty days. On the way back to camp they cut down a cluster of ripe grapes that was so big, it took two men to carry it. The grapes would show the people that the land was good for farming.

The spies reported what they had seen. "It's good land," they said. "It has grass, fields, fruit trees, and lots of water." Then their faces became serious. "But the people

who live there are very strong fighters. They have cities with great walls that would be hard to capture, and the people themselves are huge! We felt like grasshoppers next to them!"

Two of the men, Caleb and Joshua, said that didn't matter. "It's worth fighting for this land," they said. "And God will help us win it."

The people believed the ten spies who were afraid, not Caleb and Joshua. All the things God had done for them were forgotten. "Let's pick a new leader," they said. "We will go back to Egypt. At least there we were safe!"

Suddenly a great light came out of the tabernacle, from the Holy of Holies. God—who was the light—spoke to Moses. "How long will these people disobey Me?" God said. "None of them will go into the land I have promised them, except for Caleb and Joshua. Everyone twenty years old and older will die in the desert because of this. Go back into the desert. When your children grow up, Joshua and Caleb will lead them into the land I have promised them."

Because they were afraid to obey God, the people had to spend another forty years wandering around the desert!

The people didn't want to hear this either. "No," they said. "We'll go into the land and take it." They rushed up the mountain. There they were met by the people who lived in the land. Because the Israelites were not organized and ready to fight, they were beaten back into the desert.

Moses knew this would happen. These people were still thinking like slaves. They were not trained to fight. They did not know how to think for themselves or how to follow the orders of those who knew what they were doing.

Their children would grow up as free people in the desert. They would be strong and hard. They would be trained to fight for the land God had promised them.

THINK ABOUT IT

✛ *Why couldn't the people go into Canaan right away? How does this show that God was still taking care of them?* ✛

STORY 32

The Long Journey Ends

✛ NUMBERS 20:1-22:1 ✛

The people spent most of the next forty years just south of Canaan, in a land called Paran. Not much happened to them there. One by one, the older people began to die in the desert. The young people who grew up there were learning a new way of living. They were being trained as fighters. They were learning how to live as free people.

Now almost forty years later, they went back to the border of Canaan. For some reason there was no water there for them this time. The Lord told Moses to bring all the people before a big rock and to speak to the rock. Then water would flow from the rock for them.

But Moses was angry at the people. Instead of talking to the rock, he yelled at the people and then hit the rock twice with his staff. God sent water out of the rock because He knew the people needed it, but He wasn't happy with Moses.

"Because you disobeyed Me," God said, "neither you nor Aaron will enter into the promised land." Moses had always obeyed the Lord before. Just this once, he let his temper get the better of him.

Soon Aaron, who was the high priest, became sick. He and Moses went to the top of Mount Hor. They took Aaron's son Eleazar with them. On the mountain Moses took Aaron's priestly robes off and put them on Eleazar, making him the new high priest. Aaron died there on the mountain.

Once again the people tried to enter Canaan. But the Canaanites and others living near the border were still too strong for them, and the Israelites had to go back into the desert. Southeast of Canaan lived a people called the Edomites. Maybe they would let the Israelites go through their land and into Canaan. They were related to the Israelites, for one thing. The Edomites were from the family of Esau. The Israelites all came from Esau's brother Jacob. So in a way, they were cousins.

Moses sent a message to the king of Edom. "Let us pass through your land," he asked. "We will stay on the road to Canaan and not bother your people or your crops. We will even pay you for the water we drink."

But the king of Edom was afraid to let so many strange

people pass through his land with all their animals so he said no. Moses did not want to fight the Edomites because they were relatives, so the Israelites went the long way around. They traveled to the south, then east, and then north toward Canaan again.

This did not make the people of Israel happy. They began to complain again, saying they wanted to go back to Egypt. This made God so angry that He sent poisonous snakes into their camp. Many of the people died from snakebites.

The people were very sorry they had again doubted Moses and God. They asked Moses to pray to God and take away the snakes. When he did, God told Moses to make a brass snake and to put it on a high stake, where the people could see it. Then anyone who was bitten by a snake could look at the brass snake and be healed.

Now there was only one more country between the Israelites and Canaan. This country was occupied by the Amorites. Moses sent a message to their king, saying if the king would let the people walk through the land, they would harm nothing on the way.

As an answer, the king sent an army to fight the Israelites. But this time the Israelites won the battle. It was the first of many battles they would have to win to claim the land of Canaan.

Soon the Israelites were camping by the mountains of Moab. The desert was behind them. Below they could see the Jordan River and the rich, green land that God had promised them years before.

THINK ABOUT IT

+ *The brass snake God commanded Moses to make was really a* symbol, *or something that stands for something else, of Jesus Christ. What did the brass snake take away or heal? When Jesus was put up on the cross, what did He take away or heal?* +

What a Wise Man Learned from a Donkey

✝ NUMBERS 22:2-25:18; 31:1-9 ✝

The people were camped beside the Jordan River, but their work was just starting. God had promised them all of Canaan, but He didn't say they would take it without a fight.

The Israelites had beaten the Amorites, killed their king, and taken their land. But there was more to do. Moses sent an army northward into Bashan. The king there was named Og. He was one of the giants the Israelites' fathers had been so afraid of forty years earlier. After defeating Og the Israelites ruled all the land on the east of the Jordan River and north of a brook named Arnon.

South of the Arnon and east of the Dead Sea were the Moabites. These people all came from Lot, Abraham's nephew. That meant they were like cousins to the Israelites too. Their king was named Balak.

Desperate for help, Balak sent for a man named Balaam. Balaam lived far to the east of Canaan. He was a prophet who could talk to God, like Moses. The king's men asked Balaam to come with them and curse the Israelites. People who were cursed by Balaam had bad things happen to them. Balaam told the king's men to spend the night. He would talk to God and see what God wanted him to do.

That night God told Balaam not to go with Balak's men.

He also said Balaam should not curse the Israelites. "These people are to be blessed," God told Balaam.

When King Balak heard this, he sent the men back to Balaam. They promised him all the money he wanted and great honors. All Balaam had to do was curse the Israelites. Again, Balaam told the men to stay over while he talked to God.

Balaam was a decent man, but he was human. He wanted honors and money. God wasn't happy about it, but He told Balaam he could go. There was one condition: Balaam was only to say what God told him to say.

While Balaam was on his way to Moab, riding on his donkey, one of God's angels met him on the road. Balaam couldn't see the angel, though. Only the donkey he was riding could see the shining angel and his fiery sword. When the donkey saw the angel in his path, he walked off the road and went around him. Balaam hit the donkey and forced him back onto the road.

The angel appeared to the donkey a second time. This time the road was narrow, with a stone wall on each side. When he tried to go around the angel, the donkey pushed Balaam's foot into the wall. Balaam hit the donkey again.

The third time the donkey saw the angel, he fell down in

the road. Balaam hit him again and again. He didn't know why the donkey was being so stupid!

Suddenly, the donkey turned to Balaam. "Why are you hitting me?" the donkey asked his rider.

Balaam was so angry at the donkey that he didn't even wonder how the donkey was talking. "You're not walking the way you should," Balaam said to the donkey. "If I had a sword, I would kill you!"

"But I belong to you," the donkey said. "Haven't I always done what you wanted? Why are you so cruel now?"

Suddenly God let Balaam see the shining angel and his sharp sword. Balaam fell to the ground before the angel.

"Balaam," the angel said, "you are going the wrong way. If the donkey had not seen me, I would have killed you. The road you are taking will lead to your death."

Balaam promised to go back home. But the angel knew he really wanted to go to Moab and become rich. "You can go," he said. "But only say what God tells you to say."

King Balak took Balaam to the top of a mountain to see the Israelites camped below. "How can I speak against those that God has blessed?" Balaam said.

The king took Balaam to the top of another mountain above the Israelites. "I can only say what God tells me to say," Balaam told the king. "God does not change His mind. He told me to bless this people, and they will be blessed. He will lead them, and they will win the battle."

Balak was losing patience with Balaam. But he took him to a third mountain. There Balaam blessed the people of Israel a third time. "Go home!" Balak yelled to Balaam. "You were supposed to curse these people. Three times you have blessed them!"

"I told you I could only say what God gave me to say," Balaam answered. "Now listen. Israel will rule over Moab. All these lands—Edom, Mount Sier, and Ammon—will someday be ruled by the Israelites." (Balaam's prophecy would come true 400 years later when David, the king of Israel, would rule all those countries.)

Finally Balaam told Balak what he should do. Instead of fighting the Israelites, Balak should make friends with them. His people should marry their people. The king took Balaam's advice. Soon some of the Israelites married Moabite women and began to worship their idols, instead of God.

Moses knew this was worse than being defeated in battle. Soon God sent a great disease to the people, killing many of them. To save the people, Moses killed the men who were leading the people into sin, then made war on the Moabites. The Israelites beat the Moabites and the Midianites. One of those who died was Balaam, whose greed had made him disobey God and hurt the people of Israel.

THINK ABOUT IT

✝ *Balaam found a way to get the money he wanted and hurt the Israelites without directly disobeying God. But in his heart Balaam knew he hadn't followed what God wanted him to do. Have you ever felt like Balaam?* ✝

On the Edge of the Promised Land

✠ NUMBERS 26:1-4, 63-65; 32:1-42;
DEUTERONOMY 31:1-34:12 ✠

While the Israelites were camped by the Jordan River, God told Moses to count the men who were fit for war. When they had finished counting all the men over twenty years old, they found there were 600,000 of them. Adding in all the women and children, the Israelites were a good-sized nation of people.

Only three men in the entire nation were over sixty years old. All the others had died along the way or been killed in battle. Moses, Joshua, and Caleb were the only old men still living.

Moses was the oldest. He was 120 now. But God had kept him strong all those years because he was needed to lead the people.

The land the Israelites already controlled on the east of the Jordan River was good for raising animals. Two of the twelve tribes and half of another tribe were herders, not farmers. They asked Moses if they could have this land for themselves while the rest of the people went across the Jordan into the farmland there.

Moses knew this wasn't fair and wouldn't please God. Why should those two and one-half tribes be allowed to settle down while everyone else had to go on fighting? The men offered Moses a deal. They would get their flocks set up safely and built shelters for their families. Then they would go on with the others and help them fight. Only when the war was over would they go back to their own land and families. Moses agreed this was fair.

Moses' work was almost done. God told him to gather all the people together one more time and speak to them. As you remember, Moses was not going to be allowed to lead the people across the Jordan River.

Moses retold all the laws he had learned from God. He told the people to be sure they obeyed God's laws and taught them to their children. Then he sang a song of farewell and wrote down all his last words. Because God had chosen Joshua to be the new leader, Moses blessed him and turned the people over to Joshua's care.

While all the people watched and cried, Moses walked out of the camp alone. He climbed to the top of Mount Nebo and looked down at the promised land below him. Then he quietly lay down on the mountaintop and died. Because there was no one there to bury Moses properly, God Himself buried him. No man knows where God put the body of Moses, who had served Him for so many years.

No man ever lived so near to God or talked to Him like a brother until Jesus Christ came into the world many years later.

THINK ABOUT IT

✛ *Why wasn't Moses allowed to go into the promised land? (See Story 31.) How do you think he felt, up there on the mountain all alone? Even though God had punished Moses, did God still love Moses until the day he died? How do you know?* ✛

Job

In those early days there was a good man named Job who lived east of the land of Israel. He had thousands of sheep, camels, oxen, and donkeys. No one had more than Job.

Job served the Lord God and prayed to God every day. He even sacrificed animals on the altar for each of his many children, just in case one of them had sinned and not asked forgiveness.

One day when all God's angels were with Him, Satan. also known as the devil, stood before God too. God said to him, "Where have you been?"

"I have been looking at all the people on the earth," Satan answered.

"Have you seen My servant Job?" God asked Satan. "He is a good man. He does nothing wrong and loves Me."

"Why shouldn't he love You?" Satan said to God. "You protect him and make him rich. If Job were to lose everything he owns, Job wouldn't love You anymore."

"Satan," God said, "do what you want with everything Job has, but do not hurt him. You'll see."

Soon a servant came running to Job with bad news. Wild men from the desert had chased away all Job's oxen and donkeys and killed all the men working with them except this one messenger.

Another man rushed in at the same time. Lightning had struck all of Job's sheep and the men taking care of them. Only the one man had been left to bring the news to Job.

A third messenger ran in then. He had the worst news

of all. Job's sons and daughters had been eating together
in one house when a desert wind hit the house. The house
fell down on all of them and not one son or daughter was
left alive.

Job had nothing. No oxen, sheep, camels, or donkeys. He
had no children to love and care for anymore. He was no
longer rich; Job was poor, and alone.

Job fell to his face and prayed to God. "I came into this
world with nothing," he said. "I will leave it with nothing.
The Lord gave, and the Lord took away. Blessed be the
Lord." Job did not blame the Lord for his grief. He did not
curse the Lord or ask to have everything back. He blessed
God in spite of all his troubles.

The next time God saw Satan, God asked, "What did I
tell you about Job? You did him great harm, but he still
worships Me and does no wrong."

Satan said, "A man will give up anything in order to live.
Hurt his body and see if he's so perfect."

"Do whatever you want to him," God said. "But you may
not kill him."

Satan made horrible sores appear all over Job's body.
The sores were so painful that Job could only roll in the
dust and moan. "What's the use of being good?" Job's wife
asked him. "Why don't you curse God and die?"

"Do we just take the good things from God and refuse to take the bad things?" Job asked his wife. Job said nothing against God even though he was in great pain.

Three of Job's friends came by to cheer him up. In those days people believed that everything bad that happened to you was punishment for sin. If you were in trouble, you probably deserved it. Job's friends tried to get Job to remember what he had done wrong. If he would ask forgiveness, they thought he would get well.

No matter what they said, Job knew better. He had been good. There was no sin he was hiding.

Then God must be unjust, his friends said. Job said no. God was just. Job could not understand God's ways, but he still believed God was good.

Suddenly God spoke to the four men. Job was right, He said. God would always do the right thing for every man. Job's three friends had sinned by saying those things, and needed to make things right. "Go give Me an offering," God said to them. "Then Job will pray for you. For his sake, I will forgive you."

Because Job had been faithful to God, the Lord blessed him once more. He took away the sores and made Job well. Then God gave Job twice the number of animals he had owned before. Job was rich again. God also gave Job seven strong sons and three beautiful daughters. Job lived many more years under God's care, with riches, honor, and goodness.

THINK ABOUT IT

✝ *Before Adam was created Satan was an angel of God. When Satan disobeyed God he was sent away from heaven and now, although you cannot see him, he tries to get people to turn away from God. Why did Satan feel Job would turn away from God?* ✝

PART 2

God Is on Our Side!

THE FIGHT FOR THE PROMISED LAND

The Scarlet Cord

✟ JOSHUA 1:1-2:24 ✟

After Moses died God spoke to Joshua, the new leader of the Israelites. "It's time to cross the Jordan River and take over the land I promised you," God said. Then He told Joshua how big the Israelites' land would be. "Be strong," God told Joshua. "I will be with you, as I was with Moses. If you read the book of the law that I gave Moses, and do as it says, you will win."

Joshua did what God told him to do. "We will cross the river in three days," he told the people. "Be ready." Because it was springtime, crossing the river would not be easy. The Jordan River was wide and deep, and the water moved rapidly downstream. Furthermore, there were no bridges or boats. The task of transporting all those people and animals across would be hard, dangerous work.

Once everyone got across the river, there would be more problems. A few miles beyond the river was the mighty city of Jericho with its high walls. Jericho had to be taken before the Israelites could go any farther.

Joshua sent two men out of the camp on a mission. "Go into the city of Jericho and learn all you can about it. Be back in two days," he said. The two men swam the river and walked to Jericho. Once in the city someone reported the strangers to the king, and the king promptly sent men to take them prisoner.

Looking for a place to hide, Joshua's two spies went to the house of a woman named Rahab. She took them in, but someone saw them going into her house. Soon soldiers were banging on the door. Rahab quickly took the two spies up onto the roof and hid them under long stalks or reeds. When the soldiers could not find the spies, they left.

One side of Rahab's house was built into the city's wall and had a window that looked over the wall. Rahab let down a long scarlet (bright red) rope on that side of her house so that the men could slide safely to the ground. Rahab spoke to the men as they were about to leave her house. "Everyone here is afraid of your people," she told them. "We know how strong your God is. We know how He protects you. Will you save me and my family when you take this city?"

"Yes," the spies promised. "We will see no harm comes to your family. Tell your family to stay inside your house until the city is taken. We will tell our men not to harm anyone in the house with the scarlet rope hanging out the window."

When the two spies returned to Joshua, they had good news. "Everyone is afraid of us! We will be able to take this land, as God promised."

The people who lived in Canaan had good reason to fear the Israelites. For one thing, they were a large, strong nation. They were trained to fight under one leader. The

85

people living in Canaan were not a united people. Each town and each tribe had its own king. They would not join together to fight the Israelites. One by one, the Israelites would defeat each king and each city, until the whole land belonged to them.

THINK ABOUT IT

✛ *Why were the people of Jericho afraid of the Israelites? Think of God's master plan for the Israelites. Why were the additional forty years in the desert such a good thing?* ✛

STORY 2

The Walls of Jericho

✛ JOSHUA 3:1-6:27 ✛

After the spies returned from Jericho, Joshua made the camp ready to cross the river. The tabernacle was taken down and wrapped up and the priests carried it between two strong poles. All the people took down and packed up their tents too. When everyone was ready and lined up by tribe, Joshua moved them forward.

Soon they were near the banks of the Jordan River. The river was flowing free and strong. The people were sure many of them would die trying to get across to the other side.

Then Joshua called out to the priests. "Bring the Ark of

the Covenant to the front. Everyone else is to stay at least 3,000 feet behind." When the Ark of the Covenant was at the edge of the water and the people the right distance behind it, Joshua told the priests to carry the special chest into the river.

As soon as the feet of the priests touched the water, the river stopped flowing! The water coming downstream just stopped above them and piled up. The water below them kept on flowing. That left a wide space of river bottom for all the people and animals to walk over. Then Joshua ordered the rest of the people across the river. In front were the herdsmen soldiers who had claimed the land on the other side of the river. After them came all the other tribes, one by one. All the time the priests stood in the river bed with the Ark of the Covenant, keeping the water away.

Once everyone was safely across the river Joshua called the leaders of the twelve tribes together. "Go gather rocks from the river bed," he said. "Make a pillar of rock here on the shore. Make another in the middle of the river. This will help you and your children remember what God did for you this day."

When that was done, the priests carried the Ark of the Covenant to the shore. The river flowed again, as if nothing strange had ever happened there.

The people made a new camp on the plain of the Jordan River, at a place called Gilgal. This would be the main camp of the Israelites from now on, until the land of Canaan belonged to them. In this land there was grain and barley and corn for the people to eat. In fact, from then on there was no manna dropping from the skies every morning.

Now Joshua had to deal with Jericho. A good soldier, Joshua went out from the camp alone to study the city and see if he could find the easiest way in. All of a sudden Joshua saw an armed man walking toward him. Joshua called out, "Are you on our side? Or are you an enemy?"

"No," said the man. "I am the captain of the Lord's army."

Then Joshua saw the man was an angel of the Lord. He bowed down. "What does the Lord want to tell His servant?" Joshua asked the angel.

"Take off your shoes. You are on holy ground," the angel said.

Suddenly Joshua could see it was the Lord Himself, not just an angel, speaking to him.

"I have given you Jericho. I will destroy the city for you." Then the Lord told Joshua exactly what he was to do. Everything the people did for the next week came directly from the Lord.

The Israelites gathered themselves together for war. In front were the herdsmen soldiers from the east bank of the Jordan. Following them were the priests, blowing loud horns. Then came the Ark of the Covenant on the shoulders of other priests. Then came each tribe of the Israelites, marching in order. No one spoke. No one shouted. The only sound was that of the rams' horns blowing. That day they walked all around the city of Jericho once before marching back to their camp.

For the next six days they did the same thing. Every day they marched once around the city in silence, except for the blaring of the rams' horns, and returned to their camp.

On the seventh day they marched again. But this time they kept on going. Seven times they marched around the city. Then they stopped. The horns stopped. All was quiet.

Suddenly, Joshua's voice rang out: "Shout! The Lord has given you the city!"

A great cry came from all the people at once. They saw the city walls begin to shake and tremble. Piece by piece, the walls crashed down before them. Only one piece of wall still stood: the wall that formed the house of Rahab, who had saved the spies.

"Go get Rahab and her family," Joshua told the two spies. While this was being done, the rest of the soldiers went into Jericho. No one fought them. The city was theirs.

Jericho was a rich city, and now everything in it

belonged to the Israelites. But Joshua ordered everything brought to him.

The gold and silver and brass and iron was given to the priests for the tabernacle. Everything else was gathered up and burned as a sacrifice to the Lord, who had given them the city. Then the city itself was destroyed and burned and cursed forever.

And what happened to Rahab, the woman who had saved the spies? She lived with the Israelites from then on. She married a prince from the tribe of Judah, a man named Salmon. And from their marriage came children who would be the ancestors of David, a great king of the Israelites.

THINK ABOUT IT

✦ *Why did the Ark of the Covenant stop the flow of the Jordan River? (Remember: What did the special chest contain? Where was the chest housed in the tabernacle?)* ✦

STORY 3

The Wedge of Gold

✦ JOSHUA 7:1-8:35 ✦

 emember how Joshua burned all the treasures in Jericho as an offering to God? That was because everything contained in the city of Jericho belonged to God since God had conquered the city for the Israelites.

While the Israelites were taking Jericho, a man named Achan, an Israelite, found a house filled with beautiful things. There was a beautiful piece of clothing that had come all the way from Babylon and a wedge of gold and some silver. When he saw there was no one else around, Achan took these beautiful things and hid them in his tent. But God had seen what Achan had done. Achan had taken these riches for himself when they really belonged to God.

After Jericho was taken, Joshua turned to the little town of Ai on one of the hills above Jericho. The Israelites would have to conquer this town before they moved farther into Canaan. Because Ai was a small place, Joshua only sent 3,000 men to take it. To the Israelites' surprise, the men of Ai fought well and forced the Israelites to retreat. Many Israelites died in the battle.

Joshua and the Israelites were worried. Wasn't God on their side anymore? If they couldn't take a little place like Ai, how could they capture the whole country of Canaan?

Joshua prayed to God, asking what had gone wrong. God told him that one of the Israelites had stolen something promised to Him. Until the treasure was returned and the man punished, there would be a curse on the Israelites. Then God told Joshua exactly how to find out who the man was.

Early the next morning the Lord showed Joshua that Achan was the thief. As punishment, he and his family were killed by the Israelites. This taught everyone an important lesson. If they wanted God to fight on their side, they had to obey Him very carefully.

The next time Joshua sent an army to Ai the Israelites took the city. This time God let them keep everything valuable they found there.

Then the Israelites marched over the mountains to the city of Shechem in the center of Canaan. By now everyone who lived in the country was afraid of the Israelites. No

one even tried to stop them or protect their villages from them. Now that God was with them, the Israelites could not be beaten.

There were two mountains near Shechem with a small valley between them. When the people stood on the sides of the two mountains, it looked a little like a football stadium, with the playing field down in the valley. Joshua gathered all the people together there and they worshiped God. Then he read the laws of Moses to the people, from beginning to end. He did this to remind the people of all that they needed to obey if God were going to stay with them in their new home.

Afterward Joshua and the Israelites marched back to their main camp at Gilgal beside the Jordan River.

THINK ABOUT IT

✛ *The death of Achan and his family may sound very cruel to you. Think for a moment about all God had done for the Israelites. Why was God's punishment of Achan necessary for right now and for the future?* ✛

Joshua Conquers Canaan

✛ JOSHUA 9:1-11:23 ✛

News of the power of the Israelites had spread quickly, even to the mountainous region between the cities of Jerusalem and Shechem. In this region were four cities, and the people who lived there were called the Gibeonites, after the most important of the cities, a place called Gibeon. These people knew they could not defeat the Israelites, so they decided to make peace with them.

The men they sent into the Israelite camp were not honest with Joshua. They only lived a little ways from the camp, but they dressed in old clothes and carried old food with them. They wanted Joshua to think they lived far away and had traveled a long time to see him. Joshua believed them and promised not to destroy their cities or hurt the people in any way.

It didn't take long for Joshua to discover he had been tricked. He had given his protection to people who lived next door to him, not far away. The Israelites might be in danger. But a promise is a promise.

In return for his protection, Joshua made the Gibeonites servants of the Israelites. From then on the Gibeonites would cut wood, carry water, and do the hard work that needed to be done in a camp. This would leave the Israelites free to be soldiers. The Gibeonites agreed. They'd rather work hard than be killed.

The largest city near the camp at Gilgal was Jerusalem.

When the king there heard the Gibeonites had made peace with the Israelites, he contacted several other kings nearby. Remember, there was no one king over the whole area. Several of these kings decided to punish the Gibeonites for serving their enemy, the Israelites.

When the Gibeonites heard an army was marching against them, they rushed to Joshua and asked him for help. They were his servants, and Joshua had to protect them.

Joshua was a good general. He immediately gathered together his army. They marched all night over the mountains. Early in the morning he surprised the five kings. This was a very important battle for the Israelites. Here they could defeat five kings at once. And since all five kings worshiped idols, and not the one true God, it was an important battle for God too. To help the people, God sent a hailstorm down on the kings. The hailstones killed more people than the Israelites' swords. Soon all five armies were running away, with Joshua and his men right behind them. This victory gave the Israelites control of all the southern part of Canaan.

Now Joshua turned his army north and defeated all the kings in that area. Soon all the mountain areas were under Joshua's rule.

In the fight for Canaan there were six great marches and six battles. Three were on the east side of the Jordan, while Moses was still living. The other three were won by Joshua. But it would still be a long time before the Israelites could live in peace in the land God had promised them.

———————

THINK ABOUT IT

✚ *Why did the Gibeonites think they had to trick Joshua? Were they right?* ✚

———————

Caleb and the Giants

✟ JOSHUA 14:1-19:51 ✟

The great wars in Canaan were over. That didn't mean that the Israelites were the only people living there or that they owned all the cities. There were still other people there. But the Israelites had won most of the important cities in the land. They hoped they could all live peacefully in the land together.

One day Caleb and the leaders of the tribe of Judah came to see Joshua. Caleb was one of the two spies who had wanted to go into the land forty-five years before. Although Caleb was eighty-five years old, God had kept him strong and healthy. Now Caleb had a favor to ask of Joshua.

"Remember how Moses promised me I would have my choice of land when the time came?" Caleb said to Joshua.

"Yes," answered Joshua. "And you may take any land you want. Where do you want to live?"

"The city of Hebron," Caleb answered. "I know there are giants living there that I will have to drive out. And the city walls are high. But the Lord will help me."

Now there was plenty of good land Caleb could have chosen. He could have taken a city that was already controlled by the Israelites. He could have chosen rich land near the river. But he chose a city he would have to fight for, even though he was an old man.

"Fine," said Joshua. "Gather together your men and take your city."

And Caleb did just that. He drove the giants out of the

city, and his family lived in Hebron for many years. Remember, Hebron was the city where Abraham, Isaac, and Jacob had been buried hundreds of years ago. Now one of their family again owned the city where these ancient leaders of the Israelites were buried.

After this God told Joshua to divide up the rest of the land among the people. After years of living in the desert the people were finally going to have their own land. Two and one-half of the tribes had already been promised the land on the east of the Jordan River. Another tribe took land in the mountains. Another took land in the south, while others went west and north.

The tribe of Ephraim took land in the middle of the country. There they buried the body of their father, Joseph, that they had carried with them through the desert for many years.

Now all the Israelites had their own land, but they would not live in peace. Nearly all the Canaanites were still there. And in the western part of the land were the Philistines. These were a strong people, and they would cause trouble in the years to come for the Israelites.

Up to now this area had been called Canaan after the Canaanites who lived there. From now on the land would

be known as Israel or the land of the twelve tribes.

✦ *Why did Caleb choose a place he would have to fight for, instead of land that was already conquered? What did you know about Caleb before you read this story? What kind of man is Caleb?* ✦

STORY 6

The Avenger of Blood and the Cities of Refuge

✦ JOSHUA 20:1-21:45 ✦

The people of Israel had many customs and laws that seem unusual to us. They were still a rather wild people and hard to control. Their ideas of wrong and right were not the same as ours, and their tribal customs were different from our family traditions.

One of their customs was that of the *avenger of blood*. Accidents happened in the wilderness. People got angry and killed each other. When that happened, the victim's tribe appointed an avenger of blood to take revenge. This person would find whoever killed their relative and kill him in turn. If he couldn't find the person, he would kill a close relative. This happened whether the first death happened on purpose or by accident. It wasn't a fair system and innocent people often died.

Joshua knew that he couldn't order this to stop. The people hadn't listened to Moses and they wouldn't listen to him. But maybe he could change the custom in such a way to protect innocent people. After the land had been divided up, Joshua chose six cities and made them *cities of refuge*. These cities were spread around the land, so everyone was only one or two days away from one. They were also built on high places, so they could be seen from far away.

If a person accidentally killed another person (or even if he did it on purpose), he would run to the nearest city of refuge. The avenger of blood would chase after him. If he caught the man before he got to the city of refuge, he would kill him. But if the man made it safely to the city, the avenger could not do anything.

The elders of the city of refuge would look into the case and see if the murder was an accident or had been done on purpose. If it had been done on purpose, they sent the killer out of the city, and the avenger of blood usually got him. But if he had not meant to kill anyone, he was allowed to stay there and farm some land especially set aside for innocent people. He would stay there until the high priest of the nation died and was replaced by a new high priest. When that happened, he was free to go home and no one could hurt him. The six cities of refuge were Kedesh, Shechem, Hebron, Golan of Bashan, Ramoth of Gilead, and Bezer.

Now Joshua had to provide for the tribe of Levi, the one of Moses and Aaron. This tribe was a tribe of priests. They cared for the tabernacle and ran all the services there. Joshua didn't want them all living in one place. He wanted them spread across the whole land, so they could help the people keep the laws of God. So he set aside little bits of land all over the country for the tribe of Levi. A Levite would stay on one of these plots of land and farm it for most of the year and then go to the tabernacle and serve as a priest for a certain part of the year.

Joshua set up the tabernacle in Shiloh, near the center of the land. This made it easy for people to come and worship there three times a year: on Passover, the feast of the tabernacles, and the feast of Pentecost. In all the land of Israel this would be the only altar for worshiping God. Now the land God had promised the Israelites had been divided up fairly among them. Their wandering days were over.

THINK ABOUT IT

✚ *Do you think the cities of refuge was a good idea? Do you think such a system would work today? Does the story of the avenger of blood remind you of a problem we still have today?* ✚

STORY 7

An Altar Beside the River

✚ JOSHUA 22:1-24:33 ✚

The first people to leave the camp at Gilgal were those who had left their families on the east side of the Jordan River. They had kept their promise to Moses. They had fought beside all the other

men, even though they already had their own land. Now they could go to their own homes.

When these men came to the Jordan River, they stopped for a while. On the west side of the river, they built a pile of stones. They built it on a high place, so it could be seen from far away.

This made everyone across the river wonder what was going on. Had these men forgotten the law and built their own altar to God? They knew there was to be only one altar in the land. Worse, had they decided to build an altar to another god?

One man from each of the tribes to the west of the river went to talk to the men from the east. If they had broken the laws the men from the east would have to be killed.

"No, we have done nothing wrong," the men said. "This is only to remind our children that those on both sides of the river are all one people and that we all worship the same God. It's a reminder, not an altar." Now that they understood, the men from the west were happy again.

By now Joshua was almost 110 years old. He wanted to give the people some more advice before he died. So he called all the leaders of the tribes to meet him in Shechem. When they were all together, he told them their history again. He went way back to Abraham and Jacob and Moses. He told them every single thing God had done for them over the years. He said that everything they had was a gift from God.

Then he asked the people to make a choice. Would they promise to serve God forever? Or would they listen to the other people nearby and serve other gods?

"We promise to serve our God only," the people said. Joshua wrote that promise down in the book of the law, so it would be remembered forever. Soon Joshua died. As long as there were people alive who remembered the great general who had led the people of Israel into the promised land, the people were faithful to God.

THINK ABOUT IT

✟ *Why would it have been wrong for the men east of the Jordan to build their own altar? Why is a strong leader like Joshua necessary for a people like the Israelites?* ✟

STORY 8

A Present for King Eglon

✟ JUDGES 1:1-3:31 ✟

In time all the men who knew Joshua grew old and died. Soon the people of Israel forgot their own God and began to worship the idols of the Canaanites who lived around them. These little statues were on rocks, under trees, everywhere. The Israelites saw them every day.

Whenever the Israelites worshiped idols, God in His anger would turn His back on the people and let them suffer. A strong people from another country would come in and take away the land from the Israelites, making them slaves. Later a great man would rise up from the Israelites and turn them back to God. Then they would be rich and free again. This went on for over 300 years after the death of Joshua. As long as they worshiped God, everything was fine. But every time they forgot Him, they would be slaves again.

The men who brought the Israelites back to God were called *judges*. They were wise men and strong leaders. They knew how to fight.

The first people to attack the Israelites were from Mesopotamia. They ruled the Israelites for eight years. Then the Lord sent the Israelites a man named Othniel, a brother of Caleb. He led the people to freedom, and the Israelites followed God as long as Othniel lived. He was the first of the judges.

But after Othniel died the people went back to worshiping idols. Then the Moabites came in and took over the land. The king of the Moabites was named Eglon.

When the people cried to God for help, He sent them a judge named Ehud. Ehud went to see King Eglon. "I have a present for the king," he told the guards. "Let me see him." Ehud gave the king a wonderful present, then left. But soon he was back again. "I have a message for the king," he told the guards. "Let me in again." Eglon had been very happy with Ehud's present, so the guards let him in to see the king one more time.

In those days men always wore their swords outside their clothing on the right side of their body. The guards could see that Ehud had no sword hanging at his waist. What they didn't know was that Ehud was left-handed and had a dagger hidden under his clothing!

Ehud drove the dagger deep into the king's body, then left quietly by the back door. By the time the guards decided to go check on the king, Ehud was miles away.

Ehud quickly gathered together an army and drove out the Moabites, who now had no king to lead them in battle. Ehud was the second judge to free the Israelites.

Years later the Philistines attacked the Israelites. Shamgar, the third judge, met them with an army of farmers and drove them back into their own land.

THINK ABOUT IT

✝ *Why did the Israelites keep coming back to their idols? Think about the differences between idols and the one true God. Did idols ever do anything for the Israelites?* ✝

STORY 9

Deborah, Judge of Israel

✝ JUDGES 4:1-5:31 ✝

One of the times that Israel forgot God they were attacked by the Canaanites. The general of the Canaanites was Sisera, and his army was known far and wide for its iron chariots drawn by horses. The Israelites had never seen chariots and horses and they were easy to defeat. Sisera defeated all the tribes that lived in the northern part of Israel and ruled them very harshly.

All in all, Israel had fifteen judges. During this time, Deborah—the only woman judge—was leading a great part of the land. People came from all over to get her advice while she sat under a palm tree north of Jerusalem. No one had appointed her a judge or elected her. She hadn't gone to war to become a judge either. The people did what she said because they knew God was with her.

Deborah knew that the Israelites in the north were suffering under the Canaanites. She sent a message to Barak, a brave man she knew who lived in that region. She told him to gather together an army and attack the Canaanite army to the north.

Barak was a good man, but he did not think he could win this battle alone. So he sent a message back to Deborah. "I will go," he said. "But only if you come with me."

Deborah agreed to go with him. But because Barak did not trust God, she said he would not be given the honor of defeating the Canaanites. The honor would go to a woman.

Deborah and Barak collected 10,000 men for the battle. They camped on the top of Mount Tabor where they could look down on the Canaanite army. The Israelite army looked awfully small.

"Go down and fight," Deborah told Barak. "The Lord will go before you and give you the victory."

Barak and his army rushed down the mountain so fast that the Canaanites didn't have time to hitch up their horses. Without their chariots and horses, the Canaanites were just normal people, and soon the Israelites were chasing them away.

There was a little brook down in the valley. In a dry season you could walk across it, but heavy rains had made the brook deep and dangerous. As the Canaanites ran away they pushed and shoved their way into the brook. Many of them were drowned.

When the Canaanite general, Sisera, saw the battle was

lost, he ran away too. He found a tent standing all by itself in the valley and rushed to it for help. The tent was owned by a man named Heber and his wife, Jael. Heber wasn't home, but Jael was. She knew who Sisera was and motioned him into her tent. Then she hid him under a rug so no one would find him.

What was Jael thinking? Why was she saving the man who had killed and mistreated the Israelites?

Sisera, still hiding under the rug, asked Jael for a drink of water. She brought him milk instead, and soon he fell asleep (milk sometimes makes people sleepy). When he was sound asleep Jael took a hammer and one of those spikes they use to tie down tents. She crept up to Sisera and pounded the stake right through his head.

Soon Barak came by, looking for Sisera. Jael called him in and showed him the body on the floor. Jael would be treated like a hero by the Israelites from then on. As Deborah had predicted, a woman—Jael—had freed her people.

THINK ABOUT IT

✝ *You have now learned about several important women*

<hr>

STORY 10

Gideon and His Brave Three Hundred

✛ JUDGES 6:1-8:28 ✛

Once more the Israelites turned away from God to worship idols. This time the Midianites attacked them. The Midianites were Arabs from the desert to the east. For seven years they fought their way into Israel during every harvest season. They took everything the Israelites grew, leaving them nothing to eat. Then they brought their own flocks of animals in to eat the wild grasses on the Israelites' land. The Israelites' animals had no food to eat.

One day a man named Gideon was hiding some wheat so the Midianites would not find it. Suddenly he saw an angel under an oak tree. "You are a brave man, Gideon," the angel said. "Go set your people free from the Midianites."

Gideon wasn't sure he could do that. But he knew he should worship God, who had sent the angel. So he brought an offering and put it on a rock in front of the angel. The angel touched the offering with his staff and it burned up without Gideon lighting it.

The angel then told Gideon that before he fought the Midianites he first had to stop the people from worshiping idols.

Idols were usually set up on little outdoor altars. One altar was near the house of Gideon's father. That night Gideon took ten men with him and knocked down the idols by his father's house. He broke the statues into little pieces. Then he built an altar to God and used the pieces to light his offering fire.

The next morning the people who worshiped those idols came to Gideon's father. "We are going to kill your son," they said. "He destroyed our god."

"If your god is so strong," Gideon's father said, "he will punish Gideon. You don't have to. See if he does."

Of course the idols had no power over Gideon or anything else. When the people saw that nothing happened to Gideon, they turned back to worshiping the one true God.

Now Gideon gathered a great army together to drive out the Midianites. High on a mountain overlooking the Midianite army, Gideon spoke to God. He asked for a sign from God, for something he could see. He needed to know he was doing what God wanted him to do. Two days in a row God did what Gideon asked. Now Gideon knew he would win the battle to come.

But God spoke to Gideon again. "Your army is too large," God said. "Send home anyone who is afraid to fight." That day, 22,000 men left the army and went home. Now Gideon's army had only 10,000 men.

God said, "The army is still too big. Take them down to the river to drink. I will show you whom to send away." So Gideon did as he was told. As the men drank at the river, Gideon saw they drank in different ways. Most of the men put aside their shield and sword, knelt down by the river, and drank out of two hands. But there were some who kept their weapons with them and just scooped up a little water as they walked by. Out of the 10,000 men only 300 had stayed ready to fight while they drank. Gideon kept the

300 men with him. The rest he sent back to the top of the mountain.

Gideon didn't need a large army for his plan. He gave each man a lamp, a pitcher, and a trumpet. They put the lighted lamps inside the pitchers (so no one could see the lights). Then they quietly surrounded the Midianite camp. In the middle of the night Gideon yelled out, "The sword of the Lord and of Gideon!" All his men shouted at once, broke their pitchers, and let their lamps shine. Then they all blew their trumpets as loudly as they could.

The Midianites woke up, terrified. All around them they saw lights and flashing swords. The air was filled with the sound of trumpets. Thinking there were thousands of men ready to kill them, they ran off to the east, toward the desert.

But Gideon had left almost 10,000 men on the mountain above. They raced down and cut off the fleeing army, killing many. A little farther on there was a river the Midianites had to cross. There another army coming to help Gideon met them and killed their kings. The Midianites never came into Israel again.

Gideon served many years as a judge and was loved by the people. One day they asked Gideon to be their king. "We want you to rule us now as a king. When you die, your son will rule us."

But Gideon refused. "You have a king already," he said. "The Lord God is king of Israel. Only He may rule over you."

THINK ABOUT IT

✛ *Do you think the Israelites have finally learned their lesson about worshiping idols? Why do they want a king?* ✛

Jephthah's Foolish Promise

✦ JUDGES 8:33-11:40 ✦

When Gideon and the three judges after him were dead, the people returned to worshiping idols. This time the Ammonites attacked them.

These people lived to the southeast of Israel. They took over the land of the tribes that lived on the east side of the Jordan River. Finally, a man named Jephthah brought together an army to fight the Ammonites.

Before he went into battle Jephthah made a promise to God. "If you let me beat the Ammonites, whatever comes out of my house first to meet me when I come home will be Yours. I will offer it up as a burned offering to You."

Jephthah lived a long way from the tabernacle. Although he worshiped God, he didn't know God's laws very well. God had made it plain years ago what kind of sacrifices He wanted. Oxen and sheep were the normal sacrifices. God wanted no part of human sacrifices. Those who worshiped idols did that kind of thing, not the people of Israel.

Jephthah won his battle. But when he returned home the first thing to come out of his house was not a lamb or an ox. It was his only child, his daughter!

Jephthah told his daughter about his promise to God. Although she must have been very frightened, she told her father he must keep his promise to God. All she asked was to go into the countryside with her friends for two months

to prepare herself. At the end of that time she came home and Jephthah kept his promise to God: Jephthah's daughter was burned on the altar as a sacrifice.

This was the only time the Israelites had ever offered a living person as a sacrifice to God. If Jephthah had known the laws of God better, such a horrible thing would never have happened.

From these stories we can see how the Israelites lived during the time of the judges, a period of 200 years. No one man ruled over them all. Many families obeyed God's laws the best they could. But others didn't. Some of the tribes lived free. Others lived under the control of other people. Life was dangerous, and people were sometimes foolish. But through it all, God stayed faithful to His people, the children of Israel.

THINK ABOUT IT

✛ *Jephthah's daughter could have run away from her father's promise. Why did she come back to her father? How did she feel about God?* ✛

Samson

After Jephthah three other judges ruled the Israelites. They were not men of war and the people lived peacefully. But then the people turned back to their idols again.

This time the Philistines attacked them. These people lived west of Israel, by the ocean. They were a very strong warlike people and they conquered all of Israel, not just a few tribes.

The tribe of Dan lived next to the Philistines. One day an angel came to a man named Manoah. He told the man that his wife was going to have a son. "He will save Israel from the Philistines," the angel promised. But the boy must be dedicated to God. He could never drink any wine, and his hair could never be cut. This would be the sign that he was under a vow to God.

The baby was named Samson. Samson grew up to become the strongest man in the Bible.

Samson and his family lived very near the Philistines, and Samson fell in love with a Philistine woman.

One day when Samson was walking along the road to visit this young woman, a young lion pounced out of the bushes and jumped on him. Samson was so strong he killed the lion with his bare hands. He left the body by the side of the road.

A short time later Samson took the same road to his marriage feast. On the way he came to the dead lion. He saw that bees had made a nest and the lion's body was full of honey. Reaching down, he scooped up some of the honey and ate it as he walked along.

During the wedding feast everyone started telling riddles. "I'll give you a riddle," Samson said to a group of Philistines. "If you can't answer it, you owe me thirty suits of clothing." The riddle he asked them was this: Out of the eater came forth meat. And out of the strong came forth sweetness. What was the answer to Samson's riddle?

For three days the Philistines worked on the riddle but no one had the answer. The Philistines asked Samson's new wife to find the answer for them. At last Samson told her the story about the lion and the honey. She told the others, and Samson owed them thirty suits of clothing.

Samson paid his bet, but not the way the Philistines thought he would. He went out and killed the first thirty Philistines he saw, then gave their clothing to the others! Samson was so mad at his wife that he went back to his parents' house for a while.

By the time he decided to go back to his wife, her father had married her to another man. This got Samson mad again. He went out and captured all the wild foxes he could find. Then he tied them together by twos. In the middle of the rope tying them together he tied a dry piece of wood. Then he lit the wood and turned the foxes loose in the Philistine fields. The foxes ran everywhere and burned down all the crops.

Because of Samson's act of rage, the Philistines killed Samson's wife and her father. The killing continued until Samson left the area to hide for a while.

The Philistines continued to make life terrible for the rest of the Israelites. When the Israelites complained to Samson, he let them tie him up and turn him over to the Philistines. The Philistines laughed at him when they saw him being turned over by his own people. But they didn't laugh long. As soon as he was near them, Samson broke the ropes holding him. He reached down and picked up the jawbone of a donkey that was nearby. Using the jawbone as a sword, Samson killed over 1,000 Philistines that day alone.

Soon Samson married another Philistine woman named Delilah. The Philistines made her promise to find out what made Samson so strong. Day after day, she pestered him. "If you loved me, you would tell me," she said. Samson would tell her a lie every time.Every time she did what he told her, nothing happened to him. But she kept pestering him so long that he finally told her the truth.

"If my hair is ever cut," he said, "I will no longer be strong."

That night Delilah cut Samson's hair while he slept. The Philistines rushed in and captured him without a struggle. Then they blinded him and kept him tied up. They would bring him in and laugh at him whenever they felt like it. Of course, Samson's hair was beginning to grow again.

One day there was a great Philistine feast. The Philistine temple was filled with people. Over 3,000 more were standing on the roof of the temple, hoping to see Samson.

Samson leaned against a column of the temple. He quietly asked God to give him back his strength just one more time. Then he pushed on two columns with all his strength, pulling the temple down on top of himself and thousands of Philistines.

The people of Samson's tribe found his body and buried him in his own land. Samson wasn't a great judge or tribal leader. All he did to Israel's enemies, he did on his own. Maybe he could have done even more if he had been a great leader. But at the end of his life Samson asked for God's help and God was with him. With God's help Samson saved Israel from its enemies.

THINK ABOUT IT

✛ *What was Samson's biggest weakness, even when he had all his hair? What was his biggest strength, not counting his hair?* ✛

The Idol Temple at Dan

✛ JUDGES 17:1-18:31 ✛

During the time of the judges there was a man named Micah. He and his mother lived in the mountains of Ephraim near the road that ran from north to south.

Micah took 1,100 pieces of silver that belonged to his mother and made himself two idols. He set the idols up in his house and made one of his sons his priest. In a little while a young man from the tribe of Levi passed by Micah's house. The Levites all served part of the year as priests in Shiloh. But when they were not in Shiloh they had to earn their own living. This young man was looking for a job. When Micah offered him a job as his private priest, the

ung man was very happy.

One day five men from the tribe of Dan stopped at Micah's house. They were on their way north, looking for land. The tribe of Dan lived near the Philistines, and some of them wanted to move to a safer place. These five men were looking for a new home for the tribe. They knew the young priest and asked what he was doing in Micah's house, so he showed them the idols and the altar that Micah had set up.

After they left Micah the five men found a small city to the north that would be easy to capture. The land was good and far from the Philistines. When they went back to Dan and told the people about the city, part of the tribe decided to move there. In addition to wives and children and flocks, there were 600 men with shields and swords and spears.

As the little army neared Micah's house, one of the five men told them about the temple and priest in the house. They took the idols away from Micah and convinced the priest to come with them and be their priest. There was nothing Micah could do to stop them.

The people from Dan easily took the little city in the mountains. They rebuilt it and named it Dan, after their tribe. Then they built their own temple for the two idols, and the priest served the idols for many years.

The saddest part of this story concerns the young priest. Instead of serving God as he was supposed to, he was serving idols. This young man was the grandson of Moses!

Because the temple at Dan was much closer to the people in the north than Shiloh, many of them worshiped at it, forgetting about the God who had taken them out of Egypt.

THINK ABOUT IT

✛ *Pretend you are Moses. What would you say to your grandson if you discovered he was worshiping idols? What would you tell him about the history of Israelites, and about the one true God?* ✝

Ruth and Boaz

✝ RUTH 1:1-4:22 ✝

One year when food was scarce in Bethlehem a man named Elimelech took his wife Naomi and two sons and moved to the more bountiful country of Moab. The family stayed there for the next ten years. The two sons married women from Moab. By the end of the ten years Elimelech and his two sons had died in Moab, leaving behind Naomi and his sons' two wives.

Times were better in Bethlehem by now. Naomi decided to go back to her home there. Her two daughters-in-law were not Israelites, so she told them they should go back to their parents and be happy. She would be fine on her own, she said. One of the women did go away, but the other, who was named Ruth, refused to leave Naomi.

"Where you go, I will go," she said. "Your people shall be my people. And your God will be my God."

Nothing Naomi said would make Ruth change her mind, so the two women went together. All Naomi's old friends in Bethlehem were happy to see her again.

Naomi and Ruth were very poor. They had no one to look after them, and they had no land to farm. In those days farmers always left a little of their crops standing in the field while they harvested the rest. Poor people could go into the fields and take this food to feed themselves.

Ruth went into the fields of Boaz, a very rich man, to gather food for herself and Naomi. Boaz saw her there and asked his workers who she was. Boaz was a relative of Naomi's dead husband. He had heard how good Ruth was to her mother-in-law, and he liked her. He quietly told his workers to leave more food in the field than they usually did and to be kind to Ruth.

In a little while Boaz and Ruth were married. This pleased Naomi, because she loved Ruth and wanted her to be happy in her new home. Boaz and Ruth's great-grandson would be David, the great king of Israel.

THINK ABOUT IT

✦ *Naomi must have felt very sad when her husband and two sons died. How did God provide for Naomi? Did God make it easy for her? Explain.* ✦

STORY 15

The Little Boy Promised to God

1 SAMUEL 1:1-3:21

The fourteenth judge of the Israelites was an old man named Eli. He was also the high priest of the tabernacle, so he served God in two ways.

About fifteen miles away from the tabernacle

lived a man named Elkanah. He had two wives, a common practice in those times. One of them had children, but the other, a woman named Hannah, did not. Every year Elkanah and his wives would go to the tabernacle to pray.

One year Hannah prayed to the Lord for a child. "If You give me a son," she told God, "he will serve You all his life." God heard her prayer, and soon she and Elkanah had a baby boy whom they named Samuel.

When Samuel was old enough to leave his mother, Hannah brought him to Eli and told him of her promise to God. From then on Samuel lived with Eli and served God. He would help in the tabernacle and do work for Eli, who was very old by now. Every year Hannah would visit her son and bring him a new linen coat, just like the ones worn by the high priest.

It had been a long time since God had talked to anyone in Israel. Once God had spoken to Moses, Joshua, and Gideon. But there hadn't been a prophet in Israel in a long time.

One night little Samuel heard a voice call his name. He got up from his bed and went to Eli. "Yes, Eli?" he said. "You called me?"

"No," said Eli. "I didn't call you. Go back to bed."

This happened three times that night. Samuel would hear someone call his name, but it wasn't Eli.

After the third time Eli said to Samuel, "If the voice calls you again, say this: Speak, Lord, for Your servant hears You."

Late in the night the voice called Samuel once more. Samuel said the words Eli had taught him, and God gave him a message. "Eli's sons are wicked men. I am going to punish them."

Eli's sons worked with him in the tabernacle. Eli had tried to bring them up right, but he was not strict enough with them and they were not good men.

Samuel didn't want to give this message to Eli. He said nothing the next morning. Finally, Eli said, "You must tell me what the Lord said, Samuel. I need to know." The news from God wasn't good. Eli was sad to hear that his sons were going to be punished by God.

Soon, however, everyone in the country, including Hannah, had heard that God was speaking to Samuel. The people of Israel were happy to have a prophet again, and from that time on Samuel shared God's words with all twelve tribes.

_____

THINK ABOUT IT

✚ *Because God had answered Hannah's prayers, Hannah made a promise to God. We have read of others who also made promises to God. Why is a promise to God very special?* ✚

_____

The Missing Chest

✛ 1 SAMUEL 4:1-7:1 ✛

While Eli was still the judge the Philistines attacked the Israelites again, killing many men. "The Lord was not with us," those who lived said. "Let's take the Ark of the Covenant from the tabernacle with us the next time we fight the Philistines."

So they went to Shiloh and took the special chest out of the Holy of Holies and into their camp. Eli's two sons went with them to care for the Ark of the Covenant, but Eli stayed at home.

God was still not with the Israelites. Not only were thousands of them killed, but the Philistines took the Ark of the Covenant back home with them after the battle.

After the battle a messenger came running to Eli. He told him the sad news that his two sons had been killed in the battle. Then he said that the Philistines had taken the Ark of the Covenant out of Israel. Eli, who was old and feeble, could not bear this news. He dropped to the ground, dead.

The people of Israel were sad that so many of their men had died in the battle, but they were even sadder that their holy chest was gone. Because the Ark of the Covenant was the home of God, this meant God no longer lived among them.

The Philistines took the Ark of the Covenant to their city of Ashdod and set it in the temple of Dagon, their main idol. The next morning they found the statue of Dagon on the floor in front of the holy chest. They stood Dagon back up again, but the next morning, the statue was on the floor again. This time the hands and head of the idol had been cut off too.

When all the people in Ashdod came down with painful boils and sores on their bodies, they moved the Ark of the Covenant to the city of Gath. Everyone there got sick, too, so they sent it to Ekron. The people there would not let the holy chest into the city. "Send it back to Israel," they said, "before we all die."

The Philistines loaded the Ark of the Covenant onto a wagon, hitched two cows to it, and sent them off in the direction of Israel. Although the cows had calves at home to take care of, they walked straight into Israel.

The cows stopped by some fields outside the Israelite town of Bethshemesh, where the people were working in the fields. All the people saw the Ark of the Covenant on the wagon and were very happy. They broke the wagon up for its wood, set a fire, and offered the two cows as a sacrifice to God for bringing their holy chest back to them.

Remember, only priests were allowed to touch the Ark of the Covenant. This was God's law. But some of the men of Bethshemesh disobeyed this law and opened the holy chest to see what was in it. Because they had disobeyed, God sent sickness to the town and many people died there. Those who were left sent the Ark of the Covenant to another town. For twenty years the Ark of the Covenant stayed in the house of a man there. They could not take the chest back to Shiloh because after Eli died everyone left the town and no one ever lived there again.

Think About It

✝ *Why did God allow the Philistines to capture the Ark of the Covenant? How will the Ark of the Covenant find its way back to the tabernacle?* ✝

STORY 17

The Last of the Judges

✙ 1 SAMUEL 7:2-17 ✙

Samuel was still a boy when Eli died and the Ark of the Covenant left Shiloh. All alone now, he went back to his father's house in Ramah. While he was growing up the Philistines ruled Israel.

As soon as Samuel became a man, he began to travel to all the tribes of Israel. He told them all the same thing. If they would stop worshiping idols and turn back to God, God would set them free of the Philistines. When everyone had heard his message—which they knew came from God—they began to worship God again.

Samuel called everyone to a great meeting in a place called Mizpah, not far from Jerusalem. He prayed for the people and asked God to forgive their sins. Then he promised they would serve God faithfully.

The Philistines saw all the people gathered together and thought they were getting ready for war. They sent an army to drive everyone back to their homes.

The Israelites saw the Philistines coming and were frightened. It had been twenty years since their last battle with the Philistines, and they had lost that one. They didn't have any swords or spears with them. They were not trained to fight. The Philistines would kill them all. They begged Samuel to ask God for help.

After Samuel had given a sacrifice to God and prayed for His help, a terrible storm blew over them, with thunder and lightning and huge, dark clouds. This type of storm is not seen very often in the desert country, and the Philistines were afraid. They threw down their weapons and ran from the storm. The men of Israel picked up the Philistines' weapons, chased after them, and won a great battle.

The Philistines stayed away from Israel for many years after that. Samuel ruled over the people as the last of the judges. He was wise and fair, and he kept the people faithful to God. Samuel was not a man of war, and there was peace as long as he served as Israel's judge.

Think About It

✝ *Samuel gave the Israelites two very important things. What were they?* ✝

The First King of Israel

✝ 1 SAMUEL 8:1-10:27 ✝

When Samuel became an old man he made his sons judges in his place and went home to live out his life. But his sons were not fair judges. They would rule in favor of men who bribed them, not in favor of those who were right.

The people were not happy with Samuel's sons. One day they went to Samuel and complained. "We need a king," they said to him. "One who will lead us into battle and keep us strong. But we want you to choose the king for us."

Samuel didn't want to do this. He knew God was the real king of the people. He also felt a little hurt that the people were not happy with his children.

But God told Samuel not to be hurt. If they wanted a king, God said, they could have one. But first Samuel should tell them how having a human king would hurt them.

Samuel called all the leaders of the tribes together and talked to them. He said a king would take away their sons and make them into soldiers. A king would take their daughters and make them servants. He would take away part of their crops and some of their animals. "If you do this," he warned them, "there will come a time you will be sorry. You will call on the Lord for help, and He will not hear you."

But the people would not listen. God wanted the Israelites to be a quiet people, living alone in the mountains and worshiping Him. But they wanted to be a great nation.

123

God told Samuel to do as the people said and find them a king.

A young man named Saul lived in the smallest of all the tribes, the tribe of Benjamin. He was the tallest man anyone had ever seen, and very handsome, but he was just a shepherd in the mountains. One day when he was out looking for some donkeys that had wandered away, he came to Samuel's town of Ramah.

When Samuel and Saul met, God told Samuel that Saul was to be the king of Israel. This was not something Saul wanted. He was happy being a shepherd from a small tribe. After treating Saul like royalty overnight, Samuel poured oil over his head as a sign that Saul was dedicated to God. Then he let Saul go home. But before he left, Samuel told Saul many things that would happen on his trip home. By the time he was home, Samuel said, Saul would be filled with God's spirit. And that is exactly what happened, although Saul didn't tell anyone at home what had happened to him. He still did not want to be a king.

Soon Samuel called all the Israelites together for a meeting to announce the name of the new king. When he called for Saul, no one could find him. He had run away and was hiding! Someone found him and brought him before all the people. Most of the people were very pleased with Samuel's choice. Saul *looked* like a king. But some of them wondered why God had chosen such an unimportant man from a little tribe.

Before the people went home Samuel told them all the rules the king and people had to follow. He wrote them all down in a book and offered the book to the Lord. After 300 years of living under the judges, the people of Israel had a king.

THINK ABOUT IT

✛ *Do you think Saul will be a good king? Why or why not?* ✛

PART 3

The Triple Threat
of Israel:

SAUL, DAVID, AND SOLOMON

Saul and the Men of Jabesh

✣ 1 SAMUEL 11:1-12:25 ✣

Saul was legally the king of Israel, but he didn't change his way of living. He stayed in his old home and worked the same fields he had always worked. He didn't live in a palace or have servants or collect taxes from the people.

One day a messenger came to Saul from the town of Jabesh. The Ammonites on the east of Israel had attacked Jabesh. The people there knew they could not win a battle against the Ammonites, so they made a deal with them. They promised to serve the Ammonites if they would let them live. The Ammonite king agreed on one condition: In a week his soldiers would come into town and take out the right eye of every man in town.

This sounds cruel, but in those days the people of a captured town were usually killed or sold as slaves. Still, the men didn't want to lose their eyes, so they asked Saul for help.

Saul didn't have an army. He didn't even know if the people would come and fight for him. So he took the oxen he was using in the fields, killed them, and cut them into twelve pieces. He sent one piece to each of the twelve tribes, along with this message: "Come to fight with Saul and Samuel, or this will happen to all your oxen."

All the tribes sent their fighting men to Saul and Samuel, who led them into Jabesh and defeated the Ammonites. After the battle Samuel led everyone to Gilgal.

Remember, that was the place the Israelites camped while they were fighting in Canaan. Samuel reminded all the people of the great things God had done for them in the past. He had taken them out of Egypt, given them their own homes, and given them the judges. "You have done wrong to choose a king," Samuel told them. "But as long as you do right and obey the Lord, everything will go well for you. I will always pray for you and teach you the right way," he promised.

Then Samuel went back to his home in Ramah and Saul ruled as king from his home in Gibeah.

THINK ABOUT IT

✛ *Israel really had two rulers in these days, Samuel and Saul. What could Samuel do that Saul needed?* ✛

The Brave Young Prince

✙ 1 SAMUEL 13:1-14:46 ✙

The people had hoped their new king would drive out the Philistines, the warlike people who still controlled part of Israel. But because the Philistines would not let the Israelites work with metal, they had no spears, swords, or shields. Only Saul and his son Jonathan had metal weapons and armor.

Saul gathered together a small army of men. Some of them went with Jonathan and some stayed with Saul. Jonathan was a brave young man. He was not afraid to attack the Philistines, and he won a battle against them. When word of this was heard, the Philistines gathered a great army to attack Saul and Jonathan.

Saul called for more soldiers to meet him at Gilgal, and the people came. But they were frightened, and not really willing to fight. Samuel sent word that Saul could not attack until he had come to sacrifice to God and pray for the people. But it took Samuel a long time to get there. And while Saul waited, the frightened people began to sneak away from his camp. His army was getting smaller and smaller. Finally Saul was afraid to wait any longer. He offered his own sacrifice and prayed to God himself, even though he was not a priest.

While the fire was still burning, Samuel arrived. "What have you done?" Samuel cried. "If you had obeyed God, He would have kept you safe. Now God must find another man to rule this nation, someone who will obey Him."

Samuel walked away from Saul and left the camp.

Despite his disobedience, Saul and his son Jonathan won a great victory over the Philistines. While they were chasing the Philistines away, Saul gave an order to all his army. No one was to stop and eat until the day was over. They had to run and fight without food until the Philistines were all dead. Anyone who did not obey would be killed.

Saul did this so his soldiers would not stop to take the food and property of the Philistines. But the battle would have been over earlier if his men had eaten and kept up their strength. Jonathan had been in the middle of a battle and had not heard Saul's order. As he was chasing the Philistines, he stopped to eat some honey. After the battle Saul heard that his son had disobeyed him. "I made an oath," Saul said. "You must die."

But the people would not let Saul kill his own son. "He has won a great victory," they said. "You will not hurt even one hair on his head." They let Jonathan go free.

The Philistines stayed away from Israel for a long time after this battle. But the Israelites were beginning to wonder if Saul was the right man to be their king.

THINK ABOUT IT

✝ *Why were the Israelites beginning to question the choice of Saul? How do you think Samuel felt about Saul?* ✝

Saul's Great Sin and Loss

✝ 1 SAMUEL 15:1-35 ✝

Many years ago as the Israelites had just come out of Egypt a wild people of the desert, the Amalekites, had attacked them. Now Samuel sent Saul and his army after these people. God said that Saul should kill every one of these people. He was not to save anything, even their animals.

Saul went and defeated these people. But he did not kill them all, and he brought back the best of their animals. God said to Samuel, "Saul does not obey My commands. He should not have been made the king."

Samuel went to meet Saul on his way home. He saw

many prisoners and large flocks of animals. "Why didn't you kill them all, as God said?" he asked Saul.

"The people wanted to bring them back," Saul said. "They wanted to use them as sacrifices to God."

"God would rather have you obey His orders than offer Him sacrifices," Samuel told Saul. "Now He will take away your kingdom from you."

Samuel went back to his home and never saw Saul again.

THINK ABOUT IT

✝ *Why do you think Saul followed the soldiers' wishes and not God's orders?* ✝

STORY 4

The Shepherd Boy of Bethlehem

✝ 1 SAMUEL 16:1-23 ✝

S aul served as king for many more years. God was not happy with him, but He waited until the right man came along and was trained before He took away the kingdom. All this time Samuel cried over Saul whom he had loved like a son.

One day the Lord told Samuel to stop crying for Saul. "He is no longer king in My sight," God said. Then God told Samuel to go to Bethlehem and find a man named Jesse.

One of Jesse's sons would be the next king.

Samuel told everyone he was going to sacrifice and pray with the people near Bethlehem. He didn't want Saul to know he was going to find the new king. Samuel looked at each of Jesse's sons very carefully, but God did not choose any of them. "Do you have any more sons?" he asked Jesse.

"There is a boy in the field caring for the sheep," Jesse said.

When the boy, whose name was David, was brought to Samuel, the Lord told him he would be the new king. But David was only fifteen years old! The Lord told Samuel to pour oil over the boy's head. This action meant David would serve God as perhaps a great prophet or warrior. Only Samuel knew David would grow up to be king, and he told no one.

As he grew, David began to show signs of greatness. He fought lions and bears that attacked his sheep. He learned to throw stones with a sling. And while he was alone in the fields, he learned to play the harp and make beautiful music. The spirit of God was with him.

God's spirit was leaving Saul. Saul became very sad and he began to do strange things that made people think he was crazy. The only thing that made him happy was music.

One day someone told Saul about David and his music. David was brought to Saul and played his music for him. Saul felt so happy that he gave David a job so he could stay with him. David became Saul's armor-bearer. When Saul went into battle, David would go with him and carry his sword and shield until they were needed.

After a while Saul seemed to be better and David went back to his home in Bethlehem.

THINK ABOUT IT

✛ *Why didn't God let David act as the king right away?* ✛

David's Magnificent Fight

✝ 1 SAMUEL 17:1-54 ✝

Saul fought the Philistines all the time he was king. He could never chase them out of the land because they were so strong.

For days one particular Philistine, a giant of a man, had been going out of the enemy camp and yelling at the Israelites. His name was Goliath, and he was *nine feet tall*. He wore armor from head to foot and carried a spear so heavy that no one else could even pick it up. Every day he would call for one of the Israelites to come and fight him. But even Saul, who was a powerful man, knew he couldn't beat this giant.

Among Saul's soldiers were David's three older brothers. One day Jesse sent David with a message for his brothers. David had to travel amid the fighting into the camp of Saul's army.

When David heard the giant talking this way to God's army, he said *he* would go out and meet him! Saul had not seen David in years and did not know him. To Saul, David looked like a little shepherd boy. "You cannot beat this giant," Saul told David.

"The Lord helps me kill lions and bears," David said to the king. "He will help me kill this man too."

David had faith in God. He also had a plan. He walked toward Saul, carrying his shepherd's staff. When Goliath saw this boy coming toward him with a piece of wood in his hand, he laughed at him.

"You come at me with a sword and spear," David called to Goliath. "But I come with God. He can save in many ways."

David did not come too close to Goliath. He stayed out of range of his huge spear and sword. When he was just the right distance away, David reached under his clothes and pulled out five smooth stones and his sling. He hurled a stone as hard as he could, and guess what? The stone hit Goliath right between the eyes and knocked him out cold! Then David rushed up, took Goliath's own sword, and cut off the giant's head.

When the Philistines saw their giant was dead, they turned and ran. The army of the Israelites chased them, killing thousands. David had saved the Israelites from their enemies with one little stone.

THINK ABOUT IT

✚ *David was a brave young man. What else would you say he was?* ✚

Looking for Arrows

✝ 1 SAMUEL 17:55-20:42 ✝

After Goliath was dead Saul made David an officer in his army and took him home with him. David was intelligent and handsome and everyone loved him. Soon he was in charge of 1,000 men.

But Saul was jealous of David. Everyone made such a fuss over him. Could he be the one who would take the kingdom away from him? Saul knew he could not kill David himself or everyone would hate him. But he *could* have him killed by the Philistines.

Saul promised David that he could marry his daughter Michal after he had killed 100 Philistines. It was a great honor to marry a king's daughter, and David liked Michal. David didn't stop at 100: He killed 200 Philistines, and then he married Michal.

Jealous and troubled, Saul still liked to have David play music for him to calm him down. Sometimes it worked. Sometimes it didn't. Many times Saul was so upset he would pick up his spear and throw it at David while he was singing! But David was careful and always jumped aside in time.

One night Saul sent his soldiers to bring David to him. Michal knew her father meant to kill David. She let him out the back window and told him to run away and save himself. David went to Samuel and stayed with him until Saul calmed down again.

While he was hiding from Saul, David met Saul's son Jonathan, the brave warrior we read about earlier. David and Jonathan were good friends. Jonathan told David to stay away from Saul for a little while. "I will come back in three days," he said to David. "I will shoot three arrows and send a boy after them. If I tell him the arrows are near him, it is safe for you to come back. If I say the arrows are far away from the boy, you cannot come back yet."

While they were together the two young men promised to be friends forever and to never hurt each other or the other's children.

At the end of the second day, Saul was still mad at David. He wanted him brought back so he could kill him. Jonathan and the boy went out to David's hiding place and Jonathan gave the signal. David could not come back. When Jonathan sent the boy away, David came out of hiding. The two young men said goodbye and went their separate ways.

THINK ABOUT IT

✚ *Why did Saul treat David so badly? Did David ever do anything to harm Saul?* ✚

David Finds
the Giant's Sword

✟ 1 SAMUEL 21:1-22:23 ✟

D avid left the area so quickly that he didn't pack any food or weapons. On his way he stopped at Nob to find some food. The tabernacle and its priests were there at this time, but the holy Ark of the Covenant was somewhere else.

David went to the chief priest and told him a lie. He said Saul had sent him on a secret mission. He had to leave so soon that he didn't have time to pack food or weapons. Did the priests have something he could eat and perhaps a spear or a sword?

The chief priest gave David the holy bread, which was to be eaten only by the priests, and then showed him Goliath's sword, which was stored there. David took the

bread and sword and thanked the priests for their help.

David first tried to hide in the land of the Philistines, but they knew him and chased him out. Then he went to live in the wilderness, in a large cave he found there. Soon men from his tribe began to join him, and in time he had a little army of 400 men.

Saul was looking all over for David. He was sure David was planning to attack him and take away the kingdom. "Can't any of you find him?" he asked his men one day. One of the men stepped forward and said he had seen David taking food and a sword from the priests at Nob.

Saul had all the priests brought to him. "Why did you help my enemy?" he asked them.

The head priest came forward. "We did not know he had done anything wrong," he told Saul. "He said he was working for you, so we gave him what he needed."

The king ordered his guards to kill all the priests, but they refused. It would be a great sin to kill God's priests. Then Saul looked at the man who had told him about the priests. "You are the only faithful man I have. You kill them," he said.

This man obeyed the king, and then went to the city of Nob and burned the city down.

Only one priest lived, a young man who saved the high priest's clothing. He found David in the wilderness and gave him the bad news. "I should have been more careful," David said. "This is my fault. Stay here with us and be the high priest."

Everyone in the kingdom heard that Saul had killed the priests and that the new high priest was now living with David. They began hoping that David would defeat Saul and become their king.

THINK ABOUT IT

✦ *Why did the priests help David? (Think about what it means to be God's priest.)* ✦

David Spares Saul's Life

✛ 1 SAMUEL 23:1-27:12 ✛

Saul kept on searching for David, trying to kill him. One day David and his men were hiding way back in a large cave. Saul walked into the front of the cave, looked around, and lay down for a nap.

In the back of the cave the men told David, "Go kill him! God has given him to you."

"No," David whispered. "God has anointed him king. I will not kill him."

Instead, David quietly sneaked up to Saul and cut off a piece of his long robe. When Saul awoke and left the cave, David followed him for a little while. Then he called out, "My lord and king!"

Saul looked around and saw David bowing down to him.

"Why are you trying to kill me?" David asked the king. "Look at this." He held up the piece of cloth from Saul's robe. "I could have killed you today, but I didn't."

Saul's eyes filled with tears. "You are a better man than I, David. I know it is God's will that you be king. When you are, promise me you will not hurt my family."

David made that promise and Saul went back to his home.

But soon Saul began to hunt David again. One night while Saul's army slept, David and one of his men walked quietly through the camp. They found Saul asleep, his spear and water bottle by his head. David would not let the king be harmed, but he did take the spear and water bottle when they left.

David's men could not understand why David never killed the king when he could. "He was anointed king by God," David told them. "Let the Lord kill him. Or let him die in battle. Or let him die of old age. I will not kill him."

The next morning David called out to Saul again and showed him the spear and water bottle he had taken. "Send someone up to bring these back to you," he said. "I spared your life today. May God spare mine."

By now David had a good-sized army, but he needed a place to live where Saul couldn't get him. David made a deal with one of the Philistine kings and lived in a little city they gave him. He would be safe there for as long as Saul lived.

THINK ABOUT IT

+ *Why did David refuse to kill the king? (Who had appointed Saul as king?)* +

The Last Days of King Saul

✛ 1 SAMUEL 28:1-31:13 ✛

The next time the Philistines attacked the Israelites, their king told David he had to fight on their side. He was living with the Philistines, after all. David and his 600 men went and joined the army. But other Philistines did not trust David. "He will turn on us and fight for his own people," they said. They sent David and his men back to their own town. But when they got home a terrible surprise awaited them. The wild men from the desert had attacked while David was gone and had taken everything and burned the city. All their wives and children had been taken away as slaves. Even David's two wives were gone.

David chased after the men from the desert and caught them. Some of them escaped into the desert on camels, but the rest he killed. Then he took back everything that was his, and all that had been stolen from other cities. He divided all this up among his own men. Now David was a rich man.

Meanwhile, Saul was about to be attacked by the Philistine army. Samuel was dead. David was gone. And Saul knew that God was not with him anymore. He needed some help.

In desperation, Saul went to a woman—a witch—who said she could talk to dead men. He asked to speak to the spirit of Samuel, and God allowed Samuel's spirit to speak to Saul.

"Why are you bothering me?" Samuel's spirit asked Saul.

"I need help," Saul answered. "Tell me what to do."

"You did not obey God. Tomorrow you and your three sons will die," Samuel's spirit told Saul.

The next day the Philistines attacked the Israelites' camp when they were not ready to fight. Many were killed, including Saul's son Jonathan, David's friend. When Saul saw the battle was lost and his sons were dead, he killed himself with his own sword.

Saul had been king for forty years. During that entire period he had fought the Philistines. David could have helped him, but Saul in his jealousy had chased him away. Samuel could have helped him, but Saul would not obey God. After Saul's death the Philistines took over the land of Israel.

THINK ABOUT IT

✛ *God does not want us to become involved with witchcraft (the practice of witches). Why do you think God let Samuel's spirit talk to Saul?* ✛

David Becomes King

✛ 2 SAMUEL 1:1-4:12 ✛

T hree days after the battle a man ran into David's town. "King Saul and his son Jonathan are dead!" he told David.

"How do you know that?" David asked him.

"I saw him wounded and went to him," the man said. "He was going to die. He asked me to kill him, and I did." Then the man showed David Saul's crown and bracelet.

"What tribe are you from?" David asked.

"I am not an Israelite. I am an Amalekite," the man answered.

Now we know that Saul killed himself. This man was lying to David. He probably came down after the battle and stole Saul's crown and bracelet, hoping for a reward from David. But he said *he* had killed Saul.

"You have killed God's anointed king," David told the man. Because the man had either killed the king or stolen from his dead body, David ordered him killed.

Now that Saul was dead, David and his men could go back to Israel. God told David to go to the town of Hebron, where his tribe lived. They made him their king, and he served there for the next seven years.

But there was another king in Israel: One of Saul's sons was ruling over all the people in the north. He was a weak king, but Saul's uncle helped him and protected him. Saul's son ruled there for the next six years.

After that two of David's men killed this king while he slept one night. They came to David for a reward. But David remembered his promise to Saul. He had said he would not hurt any of Saul's family, and now that promise had been broken. "Take these two men away and kill them," David ordered.

THINK ABOUT IT

✝ *Two times men came to David for a reward when they killed his enemies. Instead of a reward, David had them killed. Was David a vicious man or was he following God?* ✝

The Sound in the Treetops

✝ 2 SAMUEL 5:1-7:29 ✝

Now that Saul and Saul's son were dead, the rulers of the twelve tribes came to David. They wanted David to be king over all the land. David was thirty-seven years old; he would be king of Israel for the next thirty-three years.

Israel was in sad shape when David became king. The Philistines controlled large parts of it. The Canaanites controlled other parts, including the city of Jerusalem, a bustling city surrounded by walls. David knew he had to take Jerusalem from the Canaanites if he were going to rule the land.

The Canaanites laughed at the Israelites. "You cannot take this city," they said. Then they put all their blind and crippled people up on top of the wall. "Even our blind and crippled can protect this city from you!"

David became angry. "The first man to climb to the top of this wall and kill those people will be my general," he told everyone. Everyone climbed up the wall as fast as they could to win this honor. The first to get there was a man named Joab. He was the son of David's sister. As long as David lived, Joab was the general of his army.

David captured Jerusalem and made it his home. Under David, Jerusalem became even stronger than before. People came from all around to live there, and it became the biggest city in the country.

When the Philistines heard Israel had a new king, they attacked Jerusalem. Two times David defeated them. Once God gave David the signal to attack by sending a sound in the trees above him. He drove the Philistines back into their own land and destroyed their main city. Then David went on and captured all the land the Philistines had owned. For the first time in 100 years, the Israelites had nothing to fear from the Philistines.

Now that the land was free, David wanted the Ark of the Covenant back. He built a big tabernacle in Jerusalem, then went to get the holy chest from its hiding place. The men who had been taking care of the Ark of the Covenant all this time put it on a wagon and walked beside it. But they were not priests. One time the wagon hit a bump and the chest almost fell off. A man named Uzzah reached out his hand to steady the holy chest and touched it. As soon as he did, God killed him.

This frightened David and the people. He was afraid to bring the Ark of the Covenant into Jerusalem because it might harm the people. For the next three months the Ark of the Covenant remained in the home of a nearby family. Instead of harming the family, the holy chest brought them great blessings.

At the end of that time David sent priests to get the chest. This was the way it should have been done the first time. The priests put the Ark of the Covenant in the tabernacle David had made for it, and everything was fine. The daily services began again, after many years, and the people were happy to have God living with them again.

David was now living in a great palace in Jerusalem and he thought the Ark of the Covenant should be in a great temple instead of a tent. But to be sure, he asked a man named Nathan, who was God's prophet.

God told Nathan to give David a message. "I took you from your sheep and gave you great power," the Lord said to David. "Because you have done My will, your son will follow you as king. He shall be the one to build me a house and a temple. I will give you and all those who follow a kingdom that will last forever."

This was good news for David and for us. For Jesus Christ would come from David's family, and He will rule the world forever.

THINK ABOUT IT

+ *Why did God kill the man who touched the Ark of the Covenant? Why wouldn't God let David build the temple?* +

STORY 12

The Promise to a Friend

+ 2 SAMUEL 8:1-9:13 +

D avid had to fight many battles after he took over as Israel's king. He defeated the Moabites, the Syrians, and the Edomites. After these victories Israel's land went from the desert to the ocean, from the Euphrates River down to the wilderness on the south.

When he finally was at peace, David remembered his promise to his friend Jonathan, Saul's son. He asked the people around him if they knew any relatives of Saul who were still living. They told him one of Saul's servants was still taking care of Saul's farmland. The man was named Ziba. He had become a rich man taking care of the land Saul owned.

David said to Ziba, "Are any of Saul's family still alive? I want to show them some of the kindness that God has shown me."

"Saul's son Jonathan had a son. He is still living east of the Jordan," Ziba told David.

Jonathan's son had been a little baby when Jonathan was killed. His nurse had taken him and run away to hide from the Philistines. As she ran she fell, and the baby's feet were hurt so badly that he became crippled. As a man he was unable to walk properly.

In those days kings often killed every person in the family of the king before them so no one would try to take their throne away. Maybe that is why Jonathan's son— whose name was Mephibosheth— lived so far away from Jerusalem. When he was called to David's palace, the crippled man was afraid he was about to be killed.

"Don't be afraid," David told Mephibosheth. "I loved your father, and he loved me. All Saul's lands are yours now, but you will live here with me in the palace."

Then David called Ziba, Saul's servant, in to him. "You take care of the land as before," he said. "But the harvest belongs to Jonathan's son now. You will serve him."

So the lame man was taken into the palace and treated with honor. And Ziba, with his fifteen sons and twenty servants, now served Saul's grandson.

THINK ABOUT IT

✛ *Was David taking a chance when he treated Saul's grandson so well?* ✛

The Story of a Little Lamb

+ 2 SAMUEL 11:1-25; PSALM 51 +

One time when David's army was out fighting the Ammonites David took a walk on the roof of his palace. As he gazed down into a garden below he saw a beautiful woman. When David asked a servant who she was he discovered her name was Bathsheba. She was the wife of one of David's soldiers, a man named Uriah.

David had many wives and children, but Bathsheba was Uriah's only wife. She was so beautiful that David fell in love with her. But he could not marry her because of Uriah.

David sent a message to his general, Joab. "See that Uriah is put in the middle of a fight and killed," it said. Joab did as he was told, and Uriah was killed in the next battle.

When her time of crying for her husband was over, Bathsheba was brought into David's home and later she married David. Soon they had a little son whom David loved very much.

No one but Joab knew what David had done. But God knew, and He sent the prophet Nathan to David with a message. Nathan told David a little story.

"Once there was a very rich man with lots of animals. Near him lived a poor man with only one little lamb. He loved that lamb very much and took good care of it. One day company came to eat with the rich man. Instead of

taking one of his many sheep and killing it for dinner, the rich man took the poor man's only lamb and ate it."

David was frowning. "That man deserves to die! He must give the poor man four times the worth of that lamb. You can't treat a poor man that way."

Nathan looked at David. "You are that man. You took a man's life and his wife, when you already had plenty. You will be punished for this. You will suffer, and your wives will suffer."

Then David saw how bad he had been to Uriah and begged the Lord's forgiveness.

"You are forgiven," Nathan told him. "But the baby you love so much will surely die."

Soon after, David and Bathsheba's baby became very ill. David prayed day after day for the baby's life. David stopped eating and sleeping. Day and night, he lay on the floor and prayed. But God does not change His mind, like people do. David's little baby died.

Later God would give David and Bathsheba another son. They would name him Solomon. The Lord loved Solomon, and he grew up to be a very wise man.

✦ *Why did God send Nathan to David? What might be one reason God had Nathan tell a story to David instead of telling David how bad he had been?* ✦

STORY 14

David's Handsome Son

✦ 2 SAMUEL 13:1-17:23 ✦

The prophet Nathan warned David that bad things would happen to him and his family, and they did.

David had many sons and many wives. One of his favorite sons was named Absalom. He was a very handsome man. He looked like a king should look. But he was not a good man. Once he killed one of David's other sons, and David sent him away. But when he came back later, David loved him so much he let Absalom back into his palace.

Absalom wanted to be king in place of his father. He was very sneaky about it, though. He did favors for everyone he met and treated everyone nicely. He would promise people anything they wanted. As time went by, more and more people loved Absalom. At the end of four years Absalom asked David if he could go to Hebron to worship God.

David was pleased to see his son loved the Lord. It may seem strange, but David had no idea what this man—his son—was trying to do. After all, David stayed in his palace all day. He wasn't out leading his army or talking to people as a judge. David didn't know how the people in his kingdom felt about anything.

Soon afterward word came from Hebron. Absalom had made himself the new king! David heard that many of the rulers were with Absalom, and the people wanted him as king. He didn't know whom he could trust at the palace, so he decided to escape while he could. He took a few of his servants, his wives, and his children and left Jerusalem.

David met many people as he left the city. Some of them gave him food and animals; others stayed in the city to spy for him. There were others, however, who lied to David and meant him harm. One of the trustworthy men was a guard who commanded 600 men. They were not from Israel, but they stayed faithful to David and went with him into the hills. The priests of the tabernacle loved David and said they would help him too.

As soon as David was out of Jerusalem, Absalom and all his followers took over the palace. Then Absalom made a mistake. Instead of chasing David and defeating him while he was weak, Absalom waited. He would stay there until his own army was stronger and bigger, and then he would kill his father. But many of the people in the land still loved David. While Absalom waited, David's army grew bigger and bigger.

THINK ABOUT IT

✛ *What did Absalom do to make the people love him? What did David do wrong?* ✛

Absalom in the Woods

✦ 2 SAMUEL 17:24-20:26 ✦

The people living east of the Jordan River were good to King David. They fed him and gave him a place to stay while all his friends came and joined him. Soon David had a large army around him.

When David was ready to fight Absalom, he stood by the city gate and watched his army march out. To every commander that passed him, he said, "Please, do not kill Absalom."

David's army won a great victory that day. Absalom was forced to run away from the battlefield on a donkey. As he rode through a deep wood, his long hair caught in the branches of an oak tree. The donkey kept on running, leaving Absalom hanging from the tree branches by his hair.

Joab, David's general, was told about Absalom's problem. He rushed into the woods and killed the young man, then had him buried deep in the woods. This was against David's orders, but perhaps it was the right thing to do. If he had lived, Absalom would have been a problem again. Joab thought he did the right thing by killing the king's son.

When David heard that his son was dead, he cried for days. His army came back but no one treated them like the heroes they were. David never came to say how proud he was of them or how thankful he was for their help. Everyone was sad and confused.

Finally, Joab went to talk to David. "You must stop this," he said to his king. "Everyone thinks you would be happier if we had all died, instead of Absalom. Act like a man! Treat those who fought for you with the respect they deserve. If you don't, no one will ever follow you again."

David knew Joab was right. He got up, washed his face, and went out to meet everyone coming to take him back to Jerusalem. When he was home he forgave everyone who had rebelled against him. But he was still angry with Joab for killing his son. Joab was a strong man, and David never felt he controlled him. But Joab was a faithful soldier and a good general, even though he was not a good man. Because of Joab, David's last years as king were ones of peace.

_____

THINK ABOUT IT

✦ *Was Joab right to kill Absalom? Was he right when he told David he was not behaving properly toward his army?* ✦

_____

The Angel with the Sword

✝ 2 SAMUEL 24:1-25; 1 CHRONICLES 21:1-27 ✝

Many years after Absalom's death David did something that God did not want done. He told his general, Joab, to count the number of men in the country who could go to war.

Joab did not want to do this. He knew God had not ordered it done and it would be a sin. But he did as he was ordered. Ten of the tribes had a total of 800,000 men. The tribe of Judah had almost 500,000 men.

Before the tribe of Benjamin could be counted, God sent a prophet to David. His name was Gad. Gad told David he had sinned and the people would suffer for it. He had his choice of punishments: God could send seven years of famine with no harvest; God would let David's enemies rule over them for three months; or there could be three days of illness that would kill many people.

David chose the three days of illness. He did not want other men to punish him because they were not as merciful as God would be.

The Lord's angel of death passed over the land. In three days 70,000 men died. When the angel of the Lord stretched his hand out over Jerusalem, God had pity on the people. "That's enough," He said. "Don't kill any more people."

Then the Lord let David see the angel of death standing on top of a mountain outside the city, his sword in his hand. "Lord," David cried, "I have sinned. These people have not. Punish me, not them."

Gad was sent to talk to David again. "Go build an altar where you saw the angel," he told David. So David and his men walked up to the top of the mountain. There they found a man threshing wheat on a huge rock with his oxen. When David asked to buy the place for an altar, the man offered it for nothing. He would even let David kill his oxen for the sacrifice. But a sacrifice is no good if it costs you nothing. David paid the man a fair price for the land, built his altar, and prayed to God. God heard his prayers and stopped the punishment of the people.

Think About It

✚ *We don't know why it was a sin to count the people. Can you think of any reasons it might be?* ✚

STORY 17

Solomon Is King

✚ 1 KINGS 1:1-53 ✚

When David grew old he began to collect wood and gold and silver to be used for building God's temple. God would not let David do the building because David was a man of war. But David's son Solomon would be a king of peace, and God had promised David that Solomon would build the temple. So while he lived, David stored up all that Solomon would need.

Solomon had older brothers who wanted to be king too. One of them made plans to have himself crowned king before David's death. When David heard of this, he decided to crown Solomon king right away. Solomon's head was anointed with oil. The priests blew their horns in celebration. From his bed David sent his blessing to the new king.

The brother who had tried to crown himself king ran to the tabernacle to pray and hide. But Solomon forgave him and those who had followed him, and he returned to the palace peacefully.

Soon David died. He was an old man, and he had been king of Israel for thirty-three years. He was buried on Mount Zion.

THINK ABOUT IT

✟ *Why should a king of peace build God's temple? Think of the many ways God blessed David during his lifetime (make a list).* ✟

The Wise Young King

✦ 1 KINGS 3:1-4:34; 2 CHRONICLES 1:1-13 ✦

When Solomon was crowned king he was only about twenty years old, and he had a large land to rule. That is a large responsibility for someone so young. Besides the land of Israel, Solomon ruled over all the other lands around. But he was a king of peace, and there were no wars while Solomon ruled.

Soon after he became king Solomon went to the tabernacle to pray to God. That night God came to him in a dream. "Ask for anything you want," God told the young king.

"Lord," Solomon said, "You were kind to my father, and now I am king. But I'm too young to rule all these people. I don't know enough. Please give me wisdom so I will rule them right."

God was very pleased with Solomon's request. He had not asked for riches or power or a long life for himself. He had thought of his people first. God told Solomon, "You will be wiser than any king before or after you. And I will give you riches and long life too."

Soon after Solomon had to make a hard choice. Two women came to him and asked him to judge between them. They had each had a baby. One night one of the babies had died, while the other lived. Now both women said the living baby was theirs. It was up to Solomon to decide which baby belonged to which mother.

"Bring me a sword," Solomon told his men. Then he told them, "Cut the living baby in half and give one-half to each of the women."

One of the women agreed to this. But the other cried, "No! Let her have the baby. Don't kill it."

"Give the baby to the one who would not let you kill it," Solomon said. "She is certainly the mother."

When all the people heard of this, they knew they had a very wise king.

THINK ABOUT IT

✛ *How did Solomon know which woman was the mother of the living baby?* ✛

STORY 19

The House of God

✛ 1 KINGS 5:1-9:9; 2 CHRONICLES 3:1-7:22 ✛

Solomon's great work was building the temple of God. David had collected a lot of the materials that would be needed. Cedar wood had been brought from Lebanon for the roof. Stone for the walls had been cut and the pieces trimmed to fit in the stoneyard. When it came time to build the temple, all the pieces fit together perfectly. The temple was built without the sounds of chopping and chiseling.

The temple was built very much like the tent tabernacle. It had courts and inner rooms, and the Holy of

Holies, where the Ark of the Covenant would stand. But the temple was made of stone and wood.

Solomon spent seven years building the house of God. A great service was held to dedicate the temple, with many offerings. The Ark of the Covenant was placed in the Holy of Holies. Then Solomon himself prayed that the Lord would make the temple holy.

After this the Lord came to Solomon in a dream. "I have heard your prayers," He said. "I will live in the temple. And if you obey Me, as your father did, your family will rule forever. But if you turn from Me, I will leave the temple. Then your enemies will come and destroy this house you built for Me."

THINK ABOUT IT

✝ *God promised to live in Solomon's temple, as He had lived in the tabernacle. Do you think Solomon will remain faithful to God?* ✝

The Last Days of Solomon

✝ 1 KINGS 10:1-11:43 ✝

While Solomon was king, Israel was a great nation. Solomon was very wise and knew about many things. He wrote many of the sayings in the Old Testament book of Proverbs, and he wrote more than a thousand songs. He knew about trees and animals, and things other people knew nothing about.

People came from all over the world to visit Solomon and talk to him. One of these visitors was the Queen of Sheba. Her land was 1,000 miles away from Israel. She had heard of this wise king and wanted to see him herself. When she came, she brought Solomon rare and expensive presents. They talked for a long time, and then she knew Solomon was as wise as she had heard.

All that Solomon built in and around Jerusalem cost a lot of money. Although he was a rich man, he still needed to tax the people to help pay for everything he made. And he needed workers to do his building and care for all his belongings. Soon the people began to complain.

Solomon had many wives. Some of them were not Israelites and worshiped idols. To please them, he built a temple for their idols. He even went there and worshiped the idols himself.

This made God angry with Solomon. For David's sake, God said Solomon's son would rule over one of the tribes of Israel. But the rest of the country would be ruled by one of Solomon's servants because Solomon had disobeyed God.

The servant who would rule over Solomon's kingdom was named Jeroboam. Solomon tried to have Jeroboam killed, but he escaped into Egypt and stayed there until Solomon died.

Solomon was king for forty years. When he died he was buried on Mount Zion. His son Rehoboam became the new king.

THINK ABOUT IT

✠ *How did Solomon anger God? What would his punishment be? Why was this punishment so terrible?* ✠

PART 4

Elijah, Elisha, and Others:

ADVENTURES IN THE KINGDOM OF ISRAEL

A Great Kingdom Is Divided

✠ 1 KINGS 12:1-24; 2 CHRONICLES 10:1-19 ✠

When Solomon died the people rose up against his son Rehoboam. They complained about the high taxes and heavy work they had to do for the king. Their leader was Jeroboam.

The people told Rehoboam he could be their king if he lightened the burdens his father had put on them. The wise men in Rehoboam's palace agreed with the people. But when Rehoboam asked the young princes around him the same question, he got a very different answer. These were spoiled men who were used to living off the work of others. They said Rehoboam should work the people even harder.

When Rehoboam told the people he was going to work them even harder than his father had, the people refused to make him their king. Ten of the twelve tribes broke away and made Jeroboam their king. These ten tribes were from the northern part of the country. Their new kingdom was called the kingdom of Israel.

Rehoboam was king of the land in the south. His kingdom was called the kingdom of Judah. When the other nations nearby saw this happen, they broke away from the rule of Rehoboam too. The Syrians, Ammonites, Moabites, and Edomites all set up their own kings. David had captured all these lands years ago. Now they were lost.

Rehoboam began to gather an army to fight the ten tribes that left him, but God told him to leave them alone. God did not want the Israelites to be a strong, rich people, worrying about earthly things. He wanted them to worship Him and live the way He had described in the laws given to Moses.

THINK ABOUT IT

✚ *How is Rehoboam different from his father Solomon?* ✚

The Temples of Jeroboam

✝ 1 KINGS 12:25-14:20; 15:25-32 ✝

God told Jeroboam that he should be the king of the ten tribes. If he served God and did what God wanted, his sons would rule after him.

The people from the north still went to Jerusalem in the southern kingdom to worship God. Jeroboam did not think this was good. He was afraid they would become friends with people in the kingdom of Judah and someday rejoin them. Then he would not be king anymore.

Remember how God had said there should only be one temple in the land? Jeroboam disobeyed that law and set up two more temples in the north. He even put golden idols shaped like calves for the people to worship in these temples. He told his people the trip to Jerusalem was too far for them. They should worship the idols at his temples.

One day while Jeroboam was at one of these temples, a prophet from Judah came to him. He told Jeroboam that all his altars would be destroyed by a man from David's family named Josiah. This made Jeroboam angry. He pointed at the prophet and told his men to capture him. As he pointed, his hand dried up and became useless. Then the altar fell apart, with its ashes falling onto the ground.

Jeroboam knew he had done wrong. "Please," he said to the prophet, "ask God to make my hand well."

The prophet prayed for the king, and God answered his prayer. Jeroboam's hand became better right away.

But Jeroboam did not change his ways; he and his

people still worshiped the idols. One day a prophet gave Jeroboam more bad news. "You have led your people against Me," God said through the prophet. "For that, you will be punished. Every one of your children will die. God will have the people of Israel taken away to a far land because they worshiped idols."

After Jeroboam died and his son Nadab became king, a servant killed Nadab and all other children of Jeroboam. The kingdom had been taken away from the man who led his country into sin.

THINK ABOUT IT

✤ *From this story, how do we know we can trust God? Did Jeroboam realize God's power?* ✤

STORY 3

Elijah the Prophet

✤ 1 KINGS 15:33-17:24 ✤

The kingdom of Israel in the north had many kings. Most of them worshiped idols and did not have long, peaceful reigns. One of these kings was named Omri. Omri was a strong king who made peace with the kingdom of Judah in the south. He built a city named Samaria in the middle of the kingdom and lived there. Before him, the kings had lived in many places. From now on, the king of Israel would live in the

town of Samaria.

Omri's son Ahab became king when Omri died, and he was worse than any of the kings before him. Ahab married a woman named Jezebel who brought new gods into Israel and killed all the prophets of the Lord she could find. Those who were left went to hide in caves in the mountains.

During Ahab's rule the Lord sent the prophet Elijah to him. Elijah lived in the wilderness. He wore animal skins for clothing and had long hair and a beard. One day he walked up to Ahab and said, "There will be no rain or dew here until I call for it." Then he walked away and disappeared. He hid in the wilderness and drank from a brook there. Every day God sent wild birds—black ravens—to Elijah. These birds brought him food to live on.

Just as Elijah said, no rain or dew fell on the land. Even Elijah's little brook in the wilderness went dry. How would he live in the wilderness with no water? One day the Lord told Elijah to go to a certain town. A woman there would take care of him. When Elijah found the woman she had only a little food and oil for cooking. She and her son were starving too.

Elijah promised that her barrel of grain would not be

empty until the rains came back. She would have enough grain and oil for cooking until then. The woman trusted Elijah and God. She used up the last of her food to feed the prophet and her family. When it was time to eat again, there was always enough for one more meal.

One day the woman's son became sick and died. Elijah carried the boy up to his own room and prayed that God would make the boy live again. God heard his prayer and healed the boy.

THINK ABOUT IT

✛ *How did God take care of Elijah? Think of as many ways as you can.* ✛

STORY 4

The Fire of the One True God

✛ 1 KINGS 18:1-46 ✛

For three years no rain fell in Israel. No food could grow and all the animals were dying. King Ahab knew he had to find Elijah and get him to bring the rains back. Ahab sent men to search for him everywhere, and he even asked kings of other countries to look for him. But Elijah could not be found.

In the third year of no rain, Ahab called the chief of his servants to him. Obadiah was a good man who worshiped

God and tried to do right, even though he served Ahab. When the time was right, Elijah let Obadiah find him. Ahab rushed out to meet with Elijah and ask for his help.

Elijah told Ahab to bring all his people to Mount Carmel. He was also to bring the 400 prophets who served the idol Baal and the 400 who served the idol Asherah.

When all the people were gathered together, Elijah told them they had sinned by worshiping idols. Then he gave them a strange order. They were to prepare two sacrifices. One would be for Baal and one for the Lord. Neither of the two fires would be lit. The people could all pray to Baal and ask him to light the fire for his sacrifice. Elijah would ask God to light his fire.

No matter what the people did, Baal's sacrifice would not catch on fire. Elijah laughed at them. "Try again," he said. "Maybe Baal is asleep. Maybe he's away on vacation!"

In the middle of the afternoon Elijah told the people to soak the wood under his sacrifice with water. This would make it very hard to light. Three times they poured barrels of water over Elijah's altar until it was soaking wet. Then Elijah stood before the altar and asked God to light the fire and show that He was the true God. Fire fell from the sky and lit the fire and the offering was burned up.

The people fell on their faces and cried, "The Lord is God!"

Elijah ordered the people to capture all the priests of Baal and kill them because they had led Israel into sin. Then he went up to the top of the mountain and prayed to God for rain. In a little while the sky was covered with clouds and rain fell on the land for the first time in three years.

THINK ABOUT IT

✛ *How did Elijah know that God would light the fire under his sacrifice?* ✛

Elijah and Elisha

✝ 1 KINGS 19:1-21 ✝

When Ahab told his wife Jezebel what had happened and how her priests were all dead, she was angry. Jezebel promised to kill Elijah.

No one in the kingdom dared to help Elijah. Running for his life, Elijah went south eighty miles, to the land of Judah, then even farther, into the desert to the south. Soon he was tired and hungry. He was also sad and upset. He didn't think the people would really turn away from the idols. He didn't think he should have run away either. He wished he were dead.

He lay down to rest under a little tree and fell asleep. Suddenly, he felt a tap on his shoulder. When he looked up, an angel of the Lord was there. "Get up and eat," the

angel told him. Next to him Elijah saw a warm loaf of bread and a container of water. He ate and drank, then fell asleep again. A little while later the angel woke him again. "Eat and drink more," the angel said. "You are too weak for the trip you have to make."

This made Elijah strong enough to keep on going. He walked all the way south to Mount Horeb. This was where Moses had seen the burning bush. It was where God gave Moses the Ten Commandments. Elijah found a cave in the mountain and went in there to hide and rest.

While Elijah was on Mount Horeb the Lord came to him and gave him more work to do. He was told to anoint several kings and a new prophet for the Lord. Many people would die fighting for these kings. But in the end, there would be 7,000 men left in Israel who worshiped God. This work would take the rest of Elijah's life.

Elijah went to work at once. He traveled back into the land of Judah until he found a young man named Elisha in the fields. Without saying a word, Elijah walked up to Elisha. He took off his cloak made of skins and put it over Elisha's shoulders.

Elisha knew who Elijah was. He knew what he meant when he put his cloak over him too. As Elijah was walking away from him, Elisha called out to him. "Let me say goodbye to my father and mother."

"Go ahead," Elijah said.

Elisha killed the oxen that had been plowing the field. He cooked the meat and took it back to his family as a sign that he was leaving for good. Then he ran after Elijah. Elisha had been chosen as a prophet of the Lord. He would spend the rest of his life working with Elijah and serving God.

Think About It

✛ *Why do you think God told Elijah to make Elisha a prophet? Often people mix up Elijah and Elisha. Starting*

STORY 6

The Bloody Prophet

✤ 1 KINGS 20:1-43 ✤

J ust north of the kingdom of Israel was the kingdom of Syria. Syria was stronger than Israel. When its king decided to attack King Ahab, Ahab could only raise a small army of 7,000 men. But God helped Israel in two battles against the Syrians, and Ahab's little army won them both.

The king of Syria dressed himself in rags and went to Ahab. He begged Ahab not to kill him. Ahab was so pleased to see a great king bowing down to him that he sent the king away without killing him.

Ahab had gone against God's wishes. God found a way to show Ahab he had done the wrong thing.

By this time Elijah and Elisha had trained many new prophets of the Lord. One of them said to another, "Wound me and make me bleed."

The second prophet refused and was killed by a lion because he did not obey the word of God. The prophet then asked another man to wound him. This man did as he was told. Then the bloody prophet stood by the road with his face covered and cried out to King Ahab when he passed by.

"What happened to you?" Ahab asked the man.

"I was in the battle," the prophet said. "I was in charge of a prisoner. A soldier told me that if I let the prisoner go, he would kill me. When I was busy the prisoner escaped. Please don't have me killed."

"You must die," the king told him. "Your life must pay for the life of the prisoner."

The prophet took the covering off his face, and Ahab saw he was a prophet. "Hear what the Lord says," the prophet said. "Because you let a king go that I wanted destroyed, your life will go for his, and your people for his."

Troubled, Ahab went back to his home. Now he knew he had done the wrong thing by letting an enemy go free.

THINK ABOUT IT

✛ *What would the king of Syria probably do when he got back to his own country?* ✛

STORY 7

Naboth's Vineyard

✛ 1 KINGS 21:1-29 ✛

A hab lived in Samaria, the capital of his kingdom. But he also had a palace in Jezreel. Next to his palace there was a vineyard owned by a man named Naboth. Ahab wanted that vineyard for a vegetable garden, but Naboth would not sell it to him.

174

When Ahab saw that nothing would make Naboth give up his vineyard, he went back into his palace and pouted. He wouldn't eat or see anyone. He just stayed in bed and acted like a spoiled child.

Ahab's wife, Jezebel, said to him, "Who is the king here? You or Naboth? I'll get you the vineyard you want so badly." She sat down and wrote out an order in Ahab's name, then sealed the order with Ahab's royal seal. She ordered Naboth to appear in front of a meeting of all the people. Then she ordered her servants to find two men who would swear they heard Naboth curse God and the king.

At the meeting the two "witnesses" lied, just the way Jezebel told them to. Because the people thought he had cursed God and his king, Naboth was taken out and killed. Ahab took the vineyard over and made it his own.

Some time later Ahab was riding through his new garden when Elijah the prophet appeared before him. "So you found me, my old enemy," Ahab said.

"I found you because you have done evil in the sight of the Lord," Elijah told the king. "You and Jezebel will both die for this, and so will all your sons."

Ahab knew he had done wrong, and he was sorry for what Jezebel had done and he had allowed to happen. He put on old clothing and did not eat and begged God to forgive him. God heard his prayers and said to Elijah, "He is sorry for his sin. Because of this, I will not punish him in his lifetime. But when he is dead, I will surely punish his children."

THINK ABOUT IT

✦ *Why was Ahab to suffer for what his wife had done?* ✦

STORY 8

Ahab's Final Battle

✦ 1 KINGS 22:1-40 ✦

After three years of peace the Syrians attacked Israel again, taking one of the cities on the east side of the Jordan River. The two nations of Israel and Judah were at peace with each other, so Ahab asked the king of Judah to come and help him drive the Syrians out of the land.

Jehoshaphat, the king of Judah, followed God. "Let's ask the prophets to tell us what God wants before we attack the Syrians," he said to Ahab. But Ahab followed idols, not God. He called 400 of his prophets together and these false prophets said the war should go on.

Jehoshaphat wasn't happy listening to the prophets of idols. "Isn't there a prophet of the Lord we could ask?" he said to Ahab.

"There is one named Micaiah, but I don't like him. He always brings me bad news," Ahab said.

"Let's hear what he has to say," Jehoshaphat said.

When they asked Micaiah, he told them the Lord wanted all the armies to go back to their homes. This wasn't what Ahab wanted to hear, so he had Micaiah put in prison and the armies went out to fight the Syrians.

Because of what Micaiah said, Ahab did not wear his royal clothing in the battle, the way Jehoshaphat did. He hoped the Syrians would think he was just an ordinary soldier. In those days armies would always try to kill a king in battle. If they did, all his army would run away. Even though he was not dressed like a king, Ahab was hit by an arrow, and by that night he had died from his wound.

Ahab had not been a bad king. His problem was that he listened to what his wife said instead of the Lord.

THINK ABOUT IT

✛ *Why didn't Ahab like to listen to the prophets of the Lord?* ✛

Elijah's Chariot of Fire

✝ 2 KINGS 1:1-2:15 ✝

Elijah knew his work was almost done. He set out on what would be his final journey, and he told Elisha to stay behind.

"No," Elisha said. "I will not leave you."

They traveled from place to place, visiting the prophets that they had trained together. At each place the prophets told Elisha that Elijah was going to die soon. "I know," he would answer. "Let's not talk about it." At each place Elijah told Elisha to let him go on alone. Every time Elisha said no and followed his master.

As they came to the Jordan River outside of Jericho, a group of fifty prophets from the area was following a distance behind them. At the banks of the river Elijah took

off his robe of skin and hit the river with it. The river immediately dried up in front of them, and they walked across dry land to the other side. Then the river flowed by again.

"What can I do for you before I leave?" Elijah asked Elisha.

"All I ask is that your spirit come to me in greater power than it comes to others," Elisha answered.

"That is a big request," Elijah said. "If you see me when I am taken away, you will have it. But if you don't see me leave, you won't."

As they walked along together, suddenly Elisha saw a chariot of fire, pulled by horses that also seemed made of fire. The fiery chariot swooped down between the two prophets and carried Elijah up toward heaven. Elisha saw his master lifted up and taken away from him!

Elisha picked up the robe of skin that had been left behind and turned back to the river. He was very sad that his friend had left him. "Where is the Lord God of Elijah?" he asked as he hit the river's water with Elijah's robe. As the robe hit the water, the water parted again, and Elisha walked across dry land, just as he had done before with Elijah.

The prophets who had been following the two men had not seen the fiery chariot and horses, but they did see what Elisha had done to the river. "The spirit of Elijah is with Elisha!" they cried. The great prophet of Israel was gone, but Elisha had the blessing he had requested.

Think About It

✦ *What happened to Elijah? Did he die?* ✦

The Fountain of Elisha

✝ 2 KINGS 2:19-3:27 ✝

Elisha stayed in Jericho for a while after Elijah was taken up to heaven. Elijah had lived in the wilderness, but Elisha usually stayed in cities and helped people there.

One day the people of Jericho told Elisha they had trouble with their water. The spring they got their water from tasted bitter, and the land around the spring wouldn't grow food. Elisha took a bottle of salt and poured it into the spring near Jericho. From that time the water was good and the land around grew all the crops the people of Jericho wanted.

Jehoram, Ahab's son, was king of Israel now. He was a better king than his father, but he still worshiped idols.

Since the time of David the land of Moab had been under Israel's command. Moab had its own king, but every year he had to give Israel the wool from a hundred thousand of his sheep, and the same number of rams. When Ahab died, the king of Moab tried to set his land free of Israel. King Jehoram of Israel and King Jehoshaphat of Judah, together with the king of Edom, marched south into the land of Moab to put down the rebellion.

On their way they found no water for themselves or their horses. It began to look like all three kings and their armies would die of thirst. "Isn't there a prophet of the Lord we can talk to?" Jehoshaphat asked. Of the three kings, he was still the only one who worshiped God. When Elisha was brought to them, he said the only reason he would help the kings was because of Jehoshaphat's faithfulness to God.

Elisha told the kings to dig ditches in the valley where they were camping. "There will be no rain or wind, but the valley will be filled with water. And the Lord will let you defeat the Moabites."

So the armies dug ditches all over the valley. In the morning all the ditches were filled with water and not one drop of rain had fallen.

The army of Moab could see the valley from their camp too. In the early morning sun the water seemed to be red. The Moabites thought the water was blood from a big battle among the three kings. Leaving their weapons behind, the foolish soldiers rushed into the valley to take all the things the three kings had brought with them into battle. The three armies killed all the unarmed soldiers of Moab and then went on to destroy the entire country of Moab.

This story is in the Bible, but it was also carved long ago on a stone pillar and set up in Moab by a later king.

Think About It

✚ *Why did God help the three kings defeat the Moabites?* ✚

The Pot of Oil and the Pot of Poison

✛ 2 KINGS 4:1-7, 38-44; 6:1-7 ✛

Although many in Israel worshiped idols, there were also many who worshiped God. Elisha traveled through the country, meeting these people and teaching them. They were called "sons of the prophets," and many of them became prophets too.

Because God was with Elisha, he was able to perform amazing acts, or *miracles*. Every time the people saw him do a miracle, they believed more strongly in Elisha and his God.

One day the wife of one of the sons of the prophets came to Elisha. Her husband had died owing a man some money. If she could not pay the man, he would take her sons and make slaves out of them. This was his right under the law.

Elisha asked the woman what she had in her house.

"Only one pot of oil," the woman answered.

"Go and borrow all the jars and bowls and bottles you can," Elisha told her. "Then fill all the bottles and sell the oil. You will have enough to pay the debt."

The woman did as she was told. Her one little pot of oil filled every pot and pan she could find. If there had been more pots and bottles around, they would have been filled too. All this oil came from the one little pot of oil the woman owned. She paid off her debt and had enough extra money to take care of herself and her sons for a long time.

Another time Elisha and his prophets came to an area where there was no food to feed them. They walked through all the fields, picking up anything they could find, and then they made a big stew. But one of the men had brought back some poisonous vegetables and tossed them in the pot. He didn't know they were bad to eat. As the men ate, they realized they had been eating dangerous food and called for Elisha.

Elisha took a handful of grain and threw it into the pot. When he told the men it was safe to eat from the pot, the men found the food was good because of what Elisha had done.

Another day a man brought Elisha a few loaves of bread and some ears of corn. There were a hundred men with Elisha that day, and so Elisha told his servant, "Give this to the people for their dinner."

"This little bit of food?" the servant asked. "How can this feed so many people?"

"The Lord says they shall eat and have enough. There will even be leftovers," Elisha promised. When the servant passed out the food, he found there was more than enough, even though he started with just a few loaves of bread and a little corn.

Another time Elisha was helping some people build a

house by the Jordan River. One of the men was cutting down a tree with an axe he had borrowed. As he swung the axe, the axe's head flew off its handle and sank straight to the bottom of the river. The man was upset. Iron and steel were very expensive, and the axe was not his. What could he do?

Elisha asked the man to show him where the axehead had gone into the river. When he knew where it was, he cut off a stick of wood and threw it into the water in the same place. The heavy axehead floated up to the top of the water, and the man rushed in and picked it up.

All these miracles showed the people that Elisha was a prophet of God and that what he said came from the Lord.

THINK ABOUT IT

✛ *Why do God's prophets perform miracles? What would happen if they didn't?* ✛

STORY 12

The Little Boy at Shunem

✛ 2 KINGS 4:8-37 ✛

hen Elisha traveled he often shared meals and stayed overnight in other people's homes. One woman he stayed with in Shunem had her husband build Elisha his own room, with a bed, table and stool, and candlestick. Elisha must have liked that little room of his own very much.

One day he said to the woman, "You have been kind to me. Isn't there something I can do for you?"

"No, there is nothing I need," she told Elisha.

As Elisha had been Elijah's servant, now Elisha himself had a servant and his name was Gehazi. At that moment Gehazi whispered to Elisha, "She has no son."

"A year from now," Elisha told the woman, "you will have a son."

The woman had always wanted a baby, and this pleased her very much. As Elisha said, a year later she had a baby boy. The boy grew up and became big enough to help his father in the field. One day, however, he became very sick and died. Without telling anyone, his mother ran to Elisha for help.

When Elisha saw her coming, he knew something was wrong. But the Lord did not tell him what it was until she spoke these words: "Did I ask you for a son? Why did you trick me like this?" She must have thought Elisha had given her the boy and then taken him away from her. This would seem very cruel to any mother.

Elisha ran to the woman's house and went into the room where the dead boy lay. He held the boy's cold hands and put his face on the boy's cold face while he prayed to God. Soon the boy's body began to warm up a little. Elisha cuddled the boy close to himself as he prayed some more. Suddenly, the boy sneezed! He began to breath again and his eyes opened.

Elisha called for the mother. "Pick up your son," he told her. The happy mother carried her son out of the room, thanking Elisha for saving him.

THINK ABOUT IT

✝ *Why did God through Elisha give the woman of Shunem*

STORY 13

A Little Girl's Wish

✛ 2 KINGS 5:1-27 ✛

Once there was a general from Syria named Naaman who came down with a terrible disease called leprosy. In those days leprosy could not be treated. A person with leprosy would develop ugly sores, his body parts would look deformed and might fall off, and eventually the person would die. Since people thought leprosy was very contagious, those with leprosy always lived and died alone. When Naaman caught this disease, he was naturally very frightened.

Naaman's wife had a little Israelite girl as her slave. The girl had been captured by the Syrians and taken far away from her family. But she liked Naaman and his wife. "I wish he could meet Elisha," the little girl told Naaman's wife. "Elisha could cure him."

When Naaman heard this he told the king of Syria what the little girl had said. The king loved Naaman and wanted to help him, so he wrote a letter for Naaman to take to the king of Israel. The letter said, "Please cure Naaman of his leprosy." The king of Syria thought the king of Israel could just order a prophet to do anything he wanted. The king of Israel misunderstood the letter and was very upset. "I can't cure a man of leprosy," he cried. "But if I don't, the king of Syria will make war on me!"

When Elisha heard of this, he told the king to stop worrying and send Naaman to him. After Naaman arrived in Israel, Elisha sent a message to him, telling him to wash in the Jordan River seven times.

Naaman was insulted. He thought Elisha would come to him and not just send a message. He wanted Elisha to wave his hand over him and make the disease go away. But the laws of Israel were very strict about leprosy. No one was allowed to go near a leper, let alone touch him. And Elisha knew the Lord could cure Naaman if Naaman just did as he was told.

Naaman's servants were wise though. "If the prophet had told you to do something hard, wouldn't you do it? But washing in a river is easy. Why not try it?"

So Naaman rode down to the Jordan River and washed in it seven times. Sure enough, he was healed! Now that he was no longer a leper, he could go see Elisha. Naaman offered Elisha anything he wanted in payment for curing him. But prophets never took pay for their work, so Elisha refused all the gifts Naaman offered.

"May I take some soil from this land home with me then?" Naaman asked. "I will build an altar there for God and follow God as long as I live. I will still have to go to the

idol temple with the king, but I will not worship there. Will God forgive me for this?"

"Go ahead," Elisha told Naaman.

Gehazi, Elisha's servant, was not pleased that Elisha had refused Naaman's gifts. That wouldn't stop him from asking Naaman himself! Naaman gave Gehazi two pieces of silver and two suits of clothing. Before he went back to Elisha, though, Gehazi hid the presents.

"Where have you been?" Elisha asked Gehazi when he came back.

"Nowhere," Gehazi answered.

"I saw the man leave his chariot and give you a present," Elisha said. "Because you did this, you and your children will all suffer from Naaman's disease."

When Gehazi left Elisha, his skin was already white with leprosy.

THINK ABOUT IT

✛ *Naaman obeyed the word of God and was cured. Gehazi disobeyed the word of God and was made sick. Did it matter to God where these men came from or what they were before?* ✛

Elisha's Own Chariots of Fire

✛ 2 KINGS 6:8-23 ✛

Israel and Syria were at war with each other all during Elisha's life. God allowed Elisha to be a great help to the king of Israel. Every time the Syrians planned an attack, God would tell Elisha about it, and Elisha would send word to the king. At last the king of Syria asked his nobles which of them was spying on him for the Israelites. There was no way the king of Israel could know all his plans without inside help!

"It's not any of us," his nobles said. "Elisha tells the king of Israel everything you plan."

"Then go and find this man so I can send an army to take him," the king demanded.

The Syrians learned that Elisha was staying in the town of Dothan. A great army was sent out to surround the town during the night. They were sure they had Elisha just where they wanted him.

In the morning a young servant of Elisha's looked out and saw all the horses and chariots and men with armor surrounding the town. "What will we do?" he cried to Elisha.

"Don't worry," Elisha said. "There are more men on our side than on theirs."

The young man looked out the window. He could see no Israelite army there. They were trapped!

"Lord," Elisha prayed, "open this man's eyes so he can see."

The next time he looked, the young servant saw that the mountainside was covered with horses and chariots of fire sent to keep Elisha safe. No one but Elisha and his servant could see the army of God.

Again Elisha prayed to God. "Make these men blind for a little while," he asked. When his prayer was answered, no one in the Syrian army could see clearly. They could see some things but nothing was clear. It was like they all needed glasses at once.

Elisha walked out of the town and up to the Syrian army. "You have the wrong town," he told them. "Follow me. I'll take you to the right place." Elisha led the Syrians from Dothan to Samaria, the capital of Israel. They walked right through the city gates as Israel's army gathered around them.

"Now open their eyes, Lord," Elisha prayed.

As soon as they could see, the Syrians realized they had been tricked and were in deep trouble. There was nothing they could do but surrender.

The king of Israel came out to Elisha. "What should I do to them, father?" he asked. "Should I kill them all?"

"Would you kill helpless prisoners?" Elisha asked the king. "Give them food and water and send them home to their king."

The king treated his prisoners well and sent them all back to their homes safely. After that it was a long time before the Syrians sent an army into Israel again.

THINK ABOUT IT

✚ *Do you remember the chariot of fire that took Elijah up to heaven? What might be one reason God sent chariots of fire to help Elisha instead of protecting him another way?* ✚

Four Lepers Have a Problem

✛ 2 KINGS 6:24-7:20 ✛

I n time there was another great war between the Syrians and Israel. This time the Syrians surrounded the city of Samaria. No one could go in or out. Once the food inside the city was gone, the people of Israel began to starve.

Elisha told the king not to give up the city. "Hear the word of the Lord," he said. "Tomorrow a peck of flour will be sold for sixty cents, and two pecks of barley for sixty cents." This was a great bargain, especially since there was no flour or barley in the entire city!

One of the king's men laughed at Elisha. "Maybe," he said. "If God opens the heavens and rains food down. But that will never happen."

"It will happen," Elisha said. "You will see it too. But you will not eat any of the food."

Early the next morning four lepers stood outside the city. By law, they could not go into the city. They also couldn't go far away from it or the Syrians would kill them. They were in real trouble. "Let's go to the camp of the Syrians," they decided. "The most they can do is kill us. If we stay here any longer, we will die too." So they started off toward the enemy camp.

The four lepers found the camp empty. Everything that would belong to an army was there, but there were no soldiers. The men checked around carefully and then ate all they needed of the food they found.

"We have to tell the king about this," they said.

When they got back to Samaria they called the news up to the guards who then went to the king. The king was afraid it was a trick. To be sure, he sent two men out to the camp, and sure enough, they reported back that the lepers were right. Not only was the camp full of food and treasure, so was the path along which the Syrians had run the night before.

What had happened? During the night God had sent the sound of a huge army to the Syrians. They heard chariots and horses and armor clanking. The ground seemed to move from the marching of heavily armed men. The Syrians knew the Israelite army was not that big. Someone else must have arrived to help Israel! They ran from their camp so fast that they left all their horses and donkeys tied up behind them.

Just as Elisha had said, grain was sold cheaply that day in Samaria. And what happened to the man who had laughed at Elisha? He was put in charge of all the food and was trampled to death by the starving people racing to collect food for their families.

THINK ABOUT IT

+ *Do you remember how poorly lepers were treated in those days? Why did God use four lepers to help save the city?* +

STORY 16

The Furious Times of Hazael and Jehu

+ 2 KINGS 8:7-15; 9:1-10:36 +

Years ago the Lord had told Elijah to anoint or crown a man named Hazael the king of Syria and Jehu king of Israel. But the right time to anoint kings depends on many things, and Elijah was taken away to heaven before he was allowed to complete the task. Now the time had come for these men to be anointed and Elisha began to make the necessary preparations.

One day Hazael, a prince of Syria, came to see Elisha. The king of that country was sick and had sent Hazael to ask Elisha if he would get well again.

"Yes, he will get well," Elisha said. "But he will die." He looked at Hazael sadly.

"Why are you crying?" Hazael asked him.

"Because I know what you will do to Israel," Elisha said. "You will burn their castles, kill their young men, and destroy their children."

Elisha told Hazael he would soon be king of Syria. This surprised Hazael, but he also felt pleased by the news. The very next day Hazael went into the king's room and smothered him to death, and then took over as Syria's new king. His next move was to attack Israel.

Elisha still had to make Jehu king of Israel. He sent one of his prophets to the battlefield with a little bottle of oil. "Get Jehu alone and anoint him king of Israel," he told the prophet. "Do it quietly and then come straight back here."

This had to be done secretly because Jehoram was still the king of Israel. When the prophet sent by Elisha had Jehu alone, he anointed him king. "You will destroy the family of Ahab because they killed the prophets of the Lord," he told Jehu.

Jehu was a good soldier. He knew that if he were to be king and destroy Jehoram and all the rest of Ahab's family, he would have to surprise them. He jumped into his chariot and drove as fast as he could, his men following after him. He raced toward Jezreel where the king and his mother Jezebel were staying.

King Jehoram drove out to meet Jehu, thinking he was bringing news of the battle. Jehu killed him and immediately drove into town looking for Jezebel. Although she had heard of her son Jehoram's death, Jezebel met Jehu like a queen, standing by a high window in her crown and royal robes.

"Who is on my side?" Jehu called to the people in the castle. When some of them came to look out the windows, Jehu called to them. "Throw her down!" he commanded. So Jezebel, who had ordered all God's prophets killed, was thrown out of her palace window to her death.

Jehu went on to kill all the sons of Ahab and Jezebel and all their children's children until no one was left alive in that family.

King Jehu then ordered all the priests of the idol Baal to him, telling them he was a worshiper of their god.

Hundreds of them crowded into the temple of Baal. They thought they would be rewarded for their faithfulness to Jehu. Instead, Jehu surrounded the temple with his army and had every one of the priests of Baal killed.

God sent a prophet to Jehu. "You have killed Ahab's family as God wanted," the prophet told Jehu. "And you destroyed those who worshiped Baal. Because of this, your children will sit on the throne of Israel for four generations."

While Jehu ruled Israel and Hazael ruled Syria, the Syrians took over all the land on the east of the Jordan River. They killed many of the Israelites and burned their castles, just as Elisha had said would happen.

THINK ABOUT IT

✛ *Jehu was fulfilling God's plans when he became king. What other promise of God's did he fulfill once he became king?* ✛

Elisha's Last Prophecy and the Lesson of Jonah

✠ 2 KINGS 13:1-25; JONAH 1:1-4:11 ✠

During the time that Jehu and his son ruled Israel, Hazael and his son of Syria gave Israel no peace. But when Jehu's grandson Joash became king of Israel, Israel began to rise again.

By now Elisha was a very old, sick man. When Joash came to see Elisha, he cried to see him so sick and near death. Elisha had done more for his country than all its armies.

"Bring a bow and arrow and point it toward Syria," Elisha told Joash. When he did, Elisha touched the bow as Joash sent an arrow in the direction of Syria. "This is the Lord's arrow of victory over Syria," the old man said. Then he gave Joash a strange order. "Beat the ground with your arrows."

Joash took his arrows and hit them on the ground three times. Then he stopped.

"You should have hit them five or six times," Elisha said. "Then you would have won five or six battles with the Syrians. Now you will win only three."

Soon after this Elisha died and was buried in a cave. The next spring some raiding Moabites buried one of their men in the same cave. When the body of this man touched the body of Elisha, the Moabite came back to life! Elisha was dead, but he was still powerful.

As Elisha had said, Joash defeated the Syrians three times. He took back all the cities that had been captured by the Syrians. After Joash died, his son, Jeroboam the second, was made king. He was to be the greatest of all the kings of Israel. Under Jeroboam the second, the kingdom was rich and strong. He took over nearly all of Syria and made Israel's capital the greatest city in the area.

Now that the Israelites were safe from Syria, more problems arose. Assyria, another enemy of the Israelites, grew strong. The capital of this country was a city called Nineveh.

A prophet named Jonah was living in Israel at this time. The Lord came to him and said, "Go to the wicked city of Nineveh and preach there."

Jonah didn't want to go to Nineveh. Nineveh was, after all, an enemy city and should suffer, not be saved. Instead of going there, Jonah went to the seacoast and boarded a ship going far away from Nineveh.

Of course, the Lord knew where Jonah was and what he was doing. God sent a great storm that tossed the ship around. All the people on board were sure they were going to die. While everyone prayed to their own gods to save them, Jonah, however, was sleeping soundly. "Get up and pray to your God!" the sailors told Jonah.

As the storm grew worse and worse, Jonah told the people his story. "I am the one causing your problems," he said. "Throw me overboard and you will be safe."

But the people on the ship would not throw Jonah overboard. Although they worshiped idols, they were not murderers. Instead, they prayed to God and asked Him to save them. But this did not work, either. Finally, they had no choice. Jonah was thrown overboard to save the ship. As soon as he was in the water, the storm stopped. Everyone thanked God for saving them and promised to serve Him.

And what happened to Jonah? While he was in the water, a huge fish came along and swallowed him whole! Jonah lived inside the great fish for three days before the fish spit him out on dry land.

Jonah learned a lesson from this. He now knew that some people who worshiped other gods were good people. The people on the ship had not wanted to hurt him, even though he was putting their lives in danger. He should not be so quick to hate people who were not like him. More importantly, Jonah learned that God loved all people, not just those who served Him.

Now Jonah did as he was told. He walked through Nineveh and called out, "In forty days Nineveh will be destroyed!" The people there believed Jonah. They stopped sinning and worshiped God. The people of Nineveh begged God not to destroy their city.

When God saw that the people were really sorry for their sins, He forgave them and did not destroy their city. This made Jonah look bad, though. A true prophet is never wrong. Now people would not believe what Jonah said to them. "You might as well kill me," he said to God.

But God would not do that. "Why shouldn't I have pity on a city with more than a hundred thousand children in it?" the Lord asked Jonah.

✦ *Jonah stayed in the belly of the great fish for three days. This story has special meaning when we think about the life of Jesus. Can you think what it might mean? Be sure to read the story of Jonah again after you have read the stories about Jesus.* ✦

STORY 18

The Ten Tribes Are Lost

✦ 2 KINGS 15:8-17:41 ✦

All this time the people of Israel were worshiping idols, and not the one true God. Because of this, their troubles grew worse and worse. One king ruled after another, and none of them was a good man. Most of them became king by killing the king before them. All in all, there were nineteen kings over the ten tribes of Israel.

The Assyrians grew stronger and stronger. They kept taking parts of Israel and making the Israelites their slaves.

The last king of Israel was a man named Hoshea. While he was king, the Assyrians surrounded the city of Samaria. No food or water or people could go in or out of the city for three whole years! At the end of the three years, King Sargon of Assyria took Samaria, killed the king, and captured all the people of Israel. He took them far to the east of Israel and made them slaves in many different countries. The Israelites were no longer a united people living in one country. Because they were scattered they became weak and unable to break loose of Sargon's rule.

In time the people of Israel forgot their God and worshiped the idols where they were living. They married people from these countries and spent their lives outside the land God had promised their fathers. The ten tribes of Israel were lost forever. None of them ever lived in the land of their fathers again.

And what happened to the land of Israel? A few Israelites had been allowed to stay there and farm the land for Assyria, but not many. Strangers from other countries were placed in Israel by the king of Assyria, but there were not enough people to fill the land as years before. Wild animals began to roam the countryside and lions were known to kill the new settlers. Life in Israel was very hard.

In those days people thought that each country had its own gods. The people who had moved into the land of Israel decided they needed to worship the God of that country to be safe. Although a priest was sent by Sargon to teach the strangers about Israel's God, the new settlers continued to worship other idols.

These settlers came to be called Samaritans. They put their temple of God on Mount Gerizim, near the city of Shechem. Some Samaritans still live there today.

―――――――――

THINK ABOUT IT

✛ *If ten tribes of Israel are now lost forever, how many tribes are left? Will they ever settle in Israel again?* ✛

―――――――――

PART 5

Tales of Crowns and Courage:

ADVENTURES IN THE KINGDOM OF JUDAH

Judah's First Four Kings

✝ 2 CHRONICLES 12:1-20:37 ✝

You remember that some of God's people were living south of Israel in the kingdom of Judah. When the ten tribes left to form their own country, the kingdom of Judah was very weak. At the time Judah's capital was Jerusalem, with Solomon's temple and the king's palace, and its king was Rehoboam.

Rehoboam tried to make Judah a strong country again, but he did not worship God the way his grandfather David had. The people put their little statues of idols everywhere and worshiped them.

While Rehoboam was king an army from Egypt attacked Judah. The city of Jerusalem was taken and the temple was robbed of all the gold and silver that Solomon had put there.

When Rehoboam died after ruling Judah for seventeen years, his son Abijah became king of Judah. During Abijah's rule, Judah was attacked by the ten tribes from the north. Although Judah's army was outnumbered and surrounded, God gave Abijah a victory over the army of Israel. Israel did not attack Judah again while Abijah was king.

Abijah only ruled for three years, and his son Asa became the next king. Asa was a great warrior, a builder of cities, and a wise king. During his rule a great army came up from the country of Ethiopia. Ethiopia is south of Egypt, and a long way from the kingdom of Judah. Asa and his army tried to fight off the Ethiopian army but there were not enough men in Asa's army to beat the Ethiopians. Asa called to God. "Help us, Lord," he prayed. "We fight here for You."

The Lord heard Asa's prayer and helped him defeat the Ethiopians and take back all the land from them. After the victory, Asa brought back all the treasures of the Ethiopian army and flocks of sheep, cattle, and camels.

Then the Lord sent a prophet to Asa. "The Lord will be with you as long as you are with Him," the prophet said. "But if you leave Him, He will leave you."

Asa rebuilt the altar of the temple and called his people to worship God. Then he went through the land and destroyed every idol he could find. When he saw his own mother was worshiping an idol, he would not allow her to be the queen any longer.

Asa served the Lord until he was old and sick. But then he allowed people who worshiped idols to try and heal him. Before Asa died, there were idols in the land again.

Asa's son, Jehoshaphat, was to become the wisest and strongest king of Judah. Jehoshaphat made peace with Israel, as you remember, and helped the Israelites fight the kingdom of Syria and the Moabites.

Jehoshaphat served the Lord with all his heart, and he ordered his people to serve God as well. So the people of Judah would know more about God, Jehoshaphat sent priests all over the country. They read the laws of God and taught people how to serve Him.

Jehoshaphat had great power because of his faithfulness. He ruled over Edom, the wilderness to the south, and the Philistines. He chose judges for all the cities and ordered them to be fair and not take bribes.

One time the Moabites, Ammonites, and Syrians all attacked Judah. There was no way Jehoshaphat could defeat three strong armies working together. But he was willing to try. Before sending his army out, the king and his soldiers all went to the temple to pray and ask God for His help in the battle.

One of the priests at the temple was filled with God's Spirit and gave Jehoshaphat a message from God. "Don't be afraid," God told them. "This is My battle, not yours. Go out to fight. You will see Me win the victory for you."

When the army reached the camp of their enemies, they found there was no one to fight! The Moabites, Ammonites, and Syrians had begun fighting one another in their camps. Many of them were laying dead on the ground. The rest of them were gone. The army of Judah picked up all the riches the armies had left behind and returned to Jerusalem without losing any lives.

THINK ABOUT IT

✛ *Jehoshaphat did more than order his people to worship God. He also taught them about God and read the laws to them. What will happen when you teach someone about God?* ✛

Jehoshaphat's Terrible Mistake

✝ 2 CHRONICLES 21:1-24:27 ✝

Jehoshaphat was a good man and wise king, but he did make mistakes. He allowed his son Jehoram to marry Athaliah, a daughter of Ahab and Jezebel, the wicked king and queen of Israel.

When Jehoram became king, Athaliah brought her family idols to Judah. She led all the people in worshiping her idols and made them forget their God. Then, to prevent anyone from taking away his throne, Jehoram killed all his brothers. The prophet Elijah was living in Israel at this time. He wrote a letter to Jehoram in which he gave this message from God: "You have led your people to worship idols. You have killed your own brothers who were good men. The Lord will punish you and your people. Furthermore, you will have a terrible disease no one can cure."

Soon the Edomites broke away from Judah and set up their own kingdom. The Philistines and the Arabs made war against Jehoram. They broke into his palace and took away all his treasures. Then they killed almost all of his children, leaving only the youngest one alive.

As God had promised, Jehoram came down with a very painful disease. No one could find a way to cure him, and after years of pain, Jehoram died. Everyone in Judah hated him so much that he was not buried with the other kings.

Jehoram's only living son was still a little boy. He was made king, but Athaliah, his wicked mother, was really ruling the country. After one year the little boy was killed by Jehu, who killed all of Ahab's family living in Israel. The boy had been visiting his uncle Jehoram when Jehu killed him.

This made Athaliah so angry that she had every living prince from the family of David killed. Since there was not one man left in the royal family, Athaliah made herself queen of Judah. She shut up the temple of God and led the people to worship Baal for the next six years. But the wicked queen had overlooked one baby boy from David's family. His aunt hid him in the closed temple and the priest taught him how to be a king and worship God.

When he was seven years old, this child, Joash, was brought out of the temple and crowned king by the priest. The people were so happy to see this relative of the great king David that they shouted, "Long live the king!"

The angry queen tried to get her soldiers to capture the boy king but they refused. Instead, they took her out of the temple and killed her. Then the priest and the people promised to follow God. They tore down the temple to Baal and broke up all the idols. Afterward they rededicated the temple of God. Everyone was glad to have someone from the house of David as their ruler again.

As long as the old priest lived, Joash ruled well, and his people worshiped God. Joash collected money from the people and made needed repairs on the neglected temple. But after the old priest died, others led King Joash into worshiping idols, and God was unhappy with him. The Syrians came into Judah, robbing the cities and leaving Joash sick and poor. Soon his own servants killed him and made his son Amaziah the new king.

THINK ABOUT IT

✦ *How strong a king was Joash? Why was it necessary for the old priest to remain alive?* ✦

Three Kings and a Great Prophet

✛ 2 CHRONICLES 25:1-28:27; ISAIAH 6 ✛

A maziah was the ninth king of Judah. He served the Lord, but there were times when he was not faithful. He gathered an army of 300,000 men to bring Edom back under the rule of Judah, and the Lord gave him a great victory. But when he came back to Judah, Amaziah brought back idols from Edom and began to worship them. When a prophet tried to warn him about this, Amaziah chased him away. But the prophet told the king that he was going to be punished for leaving God.

The prophet's warning came true. An army from Israel attacked Judah and took Amaziah prisoner. The warring soldiers also broke into the temple and stole all the treasures. Amaziah lived fifteen more years before he was killed by his own men and buried in the tombs of the kings.

His son Uzziah was the tenth king of Judah. Anointed as king when he was sixteen years old, Uzziah ruled for fifty-two years. Most of the time Uzziah did what the Lord liked, and the Lord helped him. Uzziah made the kingdom of Judah strong again. He won back the land of the Philistines, Ammonites, and Arabians. He built cities with strong walls and planted trees and vineyards.

But Uzziah became very proud as he got older. He wanted the power of the high priest as well as the power of a king. One day he went into the Holy of Holies to offer incense, a substance that gives off a pleasant odor when burned. This could only be done by the high priest once a year. The high priest tried to warn Uzziah, but the king would not listen to him.

Suddenly, Uzziah's forehead became white with leprosy! No one with leprosy was ever allowed in the temple because such a disease would make the temple unholy. The priests pushed Uzziah out the door as fast as they could. For the rest of his life Uzziah was a leper. He could no longer act as king or live in the palace. His son Jotham became the king and Uzziah lived in a little house all alone. When he died Uzziah could not even be buried with the other kings of Judah.

Jotham served as king for sixteen years. He served the Lord but he let the people worship idols. God was pleased with most of what Jotham did and helped him rule the people well.

The next king was Ahaz, the most wicked of all the kings of Judah. He worshiped Baal and closed the temple of God again. During his rule, the king of Israel fought Judah and killed more than 100,000 people of Judah, including Ahaz's own son. The Israelites captured many people of Judah in this war and took them home as slaves.

But a prophet of the Lord went to the Israelites and told them to set the slaves from Judah free. "The Lord gave the people of Judah to you. But do you intend to keep your brothers as slaves? You have sinned too."

The rulers of Israel gave all the slaves from Judah food and clothing and then took them to Jericho and set them free.

When the Edomites attacked Judah, King Ahaz asked the Assyrians to come and help him. They came, but not to help. Instead, they made themselves the rulers of Judah and took everything of value they could find. When Ahaz died, his people were still worshiping idols and under the power of the king of Assyria.

The year that King Uzziah died a young man named Isaiah was made a prophet of God. God told Isaiah, "You

will tell the people My words. But they will not listen to you. They will not turn to Me and be saved, no matter what you say."

"How long will it be this way, Lord?" Isaiah asked God.

"Until all the people are taken away to another land and the cities left abandoned. But one-tenth of them will come back here and start over again. They will be the seed of a new people."

THINK ABOUT IT

✛ *Poor Isaiah. God gave him work to do and then told him it would make no difference at all! But someone had to go on teaching the Word of God. How would you feel if you were Isaiah?* ✛

Good King Hezekiah

✛ 2 KINGS 18:1-21:21; 2 CHRONICLES
24:1-32:33; ISAIAH 35:1-38:22 ✛

If Ahaz were the worst king of Judah, Hezekiah was the best. He listened to what Isaiah said and obeyed the commands of God. In the first month of his reign Hezekiah had the temple cleaned and reopened. Then he decided the people should celebrate the Feast of the Passover, as they had years ago. He even sent messengers into Israel to invite the people to come and worship in the temple in Jerusalem. Most of them laughed at him, but the sons of the prophets came to the feast.

Once the people had been rededicated to God, Hezekiah started cleaning up after the idols. His men broke every idol they could find in the land, and the people turned back to God.

When Hezekiah became king, Judah and all the lands around it were under the power of the Assyrians. They each had their own kings, but every year they had to send a large amount of money to the Assyrians. Hezekiah refused to pay these taxes, and the Assyrian army came in and threatened to take Jerusalem. Hezekiah saw he could not win this battle and begged the Assyrians to forgive him.

In return for their forgiveness, the Assyrians asked for even more money. Hezekiah sent them everything he had. He sent all the gold and silver from the temple. He sent everything he could get from the people. He sent everything he owned himself.

"Not enough," said a letter from the Assyrians. "We are

going to make you slaves and send you away. Give up and go willingly wherever we send you."

Hezekiah took this letter to the temple and laid it out on the altar before God. He prayed to God for help. Then he sent for Isaiah, hoping for some good news from him.

"The king of Assyria will not come here or shoot one arrow against this city," Isaiah told the king. God had promised to protect Jerusalem, the city of David. David had been a man of God and always done His will.

Just as the Assyrian army was preparing to attack Jerusalem, another one of their enemies attacked them. The Assyrian army was forced to turn away from Jerusalem and fight somewhere else. To make sure they wouldn't be back, the Lord sent a sickness to the Assyrians that killed 200,000 of them in one night.

Before the Assyrians left Judah, Hezekiah himself became very sick. He did not want to leave his people at this time, and he had no son to take over as king. So he prayed to God to heal him and let him live a little longer. God sent Isaiah to the king with a message. Hezekiah would get well and live for fifteen more years. Within three days Hezekiah was well again, and, as God promised, he lived for fifteen more good years before he died.

_____

THINK ABOUT IT

✝ *Why was Hezekiah unable to defeat the Assyrians? Why was Hezekiah such a good king?* ✝

_____

The Lost Book in the Temple

✛ 2 KINGS 21:1-23:25;
2 CHRONICLES 33:1-35:27 ✛

Manasseh was the fourteenth king of Judah. He was more like his wicked grandfather Ahaz than his good father Hezekiah. He was only twelve when he became king, and not wise enough for the job. He turned away from God and worshiped Baal and other false gods. He would not listen to God's prophets. Some even think—but this is not written in the Bible—that Manasseh killed Isaiah.

God was angered by Manasseh's acts and sent the Assyrians back into Judah. They captured Manasseh and

took him to Babylon where he was kept prisoner for some time. This was a good thing because while he was a captive, Manasseh began to worship God again. When he was set free and sent home, Manasseh stayed faithful to God for the rest of his life. Nonetheless, he could not convince the people of Judah to give up their idols and turn back to God.

After ruling for fifty-five years, Manasseh died. His son Amon ruled for two years after him, worshiping idols and living sinfully.

The sixteenth king of Judah was Josiah. He was only eight years old when he was made king! By the time Josiah was sixteen, he decided to worship the Lord. When he was twenty Josiah began to clear away the idols, and in a short time not one idol could be found anywhere in Judah.

While Josiah's men were at work in the temple in Jerusalem, taking away idols and making the place holy, they found an old book written on rolls of leather. This was the book of the law that Moses had written years ago! The book of the law had been hidden away so long that everyone had forgotten about it. Josiah had the book read to him and he became very frightened. He knew the people had broken every one of God's laws and would suffer for it. He needed to hear the Word of God about this, so he sent his men to find a prophet.

They found a woman named Huldah who was living in Jerusalem. She told them that God was very angry at Judah and would surely punish the people. But because Josiah prayed to God and did God's will, nothing would happen until he died.

Josiah called all the people to the temple and read the laws to them so they would know them. They promised to obey God and not to worship any idols, and they did this until Josiah died.

By now the people of Israel had all been made slaves and taken away to other countries. The Assyrians were not the strong nation they once were, but they still ruled over Judah. Now that the Assyrians were weak, a great army came up from Egypt, prepared for battle. Josiah knew the Egyptians would have to pass through Judah, and since Judah was ruled by Assyria, he thought he would have to fight the mighty Egyptian army. The ruler of Egypt, in a letter, had promised not to hurt anyone in Judah on his way to Assyria, but this promise was soon broken. The Egyptians easily defeated the army of Judah, and King Josiah was killed in the battle.

THINK ABOUT IT

✙ *Why was it important that the people have the laws of God read to them?* ✙

STORY 6

Jeremiah, the Sad Prophet

✙ 2 KINGS 23:31-25:22; 2 CHRONICLES 36:1-21; JEREMIAH 22:10-12;29:1-29; 36:1-43:13 ✙

After Josiah died his son Jehoahaz became king. Egypt was ruling Judah, as we know, and the Egyptian king did not trust the new king of Judah. Jehoahaz, who had reigned only three months, was sent to Egypt as a prisoner. He would never come home again.

The king of Egypt put Jehoahaz's brother, Jehoiakim, in charge of Judah, and he turned the people back to worshiping idols. The prophet Jeremiah tried to warn the king, but this only made Jehoiakim very angry. Jeremiah had to run away and hide when the king tried to have him killed.

The Egyptians ruled the country for only a few years and then lost control of Judah to the powerful Babylonians. When King Jehoiakim of Judah tried to rebel against them, he lost his kingdom and his life. His young son was made king, but the Babylonians captured him and took him away.

Once in Judah the Babylonians, under King Nebuchadnezzar, took away many of the nobles and rulers of the people. Many of these people worshiped the Lord in Babylon and stayed true to their faith while they were prisoners there.

God gave a message to the prophet Jeremiah, who sent a letter to the captives in Babylon. "Live there peacefully," God told the people. "Have children, and let them marry there. You and your children will stay there for seventy years, but then you will come home again. Call on Me, and I will hear you. I will be with you there."

The last king of Judah, who continued to rule from Jerusalem, was named Zedekiah. He promised to be faithful to Babylon, but he soon changed his mind. Jeremiah warned him not to rebel, but Zedekiah would not listen. Jeremiah was captured and thrown into a deep, dark dungeon to die. This dungeon was filled with mud and slime and Jeremiah began to sink. One of the men in the king's court was a kind African man named Ebedmelech. He threw down a rope to Jeremiah and pulled him up to a safe and dry place in the dungeon. He could not let Jeremiah out of prison, but he could give him a better place to stay than the bottom of a slimy pit.

By now the army of Babylon had surrounded Jerusalem. Soon they captured the city and took the king and all his family to the king of Babylon, just as Jeremiah had said they would. While the king watched, they killed every one of his sons. Then they blinded Zedekiah and dragged him off to Babylon. All the rebels were killed, and everyone in the land was taken to Babylon, except for the very poorest people. They were allowed to stay in Judah.

Jeremiah was set loose. He could go to Babylon or stay behind. He chose to stay behind with the poor people. But soon he was captured by enemies of Babylon and taken to Egypt, where he would die. Jeremiah is known as the sad or weeping prophet because all his life he had seen nothing but evil come to Judah. The messages from God that Jeremiah gave the people of Judah were filled with sadness and terrible news.

King Nebuchadnezzar and the Babylonians carried away all the riches of Jerusalem and then burned the city to the ground. All that was left of the temple was a heap of ashes and black stones. Four hundred years after Rehoboam became king, the kingdom of Judah was gone.

THINK ABOUT IT

✦ *Why do you think the Babylonians took everyone home with them?* ✦

Ezekiel and the Valley of Bones

✝ EZEKIEL 37 ✝

The people of Judah were marched almost a thousand miles to Babylon. Whole families went—husbands, wives, and children—not knowing what would happen to them there. Would King Nebuchadnezzar be kind to them or kill them all?

The people of Babylon treated the captives from Judah very well. They were given land to farm, and the land was good. They raised all the food they needed and built houses for themselves. Some went into the cities and became rich. Others worked for the king and became important nobles and princes.

All the time they were in Babylon, the people of Judah remained faithful to God. They taught their children to love and serve the Lord. They sang songs about their land, so they would remember their homeland while they were away and not forget their God.

The people of Judah were called Jews now or Israelites. They were all that was left of the people Moses brought out of Egypt so long ago.

God provided for the Jews in Babylon. He sent them prophets to teach them about God. One of these was Daniel, a young man who lived in the court of the king. Another was a priest named Ezekiel, who saw wonderful visions and heard what God had planned for His people in the future.

One day the Lord brought Ezekiel to a great valley. When Ezekiel looked around him, he saw dried bones filling the valley, as if a huge battle had been fought there a long time ago. The bones were scattered everywhere. "Son of man," the Lord said to Ezekiel, "can these bones live again?"

"Only You know that, Lord," Ezekiel answered. Since not even two bones in the entire valley seemed to be connected, Ezekiel must have doubted the bones could ever live again.

"Preach to these bones," the Lord told Ezekiel. "Say I will make them live and put flesh on them, and cover them with skin. They will live, and know I am the Lord."

Ezekiel spoke to the dry bones. While he did, he heard the sound of rolling thunder. All over the valley, bones began to come together until they formed human skeletons. Then flesh began to grow on the bones, until they lay like an army of dead men on the valley floor.

The Lord said to Ezekiel, "Call the wind, son of man. Tell it to breathe on these dead men and make them alive."

As Ezekiel called the wind, the dead bodies began to breathe. They stood on their feet, an army of living men, filling the whole valley!

Then the Lord said to Ezekiel, "These bones are like the people of Israel. They seem to be lost, dead, and without hope. But they will live again. I will put life into them. They will go back to their own land and live together again."

When Ezekiel told the people of Judah about this, they knew they would go home again one day.

THINK ABOUT IT

✝ *Can you picture the scene Ezekiel saw in the valley? What sounds do you hear in the valley?* ✝

STORY 8

Daniel and the Dream of a King

✝ DANIEL 1:1-2:49 ✝

When the Jews were brought to Babylon, King Nebuchadnezzar ordered his men to choose some of them for special training. He wanted young men who were very intelligent. They would be educated by the king's wise men, and when they were ready, they would serve the king and give him advice on ruling the people of Judah.

After three years of training, four of these young men—

Daniel, Shadrach, Meshach, and Abednego—were brought to the king's palace. They were treated as honored guests and food from the king's table was given to them to eat. But the Jews had strict laws about how food was to be cooked. Very politely, the four young men refused to eat the food.

"You must eat," the chief of the nobles told them. "If the king sees that you are not looking well he will be angry with me for not taking better care of you. The king may have me killed!"

Daniel said, "Just give us vegetables and bread. See if we don't look healthy at the end of ten days." At the end of the ten days, the four men were brought to the king. King Nebuchadnezzar was pleased with them. Obviously, they were faithful in the work he gave them to do, and good leaders of other people too.

Daniel was more than a wise man. He was a prophet of God who could understand dreams. One night the king had a wonderful dream. But the next morning when he awoke he could not remember any of it. He knew there was a message for him in the dream and he wanted to know what it was.

Nebuchadnezzar called all his wise men, including the four men from Judah. "Tell me the meaning of my dream," he ordered them. How could they do that when the king couldn't even remember the dream? The king got so mad at his wise men that he ordered them all killed. Daniel and the other three men would have been killed, too, but wisely Daniel asked for a little more time.

"Let me call to my God. I know He will help me tell the king his dream and its meaning." Daniel's request was granted, and the four men prayed to God.

In the morning Daniel knew the answer. He was brought back to the king. "Idols can do nothing," he said. "But there is a God in heaven who knows all things." Then Daniel told the king exactly what his dream had been and what it meant. The king was so happy with Daniel and the other three men that he gave them many presents. Three of them were given important jobs in the kingdom. Daniel was given work in the palace so he would be near the king whenever he was needed.

THINK ABOUT IT

✝ *What do you think the food in King Nebuchadnezzar's palace must have been like if Daniel requested vegetables and water? Do you think God is trying to tell us what foods are good for us?* ✝

STORY 9

The Fiery Furnace

✝ DANIEL 3:1-30 ✝

Nebuchadnezzar had been good to the Jews, but he did not worship God. Once he had a great statue made and covered with gold. The statue was set up on a large area of flat land. Since the statue was almost a hundred feet high, it could be seen from a great distance away.

The king called all his people together to worship this new idol. Among the people were the three Jewish men we met earlier, Shadrach, Meshach, and Abednego. At the sound of trumpets and beating drums and other instruments, everyone was to bow down before this idol and worship it. If anyone refused, the king would have them killed.

For some reason Daniel was not there that day. He might have been off somewhere on the king's business. But when the time came to bow down to the idol, Shadrach, Meshach, and Abednego stood still. They would only bow down to God.

Many of the men in the king's castle were jealous of Daniel and his three friends. They were the king's favorites and had been given very important jobs. Some of these men told the king that the three had not bowed down before the golden statue.

Nebuchadnezzar had the three men brought to him. If he gave an order, everyone had to obey!

"I will have the music played again," he said to the three men. "If you bow down now, you will be saved. If not, you will be thrown into a fiery furnace to die."

"Sir," the men replied, "we have a God who is able to save us from the furnace. But if it is God's will that we die, we still will not serve your gods."

Soldiers took the three men to the huge furnace. Others fed the fire and made it as hot as possible. As the king's men opened the furnace doors, the fire was so hot that flames rushed out and burned them to a crisp. Even the men holding Shadrach, Meshach, and Abednego were

burned to death as they pushed the three Jews into the flames.

When the fire cooled off a little, the king peeked into the flames. "Didn't we throw three men in here?" he asked his soldiers. "Why do I see four?" The fourth man was the angel of the Lord who was protecting the three Jews from the fire.

The king called out, "Shadrach, Meshach, and Abednego, come out!"

The three men walked out of the furnace and stood before the king. Not one hair on their heads was burned! They didn't even smell like fire and ashes.

"The God of these men has saved them!" the king called out. "I am making a new law today. No man in my kingdom can say a word against the God of these men. If anyone speaks badly of this God, I will have them killed."

Then the king gave Shadrach, Meshach, and Abednego even more important jobs than they had had before.

THINK ABOUT IT

✚ *Shadrach, Meshach, and Abednego knew for sure that God was with them, whether He chose to save them or not. Do you think King Nebuchadnezzar believes in God at the end of the story?* ✚

The Tree That Changed a King

✝ DANIEL 4:1-37 ✝

One day King Nebuchadnezzar sent a message to all of his people that began like this: "How great are God's works! How mighty are His wonders! His kingdom is without end, and His rule is forever!"

What had happened to this worshiper of idols to make him speak this way? His letter told the whole story.

One night Nebuchadnezzar had another dream. Again he sent for Daniel, whom he knew had God's Spirit, and asked the meaning of his dream.

In Nebuchadnezzar's dream a great tree gave fruit for everyone to eat. Animals rested in its shade and birds lived in its branches. An angel of the Lord came down from heaven and ordered this great tree cut down. For seven years everyone would see the stump of this great tree and know that God rules over men and women and does as He wants.

When he told Daniel about this dream, Daniel became upset.

"Tell me the truth," the king told Daniel. "Nothing will happen to you."

"Sir," Daniel said, "you are that tree. You will be driven away from men and live in the field with the animals. You will eat grass like the animals. Seven years will go by before you know that God rules your kingdom and gives it to whomever He wants. When you know this, you will have your kingdom back."

Then Daniel told the king that if he stopped sinning and ruled properly, perhaps this would not happen to him. Twelve months went by and nothing bad happened. But one day the king looked over his great city and felt proud of himself. "I built all this," he said. "I did it alone. I am a great man."

As soon as he said this, a voice came down from heaven. "Your kingdom is gone!" Nebuchadnezzar was suddenly changed. His mind left him and he became like an animal. For seven years he lived with the animals and ate like an animal. His hair grew long and his fingernails looked like bird claws.

At the end of the seven years, his reason returned. He blessed God and praised Him, and God gave him back his kingdom.

The letter ended like this: "Now I praise and honor the king of heaven. His words are truth and His works are right. Those who walk in pride He is able to make humble."

THINK ABOUT IT

✛ *What was so wrong about Nebuchadnezzar's words, "I did it alone, I am a great man?"* ✛

STORY 11

The Writing on the Wall

✝ DANIEL 5:1-31 ✝

After Nebuchadnezzar died one king followed another. As long as Nebuchadnezzar had lived, the kingdom of Babylon was strong; after he died, the kingdom began to fall apart. One reason was that the new kings went back to worshiping their idols.

During this time other nations were growing strong. Far to the east, the countries of Media and Persia joined together under a man named Cyrus and made war on Babylon. They surrounded the city, looking for a way to capture it, but the walls of Babylon were great and high.

Inside Babylon many people did not like Belshazzar, the new king. One night they opened the gates of the city and let the Persian army surround the palace.

Inside the palace Belshazzar was having a great feast. All his nobles were with him, eating and drinking off the gold and silver that had once been in the holy temple of Judah. They did not know that they were surrounded.

Suddenly, a strange thing happened. Everyone at the feast saw a huge hand writing words on the wall of the room. No one could read the words, but everyone saw the hand. "Find me someone who can read this message!" Belshazzar called out. The queen remembered Daniel and sent for him.

Daniel had become an old man. Since King Nebuchadnezzar died, Daniel was no longer the chief

adviser of the king.

"You do not worship God the way Nebuchadnezzar did," Daniel said. "That is why this message comes to you."

"What does it say?" the king asked Daniel.

"It says 'Mene, Mene, Tekel, Upharsin.' God has counted the years of your kingdom and brought it to an end. You have been weighed and found wanting. Your kingdom will be divided and given to the Medes and the Persians."

Almost immediately, the Persians and the Medes broke into the palace. They found the king and killed him in front of everyone at the feast. The kingdom of Babylon was no more.

THINK ABOUT IT

✝ *Why was the kingdom of Babylon defeated?* ✝

Daniel in the Lions' Den

✝ DANIEL 6:1-28 ✝

Babylon now became part of the Persian Empire and was ruled by a man named Darius. Darius was very fond of Daniel, and he gave this very old prophet a position of honor and power in his kingdom. In fact, next to Darius, Daniel was the most powerful ruler in the land.

There were some people in the palace who were jealous of Daniel's power and looked for a way to get rid of him. One day some of them went to the king.

"We would like to see a new law made," they told Darius. "For thirty days no one can pray to any god or ask favors from any other person. They must all come to you when they want something. If anyone disobeys this law, they will be eaten by lions."

This law pleased Darius because it gave him great honor. Darius would be more powerful than any god. Without asking Daniel for his opinion, Darius signed the law.

What Darius did not know was that Daniel prayed to God. Three times every day, he went to a window that looked toward Jerusalem—even though Jerusalem had been burned down—and prayed to God.

The men who made up this law knew that Daniel prayed three times a day and would not stop doing it. Soon they went back to Darius and told him that Daniel was breaking the new law.

In the Persian Empire once a law was made even the king could not change it. Darius had to punish Daniel. All day Darius tried to think of a way to save Daniel. In the evening the men came back and Darius had no choice. He ordered Daniel thrown into a den of hungry lions. "Maybe your God will save you," he said to Daniel as he was tossed into the den.

That night Darius could not eat or sleep. He knew he had done a very wicked thing. In the morning he rushed to the den and called out, "Daniel, has your God saved you from the lions?"

"My Lord sent an angel to save me, sir!" Daniel called out to the king. "God saw I had done no wrong and closed the mouths of the lions."

Although Darius was happy to see Daniel alive, he grew angry with the men who had tricked him. Darius ordered these men thrown into the den with the lions. He also killed all their wives and children. That doesn't seem fair, but such punishment was done in those days when a man was guilty of a great wrong.

Darius then wrote to all the people under his rule: "May peace be given to you all! I make a law that everywhere in my kingdom men should worship the Lord of Daniel for He is the only God who can save you."

Daniel lived for a number of years after this, serving Darius and after him a ruler named Cyrus.

THINK ABOUT IT

✝ *Was Darius a wise ruler? Why or why not?* ✝

The Happy Journey

✝ EZRA 1:1-3:7 ✝

Seventy years had passed since the Jewish people were taken away from their homes and brought to Babylon. Cyrus, the Persian king, treated them very well. In fact, they were no longer thought of as outsiders. They had their own land and homes and lived in peace. Many of them had become rich, while others were important people in the government.

Do you remember what the sad prophet Jeremiah had said would happen to the Jews in Babylon? After seventy years the Jews were to return to their own land of Judah. Although many of the Jews who had come from Judah were dead, their children and grandchildren still loved the land of their ancestors, even though it was far away.

Right on time, the Lord caused Cyrus to decide to allow

the people to go back home if they wanted. He wanted the temple in Jerusalem rebuilt and the country made rich again. Cyrus would still be in charge of the land of Judah, so it made sense for him to make it a better, richer place.

But Cyrus knew that not everyone would want to go back, and he didn't force them to go. He did ask those who stayed to give money to those who went. This money would be used to rebuild the temple. The people were happy to give their money for this. Cyrus also gave those who were leaving all the treasures that had been taken from the temple fifty years earlier.

Soon 42,000 Jews and all their servants left for Jerusalem. It was a long but happy trip. When they arrived, their first task was to rebuild the altar of the old temple. That completed, the daily services began again.

From that time, there were two branches of the Jewish race. Those Jews who went back and rebuilt their homes in Jerusalem and Judah would be called *Hebrews*. Those who did not go home but spread out over the rest of the world would be known as the *Jews of the Dispersion* or the *Diaspora*. Some went to Africa and Europe. Some were in business for themselves. Others were great scholars. A great number of them would visit Jerusalem during their lives to pray in the temple and many would send money to help with the rebuilding. No matter where they lived, they knew they were still one people serving the same God.

THINK ABOUT IT

✛ *Why did God through Cyrus allow the Jews to move wherever they wished?* ✛

The New Temple

✝ EZRA 3:8-6:22; HAGGAI 1:1-2:23;
ZECHARIAH 4:6-10 ✝

The man that Cyrus put in charge of Judah, or Judea as it would now be called, was named Zerubbabel. Together with the priest Joshua, the two men worked rebuild the temple. When the first stone was laid, many cried tears of joy. Others who remembered the old temple and those who had died cried tears of sadness.

But soon the builders ran into trouble. Do you remember the Samaritans? These people worshiped God but they also worshiped idols. Some of the Samaritans were Jews from the old ten tribes. Others were Assyrians who had been brought in long ago to settle in the country. When they heard the temple was being rebuilt, they wanted to help.

Zerubbabel and Joshua did not want the help of people who worshiped idols and told them to go away. Cyrus had died, and the king who was now ruling the Persian Empire was not a friend of the Jews. The Samaritans wrote to him and warned him not to let the people rebuild the temple. If they did, the Samaritans advised, the Jews would rebel against his rule.

This king believed the Samaritans and ordered that the building stop. After a while two prophets began speaking God's Word to the people. One was named Haggai and the other was Zechariah. The prophets said it was God's will that the temple be finished. Zerubbabel and Joshua went back to work.

Soon a new king took over the Persian Empire. He was a wise man named Darius, and he wanted the temple to be built. He told the Samaritans to leave the Jewish people alone. Twenty-one years after the work started, the temple was done. The new temple was larger than Solomon's temple, but not as beautiful or as richly decorated. Further, there was no Ark of the Covenant in the Holy of Holies because the golden chest had been lost forever. But at least the people had a temple again where they could serve God.

Think About It

✤ *Why did the Samaritans want to help rebuild the temple?* ✤

Story 15

Beautiful Queen Esther

✤ Esther 1:1-10:3 ✤

When Darius died, his son Ahasuerus took his place on the throne of Persia. The new king wanted to choose a queen and he commanded that all the beautiful women from his kingdom be brought to his palace. He would choose a queen from these women.

One who was brought to the palace was a beautiful Jewish woman named Esther. She lived with her cousin Mordecai because her parents were dead. As soon as the king saw Esther, he fell in love with her, and soon they were married.

Mordecai could not visit Esther at the palace since no man except the king could enter the rooms of women. But Esther could see Mordecai from her window whenever he walked by, and they could send messages back and forth through her servants. Every day Mordecai would sit by the palace gate in case Esther wanted to send him a message.

Mordecai heard many things while he sat by the palace gate. No one paid him any attention or watched what they said when they were around him. One day he heard two men planning to kill the king. He sent a message about this to Esther. She told the king and the two men were captured.

A man named Haman soon became very powerful in the palace. Haman was given more power than other princes and the king asked his advice on everything. People would always bow to Haman as a sign of respect when he walked by. But Mordecai would not bow down to anyone but God, and that made Haman angry at Mordecai and at all Jews.

Haman went to the king and told him that there was a certain group of people in the kingdom that should not be allowed to live. He said these people followed different rules and not the laws of the king. This was not true, of course, but the king, who almost never left the palace, believed what Haman said. He told him to do whatever he wanted.

Haman made a new law and sent it to every city in Persia. It said that on a certain day all the Jews could be killed. Anyone who killed a Jew could take everything the Jew owned for himself. No one could understand why this was happening. Here was a chance to get rich and obey the law at the same time!

Mordecai heard about this law too. As soon as he could, he sent a message to Esther, telling her to go to the king and stop the murders that would soon occur.

Esther wrote back to Mordecai. "No one can go to the king without being called. I would be killed."

"You will not be safe either," Mordecai reminded her. "Maybe you have been put in the palace by God just for this reason."

Esther asked all the Jews to pray for her and fast for the next three days. She and her servants in the palace did the same.

On the third day Esther entered the throne room of the king. The guards moved toward her. Would she be killed? When the king looked at her and saw how lovely she was, he told his guards to leave her alone. "What do you want?" the king asked Esther. "I would give you half my kingdom if you asked for it."

Esther was very careful in choosing her words. "I only wanted to invite you and Haman to dinner, sir," she said. The two men came and ate with Esther. When they were done, the king asked if he could give Esther anything in return. "No," she said. "But I would be happy if you both came back again tomorrow for dinner."

Haman was very pleased to eat with the king and queen, but he was still angry at Mordecai. That day he had gallows built, or a wooden structure on which someone would die by hanging. At dinner that night Haman was going to ask the king for permission to hang Mordecai.

Before the second dinner the king remembered he had not rewarded Mordecai for saving his life some time ago. He asked Haman how a man should be honored, and when Haman told him, the king ordered him to go honor Mordecai in that way. Haman was furious at having to honor a man who would not bow down to him, but he did as he was told.

At dinner that night the king asked Esther what he could do to make her happy. "If you love me, sir," she said, "you will save my life and the lives of my people. We have an enemy who is going to kill us all."

"Who would dare to kill the queen?" the king asked.

"Our enemy is Haman," Esther said quietly.

The king was so angry with Haman that he had him hanged on the very gallows Haman had built for Mordecai! Then he gave Mordecai Haman's job, setting him over all the princes.

The terrible law was still legal though. Remember, no Persian law could be changed once it was signed by the king. The king sent out one more law. This new law allowed the Jews to defend themselves if they were attacked on that day. Because everyone knew the king was a friend of the Jews, few people tried to kill the Jews. Those who did were killed by the Jews themselves.

Jewish people today still celebrate God's mercy and the bravery of beautiful Queen Esther during the holiday of Purim.

THINK ABOUT IT

✛ *Can you think of any reason why Esther didn't ask for what she wanted right away?* ✛

Ezra, The First Scribe

✝ EZRA 7:1-10:44 ✝

Things did not go well for the Jews who returned to Judea. Ninety years after their return, Jerusalem was still only a small town. There was no wall around the city to protect it from robbers who came from the desert and took what they wanted. Their children were marrying people from other races who worshiped idols. Their grandchildren were not following the laws of God.

God raised up two men to help His people. The first was Ezra. Ezra led the people back to God and God's Word. The second man was Nehemiah. Nehemiah led the people in building a wall around the city. Once their city was safe and God blessed them, more people came to live in Judea.

Unlike most people of the day, Ezra could read and write. Most people had to have letters read to them by others. Nearly all the books of what we call the Old Testament had been written by now, but these books were not all in one place. Books were all written by hand then, and no one had a copy of the entire Old Testament.

Whenever Ezra found a book of the law, he would carefully copy it by hand. He asked others who could read and write to do the same. In time, Ezra put everything together into one book and called it the Book of the Law. Ezra's book contained all the laws of Moses and the sayings of all the prophets. When he was done, Ezra brought his book to Judea.

Ezra's helpers came with him. These men had been trained to love the law, copy it, and teach it to others. They were called *scribes*, or writers. After Ezra, there were many scribes among the Jewish people. Eventually every place of worship had its own copy of the laws. This kept the law from ever being lost or forgotten.

The Jews had only one temple for sacrifices and that temple was in Jerusalem. But now that Jewish people lived all over the world, they needed places to worship that were close to them. *Synagogues* were built as places where people could meet to hear the Word of God, to study the Book of the Law, to worship God, and to sing psalms together.

Ezra was more than a scribe; he was a man of God. Ezra reminded the people that they were a special people. They had been chosen by God and protected by God and they must live apart from other nations. They had work to do for God and could never forget His love and kindness toward them.

THINK ABOUT IT

✝ *Why were scribes important to the people of Judea?* ✝

Nehemiah and the Wall of Jerusalem

✝ NEHEMIAH 1:1-7:73 ✝

Nehemiah served Artaxerxes, the king of Persia after King Ahasuerus. As the king's cup bearer, Nehemiah poured wine for the king and saw that no one poisoned him. A king always chose a trusted friend for this job.

One day Nehemiah received terrible news of his beloved city Jerusalem. He heard that Jerusalem was still a struggling town with no walls. Life was dangerous in an unwalled city and the people living there were very poor.

Nehemiah became so sad that the king was concerned. When he asked what was the matter, Nehemiah told him about Jerusalem and then he asked the king if he could go

there and rebuild the city walls.

King Artaxerxes agreed that Nehemiah could go. He gave him letters that said he could have all the building materials he needed. He even sent a company of horsemen and guards to protect Nehemiah and help him with his work.

When Nehemiah arrived in Jerusalem, he convinced the people to rebuild the city's walls. Each family in the city was in charge of one section of wall. Some built large pieces of the wall while others only built right in front of their own houses. Slowly, the wall began to grow.

Building the wall was not safe work. Because there were those in the land who wanted to keep Jerusalem weak, the men who worked on the wall always carried weapons and Nehemiah set guards all around the wall. Nehemiah and his crew worked so hard and so fast that the wall was done in only fifty-two days! The gates were hung and guards took their places inside the wall. Now that Jerusalem was safe from its enemies, the once proud city could become strong again.

_____

THINK ABOUT IT

✝ *Why did King Artaxerxes approve of Nehemiah's mission?* ✝

_____

So Everyone May Understand

✝ NEHEMIAH 8:1-13:31; MALACHI 1:1-4:6 ✝

When the wall was finished, Nehemiah called all the Jews in the land to Jerusalem and asked Ezra to read the Book of the Law to them. The people spoke many different languages, and most of them could not understand what was being spoken. Realizing the problem, Ezra had men stand next to him who spoke many languages. He would read a part of the law and they would translate it into another language. This way everyone understood what had been read.

After the reading everyone went home and had a great feast. They were happy they could hear God's Word and learn the laws He had given them.

The next day, all the Jews met again. They confessed their sins and the sins of their fathers who had worshiped idols. Then they made a promise that they would always keep God's law. They wrote this promise down, and all the rulers signed it for the people.

Jerusalem grew large and strong. Jews living in other countries came to live and work in Judea. Soon the land was filled with people. The hills were covered with vineyards and olive groves and the plains with fields of grain.

As the Old Testament ends, the prophet Malachi writes these words: "Thus saith the Lord, Behold, I will send my messenger, and he shall prepare the way before me." Of whom was Malachi speaking?

THINK ABOUT IT

✛ *Why is Jerusalem growing strong again?* ✛

242

PART 6

A World Is Saved!

GOD SENDS HIS SON TO EARTH

An Angel by the Altar

✝ LUKE 1:1-80 ✝

When the New Testament begins, Judea is under the control of the Roman Empire. A man named Herod of Judea is the king ruling the country for the Romans. The temple built by Zerubbabel was very old by now, and was being rebuilt by King Herod.

One day an old priest named Zacharias was in the temple serving God. He suddenly saw an angel of the Lord standing by the altar and he was very afraid. "Don't be afraid," the angel told him. "I bring you good news. Your wife will have a son named John. He will lead many people to the Lord."

When Zacharias returned to his home, he told his wife Elisabeth about the angel. She was very old too. But she was happy to hear she would have a son who would serve the Lord.

About six months later the same angel went to see a woman in the city of Nazareth. She was a cousin of Elisabeth. Mary was engaged to be married to a man named Joseph, a carpenter, who came from the family of David the king.

"Mary," the angel said, "you are to be blessed by God. He is going to give you a son named Jesus. He will be called the Son of God and will rule over His people forever."

Then the angel told Mary that her cousin Elisabeth was going to have a great son too. When the angel left Mary traveled to Elisabeth's home to see her and stayed with her for almost three months.

Just as the angel said, Elisabeth gave birth to a son and named him John. He was dedicated to God and grew up in the desert south of Judea.

THINK ABOUT IT

✝ *Do you know who these two babies will grow up to be?* ✝

The Manger in Bethlehem

✟ MATTHEW 1:18-25; LUKE 2:1-39 ✟

Soon after Joseph and Mary were married, the Roman emperor ordered everyone to return to the towns their families came from. The emperor wanted to know how many people were in the kingdom and to what family everyone belonged. Mary and Joseph were both from David's family, so they traveled to Bethlehem, where David had been born.

Everyone in the kingdom was traveling far from their homes. They all needed places to eat and sleep, and soon the few inns in each area were full. When they got to Bethlehem, Mary and Joseph could not find a place to stay. Finally a man let them stay in his barn (called a manger) with the cattle. This manger wasn't a fancy place, but the animals helped keep it warm, and it was out of the weather. While they were staying there, Mary had her baby.

That night some shepherds were taking care of their sheep in a field near Bethlehem. Suddenly a great light shone from the sky and an angel of the Lord stood before them. "Fear not," the angel told them. "I bring you good news. This day in Bethlehem, the city of David, a Savior has been born for you. Go look for Him. He is a newborn baby, lying in a barn at the inn."

Then the sky above the shepherds was filled with angels that praised God and sang, "Glory to God in the highest. And peace to men on earth."

The shepherds hurried to the inn and found the baby boy in the manger. They told Mary and Joseph what the angels had said to them and praised God for the good news they had heard.

After the first child was born into a family, the Jewish people always took the baby to the temple and offered a sacrifice to dedicate the baby to God. When Jesus was forty days old Joseph and Mary took Him to the temple. Joseph could not afford to sacrifice a lamb so he bought a pair of young pigeons and gave them to God as thanks for the baby Jesus.

While they were at the temple, an old man named Simeon rushed in. God had told Simeon that he would not die until he had seen the Savior (the *Messiah*) promised to the Jewish people. That day the spirit of the Lord told him to go to the temple. When he saw Jesus, Simeon took the little baby in his arms and thanked God for allowing him to see the Savior in his lifetime. Then Simeon blessed the baby.

A woman named Anna, who was a prophet, came into the temple at that very time. She too saw that Jesus was the promised Savior, and she gave thanks to God for the little boy He had sent.

Think About It

✛ *How many people did God tell about the baby Jesus and what He would grow up to be?* ✛

The Wise Men Follow a Star

✛ MATTHEW 2:1-23 ✛

J oseph, Mary, and Jesus were in Bethlehem for some time, staying in a room at someone's house. There they had more visitors.

Before Jesus was born a new star began to shine in the sky far east of Judea. Wise men lived there who studied the stars. They believed this star meant that a new king was about to be born far away to the west of them. They packed up gifts fit for a king and traveled toward the star on their camels, hoping to meet the king.

When the wise men reached Judea, they thought everyone would know about the new king. But no one could tell them anything. King Herod heard about these men and

had them brought to him. Herod didn't know about a new king: He thought *he* was the king. If someone else were claiming to be king, he wanted to know about it.

Herod called for his own wise men. "Tell me where Christ, the King of Israel, is supposed to be born," he demanded.

The men searched the holy books and came back with their answer. "He is to be born in Bethlehem."

Herod told the wise men from the east to look in Bethlehem. "If you find him, come back and tell me where he is," he said. "I want to go and worship him too."

The wise men went to Bethlehem and found the baby Jesus. They unpacked their expensive gifts of gold and sweet spices and gave them to Him. Then they bowed down and worshiped the new king. That night God in a dream told the wise men not to go back to Herod but to leave the country by a different way. They obeyed the Lord, and Herod did not learn where Jesus was.

After the wise men left, the Lord in a dream spoke to Joseph. "Get up and go to Egypt. Herod will try to kill the baby." In the middle of the night, Joseph, Mary, and Jesus left Bethlehem and began the long trip south to Egypt.

Herod waited for the wise men to come back, but they never did. He would have to take care of this baby king himself. Since he couldn't find the baby, Herod gave a cruel order. All baby boys under the age of two were to be taken away from their mothers and killed. That would take care of Herod's problem. He did not know that the baby he was looking for was safe in Egypt.

Soon after, the angel of the Lord told Joseph it was safe to go home again. King Herod had died, and his kingdom had been divided between his children. Instead of going back to Bethlehem, which was ruled by a cruel son of Herod, Joseph and Mary and Jesus went to their old home of Nazareth. The king that ruled there was not as bad as the one in Bethlehem, and the young child would be safer there.

The family stayed in Nazareth for many years. As Jesus grew, the family of Mary and Joseph grew as well and other sons and daughters were added to their household.

THINK ABOUT IT

✦ *The wise men and Herod thought Jesus was going to grow up to become the kind of king Herod was, one who ruled a kingdom on earth. What was different about the kingdom Jesus would rule?* ✦

STORY 4

In His Father's House

✦ LUKE 2:40-52 ✦

The Bible does not tell us much about Jesus' life as a boy. We know Joseph was a carpenter, so he was not rich. Jesus probably lived in a one-room house and slept on mats on a dirt floor.

Twice a week Jesus would go to the synagogue in town with Joseph to worship God. He probably studied the Old Testament and learned to read and write. In those days most Jewish boys learned the entire Old Testament by heart.

When Jesus was twelve years old he traveled to Jerusalem with his family and other people from Nazareth to celebrate the feast of the Passover. This was the first time Jesus had been to the temple and seen all the people and ceremonies there. He loved it, and wanted to learn all He could while He was there.

When it was time for the family to leave Jerusalem, Jesus stayed behind in the temple. There were many people traveling together back to Nazareth, and it took a while for Mary and Joseph to realize Jesus was not with the group. They hurried back to town to find Him.

They looked for Him for two days. Where could He be? They asked everyone they knew in town if they had seen Jesus. Maybe He was visiting some of their relatives or playing with friends. On the third day they went to the temple. Maybe they were going to pray to God to help them find their son.

There in the temple was Jesus, sitting with the teachers of the law. He was listening to what they said and asking many questions about the law. Everyone around Him was surprised by how much He knew.

Mary was very upset with Jesus by now. "We have been looking for You for days!" she told Him. "Why are You acting like this?"

"Why did you have to look everywhere for Me?" Jesus asked Mary and Joseph. "Didn't you know I would be in My Father's house?"

Remember, the Jewish people believed that God lived in the temple in Jerusalem. Mary and Joseph weren't too sure what Jesus was talking about, but they were happy to find Him.

The years went by, and Jesus grew into a fine young man. He was loving and smart, and everyone who knew Him liked him very much. When Joseph died, Jesus took care of Mary and the rest of the family by working as a carpenter. He stayed in Nazareth with his family until he was thirty years old.

THINK ABOUT IT

✝ *How would your parents feel if you disappeared in a*

large city for three days? Why should Mary have expected something unusual to happen to Jesus? ✝

STORY 5

The Prophet in the Wilderness

✝ MATTHEW 3:1-17; MARK 1:1-11; LUKE 3:1-22 ✝

Jesus had never met Mary's cousin's son John. Jesus lived in the northern part of the country, and John lived in the desert far to the south.

John did not live the way most people lived. He dressed in clothes made of camel's hair and skins. He ate dried locusts and wild honey. But the spirit of God was with John, and he became a great prophet.

It had been 400 years since the last prophet had been sent by God. When the people heard that John was speaking the words of God, they came from all over the country to hear him and learn God's will. He gave everyone the same message: "Do right. Stop living sinful lives and give yourselves to God." Then he would take those who wanted to change into the Jordan River and wash away their sins as a sign that God had forgiven them.

Some people thought that John must be the Messiah. The Jews had been waiting for the Savior or Messiah to come for years. But John said he was not the one they were

waiting for.

Jesus went to listen to John too. As He came near, God told John that this was the Savior. Jesus asked John to baptize Him.

"I should be baptized by You," John said Jesus.

"No," Jesus answered. "This is the right thing to do."

So John baptized Jesus in the Jordan River. As Jesus came up out of the water, John saw the heavens open above Jesus' head. The spirit of the Lord came down to Jesus in the form of a dove and landed on Him. And John heard God's voice say, "This is My beloved Son. I am very pleased with Him."

John told everyone there that Jesus was the Son of God, the Messiah.

THINK ABOUT IT

✝ *A prophet brings people news from God. What news did John have for the people of Judea?* ✝

Jesus Is Tested

✚ MATTHEW 4:1-11; MARK 1:12, 13;
LUKE 4:1-13; JOHN 1:29-51 ✚

After God's spirit came to Him, Jesus went into the desert to pray and learn what God wanted Him to do. He was there for forty days with nothing to eat or drink. At the end of that time, Jesus was feeling very weak.

While Jesus was weak from hunger and thirst, Satan the devil appeared to him. "If You are the Son of God," Satan said, "why don't You turn these rocks into bread and eat them?"

Jesus knew He could do this if He wanted. But this was not the reason He had great powers. His job was to help others, not Himself. He refused to do what Satan said.

Then Satan led Jesus to Jerusalem and took him to the top of the temple. "The book of Psalms says angels will take care of the Son of God. Throw Yourself off this roof. See if the angels save You."

Jesus was not going to test God's strength and power. He knew God could save Him if He jumped, but it wasn't right to test God like that.

Then Satan took Jesus to the top of a high mountain and let Him see all the countries in the world. "All this will be Yours if You worship me," he said.

But Jesus knew only God deserves to be worshiped, and He sent Satan away from Him. Once Satan was gone, God sent angels with food and water for Jesus.

Jesus went back to the Jordan River where John the

Baptist was still preaching. As John saw Jesus coming, he cried out, "Behold the Lamb of God, who takes away the sin of the world! This is the one I have told you about. This is the Son of God."

Two men who had been with John wanted to know more about Jesus. When He left the riverside, they followed Him and talked with Him. By the end of the day they were sure Jesus was the Messiah, the Christ they had all been awaiting. The names of these two men were Andrew and John. They were the first men after John the Baptist to believe Jesus was the Son of God.

Andrew went and found his brother Simon and brought him to see Jesus. When He saw Simon, Jesus gave him a new name. "You will be called the Rock." The name Peter means rock in Greek, so Simon became Simon Peter from then on.

The next day Jesus started back toward His home in Galilee. On the way He met a man named Philip who lived in the area of Nazareth. "Follow Me," Jesus told Philip. Philip found a friend named Nathanael and asked him to join them.

But Nathanael had questions. First of all, he wondered why the Messiah would come from such a tiny town in a tiny province. Philip convinced Nathanael to at least come and meet Jesus. Maybe then he would believe.

As Nathanael approached, Jesus called out to him. "Here comes a real Israelite, a man with no sins."

"How do You know about me?" Nathanael asked Jesus.

"I saw you standing under the fig tree before Philip came to you," Jesus answered.

No regular man could do that. No regular man could just look at another and know if he were good or sinful. Nathanael was convinced: Jesus must be the Son of God.

Jesus now had five followers. These men, and others who would join them later, would stay with Jesus and learn from Him. They would be called *disciples*.

THINK ABOUT IT

✛ *Why did Satan want Jesus to prove He was the Son of God? Why did Jesus refuse to do the things Satan asked Him to do?* ✛

STORY 7

The Wedding Feast in Cana

✛ JOHN 2:1-3:21 ✛

A few days later, Jesus and His five followers went to a wedding in the city of Cana. Jesus' earthly mother Mary was there too. She was a friend of one of the families.

At that time in Israel wedding parties sometimes went on for days after a marriage. Guests who came from far away would stay over and celebrate with food and drink. While there were still guests there the family giving this party ran out of wine. To run out of wine while the wedding party was still going on could be embarrassing for the host, so Mary told Jesus about the problem.

Jesus told Mary that it was not time for Him to perform miracles. But Mary knew Jesus could help if He wanted to, and she hoped He would help out her friends. Mary went to the servants in charge of the wine and said they should do whatever Jesus instructed.

Six mammoth stone jars were in the room. They were meant for water, not wine, and Jesus told the servants to fill the jars with water. Then Jesus told them to draw out some of the water and take it to the man in charge of the party. When they went to take out some of the water, they saw the water had been changed into wine! And it was very good wine too.

This was the first time Jesus let others see Him use His power to do what no one else could do. Acts like this are called *miracles*. Jesus performed miracles to show people the power of God.

When the feast of the Passover was near, Jesus and His disciples went to the temple in Jerusalem to worship. People came from all over the land to Jerusalem to give sacrifices of thanksgiving.

Many of these people had different money from that which was used in Jerusalem. Just like countries today, each area had its own type of money. In Jerusalem the outsiders' money had to be changed into local money, and there were people in the temple that did just that. Also, most people bought the animals they would sacrifice in the temple, instead of bringing them from home. An animal that was to be sacrificed had to be perfect, so it was easier to buy one in the temple. The temple area was filled with sheep and oxen and doves and money changers. It looked more like a market than a temple of God.

When Jesus saw all this going on in the temple, He became angry. He took a piece of rope and, using it like a whip, chased all the money changers and animal sellers out of the temple. The rulers of the temple were not happy about this. They made money from all these people.

"Who are You to do things like this?" they asked Jesus. "Prove to us that God has given You the right to do this."

Jesus said to them, "Destroy this temple, and in three days I will raise it up."

"It's taken forty-six years to build this temple," they said. "And You think You can build it in just three days?"

Jesus wasn't talking about the temple in Jerusalem. He was talking about His own body, which was God's temple. Later, when He rose from the dead after three days, His disciples would remember what He said and understand what He meant that day in the temple.

While Jesus was still in Jerusalem one of the rulers of the Jews came to see Him. He came at night. Maybe he was afraid to have the others know about his visit. This man was named Nicodemus. He asked Jesus what he had to do to be saved from his sins.

Jesus answered, "Unless a man is born again, he cannot see the kingdom of God."

Nicodemus didn't understand what Jesus meant. He didn't see how someone could ever be born again once they were alive.

"Unless a man is born of water and spirit," Jesus went on, "he cannot enter into God's kingdom." Jesus meant that we need to be baptized: God must put His spirit in us if we are to be His children. "God did not send His Son to judge the people of the world, but to save them."

As you can see, not everyone who talked to Jesus understood what He meant.

STORY 8

The Stranger at the Well

✛ MATTHEW 14:3-5; MARK 6:17-20; LUKE 3:19, 20; JOHN 3:22-4:42 ✛

The Samaritans and the Jews had been enemies for hundreds of years. Although they all worshiped God, they did it in different ways. A Jew would not talk to a Samaritan if he met one. Most Jews would not even walk through the Samaritans' land.

Jesus and His followers were on their way from Jerusalem to Galilee. Instead of walking around Samaria, Jesus decided to go through it. One morning Jesus stopped to rest at Jacob's well. This well had been dug hundreds of years ago but still contained good water. His disciples went to a nearby village to buy some food, leaving Jesus alone. Jesus was very thirsty, but He had no jar or bucket to lower into the deep well.

When a Samaritan woman came to the well for water, she brought her rope and a water jar. Jesus asked if she would give Him a drink of water.

Now she could tell by His clothing that Jesus was a Jew. She wondered why He was even talking to her.

"Whoever drinks from this well will be thirsty again," Jesus told her. "I give water that leads to everlasting life."

"Sir," the woman said, "give me some of this water. Then I will not have to come all the way to this well."

Jesus looked at the woman. "Go home and bring your husband here," He told her.

"I have no husband," she said.

"I know. You have had five husbands. You are not married to the man you live with now."

How could this stranger know all about her life, she wondered. He must be a prophet of God to be so wise. "I know the Christ is coming," she said. "He will teach us about everything."

Jesus said to her, "I am the Christ."

Just then the disciples came back and saw Jesus talking with the Samaritan woman. The woman was so amazed at Jesus' words that she rushed off to her village to tell everyone there about this man who said He was the Christ. She had forgotten to draw her own water and even left her water jar by the well.

Soon the woman came back with a crowd of people from her village. They asked Jesus to stay with them for a few days and teach them about God. Many of the people believed in Jesus and knew that He was the Savior of the world who had been promised to them.

THINK ABOUT IT

✚ *From this story, what have the disciples learned about Jesus?* ✚

Jesus Returns to Nazareth

✝ JOHN 4:46-54; LUKE 4:16-31 ✝

When Jesus returned to Galilee the news spread quickly. This made one man very happy. He was a nobleman in the court of King Herod, and his son was dying. The man rode all night and came to Jesus early in the morning. "Please come and save my son," he begged Jesus.

"Go home," Jesus said. "Your son will live."

The man believed Jesus. He did not beg Jesus to go with him; he did not race home to see if his son was better. If Jesus said his son would live, the man was sure he would. He had *faith* in Jesus. On the way home one of his servants met him and said the boy was better.

"When did he begin to get better?" the man asked.

"At seven in the morning the fever left him," the servant replied. That was exactly when Jesus had told the man his son would live.

Jesus had come to Galilee to preach to the people. He thought He would begin in His own town of Nazareth. He had many friends there, people He had grown up with, and He wanted them to hear the good news of God's salvation first.

On the Sabbath Jesus went to His old synagogue in Nazareth. The place was filled with people, people who wanted to see Jesus perform a miracle for them. No one was interested in the kingdom of God or forgiveness of their sins. They wanted to see something special. They wanted a show!

Jesus began to tell them how He had been sent to save the world from sin and to tell everyone about God's goodness. Soon people began to squirm and whisper. They didn't want to hear all this!

Jesus saw they were getting bored. "I know you want to see a miracle from Me. Remember the prophets of long ago? They didn't do miracles in front of their own people. Elijah didn't do miracles for the widows in his land. But he did for one outside his own country. Elisha only cured one leper, and he was a Syrian."

The people became angry at Jesus. He would do miracles for strangers, but not for them, His old friends? They pushed Him out of the synagogue and took Him to the top of a hill. If He had not slipped out of their grip and disappeared, they would have thrown Him over the cliff!

Jesus left Nazareth, knowing He could not help His own people, and walked to Capernaum. He would teach the people there instead.

THINK ABOUT IT

+ *What are the differences between the nobleman and*

the people of Nazareth? (The nobleman wanted Jesus to perform a miracle, and so did the Nazarenes.)

A Net Full of Fish

✛ MATTHEW 4:18-22; MARK 1:16-34;
LUKE 4:33-5:11 ✛

Four of Jesus' disciples had traveled with Him to Jerusalem and back. But now in Galilee they were home, and they went back to their families and their fishing.

One morning Jesus came to the edge of the Sea of Galilee. A great crowd of people was following Him, wanting to hear Him speak. On the shore nearby were two boats. One belonged to the disciples Simon Peter and Andrew. The other belonged to two other disciples, James and John. The four men were nearby, working on their nets.

Jesus asked Simon Peter and Andrew to row Him out a little from the shore so He could talk to the people without being pushed and shoved. Later, when the people left, Jesus told the two men to row out into deeper water. "Let down your nets and catch some fish," He said.

"Master," Simon Peter said, "we have been fishing all night. We caught nothing. But if You say so, we will let down the net again."

Soon the net was so full that the two men could not pull it up! Their little boat was in danger of turning over. They called to James and John for help. Even then, the catch was almost too big to be brought in.

When Simon Peter saw this, he bowed down before Jesus. "Lord, I am full of sin. I am not worthy of all this! Leave me, Lord."

"Don't be afraid," Jesus told him. "Stay with Me. I will make you fishers of men." From then on, Simon Peter, Andrew, James, and John gave up fishing and stayed with Jesus all the time.

Jesus would speak in the synagogue every Sabbath, teaching the people about God. One Sabbath a man came into the synagogue who had an evil spirit living inside him. While Jesus was preaching, this man, or rather, the evil spirit inside him, interrupted the service.

"Leave us alone! I know who You are. You are the Holy One of God!"

Jesus spoke to the evil spirit living inside this man. "Be quiet and come out of this man!" He said.

The spirit threw the man down and the poor man appeared to be torn apart. But the spirit obeyed Jesus and left the man there on the floor, alive and well.

Everyone who saw this was amazed. "This man has power over evil spirits!" they said.

After the meeting Jesus went to the house of Simon Peter and found Simon's mother-in-law sick with a high fever. When Jesus touched her hand lightly, the fever left her. She was so well that she was able to make dinner for everyone that day.

That evening, when the Sabbath was over and people could work again, many of them came to Jesus with their sick friends and relatives. Jesus healed them all.

THINK ABOUT IT

✢ *Why was Simon Peter so afraid when Jesus did a miracle for him?* ✢

Healed by Him

✛ MATTHEW 8:2-4; 9: 2-8; MARK 1:40-45;
2:1-12; LUKE 5:12-26 ✛

Before it was light the next day, Jesus left Simon's house and wandered away to be alone with God and pray. When everyone else woke up and found Him gone, they went looking for Him. "Everyone is looking for You," they said when they found Him. "Come back into the city with us."

"No," Jesus answered. "I must leave here. There are other places I must preach. That is why I have been sent."

Jesus went to all the towns in that part of Galilee, preaching, healing, and casting out evil spirits. His disciples all went with Him, and great crowds followed them everywhere.

One day a leper came to Jesus. Remember how the Jews were forbidden to touch a leper or to be anywhere near one? This poor man said to Jesus, "I know You can make me well if You want."

"I am willing," Jesus said. Then He reached out His hand and touched the leper. "Be clean," He said. In an instant the disease left the man. "Do not tell anyone about this," Jesus told him. "Go to the priests and let them see you are cured. Then offer the proper sacrifices."

Jesus said this because He knew more people would come to Him for healing if the leper told of this miracle. Jesus had come to preach to the people and teach them. As much as He liked to cure people, His real job was to save them from their sins.

But the leper was so happy that he could not keep his

secret. Soon more people followed Jesus than ever. He had no time to preach or teach, and He could never get away by Himself.

One evening a huge crowd filled the house where Jesus was staying. Under a roof in the courtyard that was there to give shade, Jesus was trying to teach. All of a sudden the roof above Jesus was removed and a sick man was lowered down in front of Jesus! "My son," Jesus said to the sick man, "be happy. Your sins are forgiven."

Not everyone in that crowd was a friend or follower of Jesus. There were Pharisees there too. These men followed God's written laws exactly. They thought doing this made them better than normal men. They were watching Jesus very carefully, hoping He would do something against the laws so they could accuse Him.

When they heard Jesus forgive the sick man's sins, they thought they had caught Him breaking the law. Only God could forgive sins. Not even the most special prophet in the world had that power, according to the law.

Jesus knew what these men were thinking. "I do have the power to forgive sins," he called out to them. Then He said to the sick man who had been lowered down, "Rise up. Take your bed, and go home."

At once the man stood up and carried off his bed. Jesus had the power to heal, and more important, the power to forgive sins.

THINK ABOUT IT

+ *Did the leper ask Jesus to cure him? What did he really say to Jesus?* +

STORY 12

By the Bubbling Waters

+ MATTHEW 12:1-14; MARK 2:23-3:6;
LUKE 6:1-11; JOHN 5:1-18 +

O nce again it was time for Jesus to go to Jerusalem for the feast of the Passover. While He was there Jesus passed by what was known as the pool of Bethesda. Every once in a while the water of this pool would bubble up like a spring. People believed the bubbling of the water could cure illnesses. Sick people would stay by the pool, waiting for it to bubble, and go into the water.

On the Sabbath Jesus saw a man who had been a cripple for almost forty years sitting on a porch by the pool. The man had no one to help him get into the pool and besides that, he was always pushed aside by others. When he told Jesus all this, Jesus said to him, "Get up. Take your bed with you and walk."

The man felt his legs grow strong again. He picked up the mat he had been sitting on and walked off. But as he did, some Pharisees nearby called out to him. "Stop! You know you cannot do any work on the Sabbath. You can't carry your bed like that!"

"The man who healed me told me to pick up my bed and walk," the man said, going on his way. When he met Jesus again later at the temple, he told the Pharisees that Jesus was the one who had healed him.

The Pharisees reminded Jesus that it was illegal to heal on the Sabbath. Jesus replied, "My Father works every day to do good things for people. So do I."

This made the Pharisees angry. Not only was Jesus working on the day no one was allowed to work, but He was talking like He was the Son of God. We know that is just what Jesus was, but talking like that was considered a sin to the Jewish people.

After Passover Jesus and His disciples returned to their homes by the Sea of Galilee. One Sabbath they walked through a field of ripe grain. Because they were hungry they took some grain from the field and ate it as they walked. It was legal to do this, but not on the Sabbath. Again the Pharisees who were watching Jesus reminded Jesus of His supposed sins. Jesus reminded the Pharisees that David had eaten bread from the temple when he was running away from Saul. And the priests in the temple worked on the Sabbath too.

Another Sabbath Jesus healed a man's hand while He was in the synagogue. This time Jesus told the Pharisees that it was right to do good things for people, no matter what day it was.

We know Jesus was right. A person should be able to do good things any day of the week. But many years ago God had told the Jews to keep the day of rest holy and not do any work on that day. Legally, Jesus was breaking the law. But in another way, He was obeying God's greater law. The Pharisees could not understand Jesus' ways. They began to see Jesus as a criminal, not the Son of God.

THINK ABOUT IT

✤ *We have a Sabbath day too. What do we call it? Think of good ways to spend a Sabbath day.* ✤

STORY 13

The Sermon on the Mount

✤ MATTHEW 9:9-13; 5-8; MARK 2:13-17; LUKE 5:27-32; 6:12-49 ✤

The Roman Empire collected taxes from the people of Judea, as all governments do. Certain men were given the job of collecting these taxes, and many of these tax collectors were dishonest. They kept some of the money they collected, or they took too much money. The Jews hated and distrusted all tax collectors.

One day Jesus walked by one of these men. His name was Matthew, and he was a good man, not a crook. Jesus looked at this man and said, "Follow Me." Right away,

Matthew walked away from his work and went with Jesus.

After he joined Jesus, Matthew gave a party at his home. He invited Jesus and the disciples and some of his other friends. The people Matthew invited were not rich and famous. Some of them were considered sinners by the Jewish people.

The Pharisees thought Jesus was wrong to be with these people. "I came to help those who know they are not perfect and want to be better. Not those who think they are holy," Jesus told His disciples.

One evening Jesus walked to the top of a mountain to pray. He stayed there the whole night. In the morning, in front of a crowd of people that followed Him everywhere, Jesus chose twelve men to stay with Him and help Him teach about God. Some of these men had been with Him before and some were new. Many years later these men would begin to tell the world about Jesus; they would write about Jesus' life and teachings in the New Testament.

Still on the mountain, Jesus sat down and the twelve disciples stood beside Him. To the great crowd in front Jesus gave a speech, a speech recorded by Matthew, the former tax collector. The speech has been called the

Sermon on the Mount. Here are the first three verses of the Sermon on the Mount (Matthew 5:3-5, KJV):

Blessed are the poor in spirit: for theirs is the kingdom of heaven.

Blessed are they that mourn: for they shall be comforted.

Blessed are the meek: for they shall inherit the earth.

THINK ABOUT IT

✛ *If you could help people be better, whom would you help? Those who were already okay, or those who needed help the most?* ✛

STORY 14

A Captain's Faith

✛ MATTHEW 8:5-13; LUKE 7:1-17; 36-50 ✛

In the city of Capernaum lived a Roman soldier who was a good man. He loved the Jews because they had taught him about God and he had even built a synagogue for them. This man was in charge of a hundred other soldiers. He was an important man, even though he was not a Jew.

When this man's servant became very sick, he went to the synagogue and asked the leaders there if they would talk to Jesus about the sick servant. He did not feel he should speak to Jesus himself. That would be asking too much, he thought. Because they liked this soldier, the

271

synagogue leaders agreed. "He is a good man," they told Jesus. "He loves our people."

Jesus agreed to go to this man's house and help his servant. As usual, there was a great crowd of people around Jesus. All of them were looking forward to seeing Him perform this miracle.

Then the soldier sent a message to Jesus. "Lord, do not bother to come to my house. Just say the word, and I know my servant will be healed. I am a soldier. When I tell my men what to do, they do it. You have the same power. If You say my servant is to be healed, I know he will be."

"This man has more faith than I have ever seen!" Jesus said when He heard this message. He sent a message back to the soldier. "Because you believed in Me, you have your wish." That same hour the soldier's servant was healed.

The next day Jesus went to a city called Nain. Near the city gate a company of people came toward them carrying a body to be buried. A poor widow was crying for her only son who had died. Now she would have no one to provide for her.

Jesus was sad to see this. He told the woman not to cry and touched the wooden frame that held her son's body. Immediately, the young man sat up and began to speak! Soon everyone in the area knew that Jesus had the power to bring the dead back to life.

While Jesus was traveling through this area one of the Pharisees invited Him to come and eat at his house. This man did not love Jesus or believe in Him. He was hoping to see Jesus do something wrong. When Jesus came to his house the man did not even have Jesus' feet washed. A host always had the feet of his guests washed. In those days, people wore sandals and their feet were always dusty. It was impolite not to have servants ready with water and a towel.

While Jesus was sitting at the table, a woman came in. She carried a container of expensive oil used to anoint people of high rank. She sat down beside Jesus and washed His feet with her tears. Then she poured the expensive oil over His feet and rubbed it in.

Now this woman was a sinner. Everyone knew her, and she did not live a good life. The Pharisee was upset by this. First, he didn't want this woman in his house. Second, why didn't Jesus know this woman was a sinner?

Jesus told the Pharisee a story. "A man loaned two men some money. One owed him very much. The other only owed him a little. When neither man could pay his debt, the man cancelled both debts. Now which man do you think will love him the most?"

"The one who owes him the most will, of course," the Pharisee answered.

"That's right," Jesus said. "This woman gave Me great honor, while you gave Me none. You don't feel you owe Me anything, and so you don't love Me. But she feels she owes Me everything, and she loves Me very much."

Jesus turned to the woman. "Your sins are forgiven," He told her.

Those around the table who did not know Jesus began to whisper to each other. "Who does this man think He is? Only God can forgive sins!"

THINK ABOUT IT

✝ *Why did Jesus say the soldier had more faith than anyone else He had seen? What had the soldier done that was so unusual?* ✝

By the Sea

✛ MATTHEW 13:1-53; MARK 4:1-34;
LUKE 8:4-18 ✛

J esus often talked to the people while He sat in Simon Peter's boat a little out from the shore. That way everyone could see and hear Him and He would not be crowded too closely.

Jesus often told the people stories instead of giving them sermons. Everyone loves a good story. But not everyone understood Jesus' stories, because He never really explained them to the people. Jesus wanted His listeners to think about the stories and discover the truths in them for themselves.

Sometimes even the twelve disciples didn't understand Jesus' stories. Jesus would explain the stories for them, though. If they were going to teach other people, the disciples needed to know exactly what Jesus meant.

One of the stories Jesus told was about a farmer who planted grain in his field. This farmer had an enemy who hated him, and after the field was seeded this enemy came in the night and planted weeds in the man's garden.

Soon both the grain and the weeds began to grow. The men who worked for the farmer asked him if they should go pull out the weeds. "No," the farmer said. "If you do that, you will also pull out some of the grain. Let them both grow together."

When the grain was ripe and ready for picking, the farmer sent his men out into the field. "First pull all the weeds," he told them. "Bundle them up and burn them. Then go back and harvest the grain that is left in the field."

This is one of the stories Jesus had to explain to His disciples. "Both good and evil people live together in the world," He said. "Just like the good grain and the weeds in the farmer's field. At the end of the world God will send His angels to pick out the evil people of the world, just like the weeds were picked from the field. They will be gathered together and thrown into the fire. The good people will then be the only ones in the world. They will be brought to God for their reward."

THINK ABOUT IT

✢ *What do you remember the best? What a teacher tells you, or what you discover for yourself? This is why Jesus never explained His stories to the people.* ✢

STORY 16

"Peace, Be Still"

✝ MATTHEW 8:18-34; MARK 4:35-5:21;
LUKE 8:22-40 ✝

Jesus had very little time to be alone and to rest. All day and into the evening crowds of people were always following Him, wanting to be near Him.

One evening when Jesus was very tired He and His disciples got in a boat and began to row across the Sea of Galilee to the other side. Jesus was so tired that He fell asleep on the way. Suddenly a great storm blew up and the little boat was tossed around. The disciples were sure they were going to be killed. Despite the powerful winds and crashing waves, Jesus was still sleeping. In desperation they called to Jesus and woke Him up.

When Jesus saw the storm and the fear in His disciples, He spoke to the water. "Peace, be still!" He said. Immediately, the water became smooth and the storm passed over them.

Then Jesus looked at His disciples. "Why were you afraid?" He asked them. "Why do you have so little faith in Me?"

As soon as they reached the other shore, a man came rushing to meet them. This man had many evil spirits living in him. He was so wild that people had tried to chain him up but the spirits had broken the chains. No one wanted to be around him. He had to live alone in a cemetery.

As Jesus was telling the evil spirits to leave the man, the evil spirits spoke to Jesus. "If we must go," they said, "can we go into those pigs?"

Jesus saw there was a large number of pigs on the hill above the lake. The Jews were not allowed to keep pigs or eat them, so Jesus gave the spirits permission to take the pigs in place of the man. When they did, the pigs rushed down the hill to the lake and were all drowned.

As Jesus was getting ready to go back across the Sea of Galilee, the man He had healed asked to go with Him. "No," Jesus said. "Stay here and tell everyone how the Lord was merciful to you and showed you great things."

THINK ABOUT IT

✝ *We are all frightened at times. What does the story of Jesus calming the storm teach you about fear?* ✝

STORY 17

Raised from the Dead

✝ MATTHEW 9:18-38; 10:1-42; MARK 5:22-43;
LUKE 8:41-56; 9:1-5 ✝

When Jesus and His disciples returned from the other side of the sea, there was still a crowd of people waiting for them. One of them pressed forward and fell at Jesus' feet. He was Jairus, one of the chief men of the synagogue.

"Master," he said, "please come to my house at once! My little daughter is dying. But if You will come and touch

her, I know she will live."

When Jesus agreed to save the girl, the crowd followed closely behind Him. People jostled and shoved to get closer to Jesus and hear every word He said.

One of these people was a woman who had been sick for years. No one had been able to help her, but she knew Jesus could. If only she could get near Him and just touch His robe, she knew she would get well. She moved closer and closer. Finally, she reached out one hand and barely touched Jesus' robe. Immediately, she was healed.

Jesus knew that someone had touched Him. Even though Jesus knew who had touched His robe, He stopped anyway and asked who it was. His disciples said, "There are so many people here. It could have been anyone."

"I felt some power go out of Me," Jesus said.

Slowly, the woman came forward. She was afraid she was going to be punished for touching Jesus. "It was me, Lord," she said softly.

"Don't be afraid," Jesus told her. "Your faith has healed you. Go in peace."

Meanwhile, Jairus was getting worried. If Jesus did not hurry up a little, his daughter would die. Sure enough, word came from his house that his daughter was dead.

Jesus heard this and told Jairus not to worry. "If you have faith, she will be well," Jesus said to the worried father. Soon they came to Jairus' house. Jesus only allowed Peter, James, John, and the girl's parents to come with Him to the girl's room. Only they saw Him reach out and take hold of her hand. "Little girl, get up," Jesus said. She awoke, and Jesus told her parents to give her a little food. "Do not tell anyone about this," He told them. If everyone in the country knew Jesus could bring dead people back to life, He would have no time to teach at all. Everyone would want Him to save their loved ones who had died.

Jesus knew He could not teach everyone by Himself. There were just too many people to talk to and too many to heal. So He sent His disciples out in pairs. He gave them the power to heal the sick and cast out evil spirits. He told them to tell everyone about God's goodness and power so the people would ask forgiveness for their sins.

THINK ABOUT IT

✛ *Can you imagine seeing Jesus bring Jairus' daughter back to life? Why did Jesus only allow a few disciples to witness that event? Why not more people?* ✛

A Terrible Wish Is Granted

✝ MATTHEW 11:2-19; 14:1-12; MARK 6:14-29;
LUKE 7:18-35 ✝

All the time Jesus was around the Sea of Galilee, John the Baptist was in the king's prison. Most of John's followers had gone to be with Jesus. A few came to prison and told John what Jesus was doing. John sent two of them to ask Jesus this question: "Are You the Savior? Or should we look for someone else?"

When these two men found Jesus He was busy healing people. They saw Him help blind people see again. They saw Him freeing people from evil spirits. And they listened to His words when He taught the people.

When Jesus had finished for a while, He said to the two men, "Go tell John what you saw today. A person who believes in Me is blessed."

Then Jesus talked to the people about John the Baptist. Jesus said that John was more than a great prophet; John the Baptist came to make people ready for the coming of Jesus. This made the people happy. Many of them knew John and had been baptized by him.

Soon after, King Herod gave a great birthday party for himself. His wife hated John the Baptist because he said she was a sinner. She was the one who had him put in prison. At the party one of her daughters danced for Herod. As a reward, King Herod promised her anything she asked. The girl went to her mother. What should she ask the king to give her?

When the girl went back to Herod, she asked for the head of John the Baptist! Herod didn't want John killed, but he could not go back on his promise. So John the Baptist, one of the greatest men who ever lived, died because of a dancing girl's request.

THINK ABOUT IT

✛ *John had been in prison all the time Jesus was doing His miracles so he had never seen Jesus healing the people. Why do you think he sent the men to ask Jesus if He were the Savior?* ✛

STORY 19

Five Loaves and Two Fish

✛ MATTHEW 14:13-36; MARK 6:30-56; LUKE 9:10-17; JOHN 6:1-71 ✛

The twelve disciples came back and told Jesus what they had done while they were away preaching and healing. There were more people than ever around Jesus now.

"Let's get away for a while," Jesus said to His disciples. They rowed across the lake to a quiet place on the other side where no one lived. But the people saw where they went and walked around the lake and found them. When Jesus saw how much they wanted to hear Him, He took pity on them and healed those who were sick.

The day was ending and there was no food in the lonely place they were standing. The disciples asked Jesus to send the people away before it got too late for them to find food for themselves.

"They can stay," Jesus told them. "You can feed them."

The disciples knew they did not have enough money to buy food for all the people. More than 5,000 men were with them, and there were also women and children. Andrew hurried up to Jesus. "There is a boy here who has five loaves of bread and two fish," he said. "But that won't be nearly enough."

"Have them sit down in groups of fifty and 100," Jesus told the disciples. When the crowd was sitting, Jesus took the bread and fish, blessed them, then divided the food among the disciples. "Go feed them," He said.

As the disciples gave out the food, the little bit they had never ran out. Soon everyone had all they wanted to eat and there were still twelve baskets of food left over! Jesus had performed another miracle.

The people all saw that Jesus could give them the food

they needed. This was the kind of king they wanted! They called Jesus to rule them as their king. The disciples felt the same way. Jesus was a king, but not an earthly one like they wanted. He did not want to rule a country. He wanted to rule people's hearts and souls.

Jesus told the crowd to go home. Then He made the disciples get back in the boat and row themselves across the lake while He stayed behind. When everyone was gone Jesus climbed to the top of a mountain to pray alone.

While He was praying, a storm blew across the lake. The sky was dark and the waves were high. Jesus could see that the disciples' boat was in danger. Jesus went down to the lake and walked across the water, as if He were walking on dry land, until He reached the boat.

When the disciples saw Jesus walking on the water they thought He was some kind of spirit or ghost and they cried out in fear.

"Don't be afraid," Jesus called to them. "It's Me."

"Lord," the disciple Simon Peter, better known as Peter, called. "Let me walk across the water and come to You."

"Come," Jesus called back.

Peter jumped off the boat and began to walk on the water, just like Jesus. But the waves were tall, and soon Peter began to be afraid. *People can't walk across water like this,* he must have thought. And since he didn't believe he could do it, he couldn't. Peter began to sink into the water, calling out for Jesus to help him.

Jesus pulled Peter to Him and shook His head. "Why didn't you believe Me? Your faith was not strong enough."

As soon as Jesus and Peter were back in the boat, the storm left and the waves were still.

The next time Jesus went to the synagogue the people there asked Him to feed them again, the way He had on the other side of the lake. "Don't ask for food to eat. Ask for the food of everlasting life that the Son of man can give you," Jesus said to them.

When the crowd saw that Jesus would not work miracles

just to please them, the people began to leave Him. A few days before they wanted to make Him their king. Now they were going away.

"Will you leave Me too?" Jesus asked His disciples.

Peter answered for them all: "You are the only one who can give us everlasting life."

THINK ABOUT IT

✝ *Why did the crowd of people want to make Jesus their king? What did Jesus want?* ✝

STORY 20

A Mother's Prayer

✝ MATTHEW 15:21-39; MARK 7:24-8:26 ✝

Afterward Jesus did not preach to crowds anymore. He had so much to teach His disciples, and He knew the time was coming when He would have to leave them. They would go to a new place and stay there a while, then leave when the crowds found them.

But although He did not want to talk to crowds of people anymore, Jesus still healed people who came to Him. He made them promise not to tell anyone what had happened. But people always need to tell others when a wonderful thing happens to them. Most of these people told others, and then the crowds would come looking for Jesus again.

During this time Jesus healed the daughter of a Canaanite woman. The disciples had wanted to send her away since she was not a Jew, but her faith was so strong that Jesus did as she asked. This helped the disciples learn that God loves all people, not just the Jews.

In another place Jesus healed a man who could not hear or speak. Soon another crowd gathered around Him. This was in the desert where there was no food, and it had been three days since the people had eaten anything. Jesus felt sorry for them. Just as He had done before, Jesus fed everyone with a few small loaves of bread and some fish. This time Jesus fed 4,000 men and the women and children who accompanied them.

THINK ABOUT IT

✝ *What would happen to Jesus' disciples if Jesus left them before He had finished teaching them?* ✝

STORY 21

The Glory of Jesus

✝ MATTHEW 16:13-17:23; MARK 8:27-9:32;
LUKE 9:18-45 ✝

J esus led His disciples to a city at the foot of Mount Hermon. One day He asked them, "Who do people say I am?"

"Some say You are John the Baptist risen from

the dead," they told Him. "Others say You are the prophet Elijah or Jeremiah."

"Who do you think I am?"

Peter gave his answer. "You are the anointed one, the Christ. The Son of the living God."

"God told you that, Simon Peter," Jesus said. "You are Peter the Rock. And on this rock I will build My church. All the powers of the earth will not defeat it."

Jesus said this because the answer Simon Peter gave is what everyone in the Christian church believes about Jesus. He is the Son of God, the Savior of humankind.

Then Jesus told His disciples what was going to happen in the next few months. "We are going to Jerusalem," He said. "The people there will refuse the Son of man [this was what Jesus called Himself]. He will suffer many wrongs from the rulers and priests. And He will be killed. But on the third day He will rise from the dead and live forever."

The disciples did not want to hear this. They wanted Jesus to be their king on earth. They could hardly think of Him dying. They could not understand how He could rise again after that.

About a week later Jesus took Peter, James, and John up to the top of Mount Hermon with Him. He went off a little ways to pray. The three disciples fell asleep while they waited.

While Jesus prayed a great change came over Him. His face began to shine like the sun. His clothes became as white as snow.

The disciples woke up and saw Jesus like this and were amazed. They saw two men talking with Jesus. One of them was Moses and the other was Elijah. When Moses and Elijah left Jesus, the disciples jumped up. Peter said, "Lord, it's a good thing we were here! Let's make three tabernacles here. One for you, one for Moses, and one for Elijah."

While Peter was speaking a bright cloud fell over them all. The men couldn't see Jesus anymore. Out of the cloud

they heard the voice of God speaking to them. "This is My beloved Son. I am very pleased with Him. Listen to Him!"

This frightened the disciples so much that Jesus had to go to them and tell them everything was all right. As they walked back down the mountain together, Jesus warned the three disciples not to tell anyone what they had seen. They couldn't even tell the other disciples.

Jesus kept trying to tell the disciples what was going to happen soon. "The time is coming when the Son of man will be killed. After that He will rise on the third day." But the disciples just couldn't understand what Jesus was trying to tell them.

THINK ABOUT IT

✝ *Because Jesus was the Son of God, He knew everything that would happen to Him in the future. Although Peter said Jesus was the Son of God, why didn't the disciples understand or accept what Jesus was telling them?* ✝

STORY 22

In the Arms of Jesus

✝ MATTHEW 17:24-18:35; MARK 9:33-48;
LUKE 9:46-50 ✝

One day Jesus heard His disciples talking with one another as they walked along. They were arguing about which of them would have the highest place when Jesus became the king. When He asked what they were talking about, they were embarrassed and said nothing.

Jesus said to them, "If one of you wants to be the most important, he must serve others now." Then He took a little child in His arms. "Whoever is gentle, and kind, and willing to be taught—like this little child—will be first in My kingdom. Anyone who takes care of a little one like this takes care of Me."

Then Jesus told them the story of the unkind servant. Once a servant borrowed a large amount of money from his king. When the time came to repay the money, the servant did not have it. He begged the king to be patient while he saved up enough to pay him. The king was kind to his servant and forgave the whole debt. He would not have to pay back one cent he had borrowed from the king.

This same servant had loaned money to another man. When he demanded the money back, the second man could not pay him. Instead of forgiving the debt or giving the man more time, the servant had him thrown into jail until he could pay his debt.

The king heard about this and was very angry. He had forgiven a large debt this servant owed him, but the servant would not forgive a little debt that someone else owed him. The king had the servant thrown into jail until all he owed him was repaid.

Jesus told His disciples, "God has forgiven all your sins. In the same way, you must forgive those who sin against you."

THINK ABOUT IT

✚ *We think of the disciples as great men. But in this story they seem like ordinary people. What must happen for these ordinary men to become great men of courage?* ✚

STORY 23

At the Feast of Tabernacles

✚ MATTHEW 8:19-22; LUKE 9:57-62; 17:11-19; JOHN 7:2-52 ✚

J esus and His disciples were on their way to Jerusalem to celebrate the feast of the tabernacles. On their way they went through Samaria, the country of the Samaritans, the people who hated the Jews. When the Samaritans saw they were Jews on their way to Jerusalem, they refused to let them come into their village.

This made the disciples angry. "Can we call down fire from heaven and destroy the village?" James and John asked Jesus.

"I have not come to destroy people," Jesus answered, "but to save them."

They went on to another village to find a place to sleep. Outside this city's gate they saw ten men who had leprosy. When the men asked Jesus to cure them, He told them to go show themselves to the priests. That is what lepers had to do when they were cured, before they could be let back into the city. The men believed they would be cured by the time they got to the priests, and so they were.

Nine of the men went back to their families right away after seeing the priest. The tenth man went looking for Jesus. He fell down before Jesus and thanked Him for curing him. Jesus was upset that only one of the ten had come back to thank Him.

While Jesus was in Jerusalem He stayed with friends. Martha, her sister Mary, and their brother Lazarus were always happy to see Jesus when He came to town. They loved one another very much. One day while He was at their home, Mary sat by Jesus and listened to Him talk. That left Martha all alone in the kitchen to do the cooking. She was upset by this and went to Jesus. "Lord," she said, "it is not right that Mary sits with You while I do all the

work. Tell her to come help me."

Jesus told her, "Martha, you worry too much about unimportant things. Mary knows what is important."

THINK ABOUT IT

✛ Why wasn't Jesus upset that Mary was listening to Him instead of helping in the kitchen? (Remember: Jesus knows what is in each of our hearts.) ✛

STORY 24

With Clay on His Eyes

✛ JOHN 9:1-41 ✛

One Sabbath Jesus and His disciples were walking through Jerusalem when they met a blind man. The disciples asked Jesus why the man had been born blind. Had he sinned? Or had his parents sinned? In those days people thought all sickness came from sinning.

"No," said Jesus. "This man was born blind to show God's power." Then Jesus mixed a little clay from the ground and put it over the man's eyes. "Go to the pool of Siloam and wash," He ordered.

When the man did this he was able to see. All the man's friends were amazed when he went to them and told them how he was cured. But the Pharisees were not happy. "This man has worked on the Sabbath," they said. Then they went see the healed man. "God has healed you," they told him. "Not the man you are talking about. He is a sinner."

"I don't know if He's a sinner or not," the healed man said. "But I do know He is the one who cured me. Why do you keep asking me questions about Him?"

"Because we don't know Him," the Pharisees said.

"You are the leaders of the people, but you know nothing about this man? You call Him a sinner, but God does not hear sinners. If this man were not from God, He could not have healed me."

Because of what he said, the man was not allowed to worship in the synagogue anymore. Jesus heard this sad story and found the man again. "Do you believe in the Son of God?" He asked the man.

"Who is He?" the man asked.

"You have seen Him, and He is now talking to you."

"Lord, I believe in You," the man said, bowing down before Jesus.

THINK ABOUT IT

✛ *The blind man was brave to say what he felt to the rulers of the people. Why was he not allowed to enter the synagogue anymore?* ✛

The Good Samaritan

✤ JOHN 10:1-41; LUKE 10:1-37 ✤

While in Jerusalem Jesus told the people the story of the good shepherd. "I am the good shepherd," He said. "Just as a shepherd knows every one of his sheep, I know mine, and they know Me. I know the Father, and He knows Me. And I lay down my life for My sheep."

The people did not understand what Jesus was saying, but they did hear Him say that God was His Father. That made them angry. The crowd threw stones at Jesus and even tried to capture Him, but Jesus escaped and left Jerusalem.

Time was growing short for Jesus. He sent seventy disciples out into the countryside to preach about God, giving them the power to heal and control evil spirits in His name. The seventy came back later, amazed at what

they could do for people when they spoke in Jesus' name.

At that time a scribe came to see Jesus. He was a man who knew all the Jewish laws and spent his life studying and writing about them. "Master," he said to Jesus, "what do I have to do to live forever?"

"You know the law," Jesus said to him. "What does it say?"

"The law says we must love God with all our heart and soul and mind. And we are to love our neighbor as we love ourselves."

"That's right," Jesus said. "Do that, and you will have life forever."

"But who is my neighbor?" the scribe asked.

To answer him, Jesus told a story. A man was traveling from Jericho to Jerusalem. On the way a band of robbers attacked him. They took all he had and left him by the side of the road, almost dead.

A priest on the road saw the man, but he would not stop to help him. Then a Levite went by. He walked around the man too. But when a Samaritan came by, he stopped and helped the man. He took the man to the nearest inn and paid the people there to take care of him until he was well again.

"Which of the three men acted like a neighbor to the traveler?" Jesus asked the scribe.

"The one who took care of him," he answered.

"Go and do likewise," Jesus said.

Jesus had taught the scribe that our neighbor is anyone who needs our help, no matter who he or she is.

THINK ABOUT IT

✝ *In His story to the scribe Jesus said the Samaritan who stopped and cared for the wounded man was better than the priest and Levite who didn't. Why did Jesus choose a Samaritan as the best example? Who are your neighbors?* ✝

At Lazarus' Tomb

✝ JOHN 11:1-55 ✝

Do you remember Mary, Martha, and Lazarus, Jesus' friends who lived near Jerusalem? One day Jesus heard that Lazarus was very sick. Jesus decided to go to Lazarus, but His disciples weren't happy about that. The last time they had been in Jerusalem the people had tried to kill Jesus.

Jesus stayed where He was for the next two days. As they were getting ready to go to Lazarus, word came that Jesus' friend had died. By the time they got to the little town where Lazarus had lived, he had been dead four days and was buried in a tomb.

All the friends of the family were there to comfort Mary and Martha. As soon as she saw Jesus coming, Martha ran to meet Him. "Lord, if You had been here, my brother would not have died!" she cried.

"Your brother will rise again," Jesus told Martha.

"I know he will rise at the end of the world when the dead are raised."

"Martha, I am the resurrection and the life. Whoever believes in Me—even if he is dead—will never die. Do you believe Me?"

"Yes, Lord," Martha said. "You are the Christ, the Son of God."

They took Jesus to the place where Lazarus was buried, and there Jesus cried for His friend. Jesus then ordered the stone that covered the opening of the tomb be taken away. Jesus lifted His eyes toward heaven and thanked God for hearing His prayers. "Lazarus," He called into the tomb, "come out!"

Lazarus, still wrapped in his burial clothes, walked out of his tomb, alive and healthy.

Once again Jesus had raised the dead, and once again, because of this miracle, many of the people in the crowd believed in Him.

When the Pharisees and other religious rulers heard of this, they were upset. "If we don't stop this man," they said, "everyone will believe in Him. They will try to make Him their king, and the Romans will come and kill us all. *We* will have to kill Him."

Jesus knew what they were planning. But it was not time for Him to die yet. He took his disciples and went into the land east of the Jordan River to preach to the people there.

_____

THINK ABOUT IT

✛ *How was Martha different from the people at Lazarus' tomb who saw Jesus perform a miracle? (Remember what Martha said to Jesus before He went to Lazarus' tomb.)* ✛

_____

STORY 27

The Prodigal Son

✛ LUKE 12:1-15:32 ✛

Jesus and His disciples traveled around the land on the east side of the Jordan River. He had not been there before, but His disciples had gone there and told everyone about Jesus. Great crowds of people

gathered around Him while He taught there.

Jesus told these people many stories about the right way to live and treat other people. He spent time with people who needed His help. Jesus had been sent to heal and save those who needed help, not those who were already leading good lives.

One story Jesus told was about the prodigal son. A prodigal is someone who spends everything he or she has. There was a man who had two sons. The younger son, the prodigal, went to his father and asked him to give him his inheritance now, instead of when he died. The son took this money, moved away from home, and lived like a rich man for some time. But soon the money ran out, and the boy had no way to support himself.

One day the son was feeding another man's pigs to make a little money. Since the Jews had nothing to do with pigs, no one else wanted to do this job. The young man was dirty and hungry.

At that point the son remembered how good life had been at home. He decided he would go back and beg his father to forgive him. He would do whatever work his father wanted him to do. Anything would be better than taking care of someone's pigs!

When his father saw the son coming home, he ordered a big feast prepared. He gave the boy clean clothing, sandals for his feet, and his own ring to wear. "My son was dead," the father said, "and now he is alive. He was lost, and now he has been found." The father was so happy to have his son back that he did not yell at him or tell him how foolish he had been.

Like the father of the prodigal son, God is our Heavenly Father who will always forgive us when we have sinned.

THINK ABOUT IT

✝ *In the story the older brother gets mad when his father is so happy to see his younger brother come home. This older brother had stayed with his father and worked for him all the time his brother was playing. Does the father love him as much as he loves the other son?* ✝

STORY 28

The Poor Rich Man, and the Rich Poor Man

✝ LUKE 16:1-31-18:1-34; MATTHEW 19:13-30; 20:17-19; MARK 10:13-34 ✝

Jesus once told a story about a very rich man who had everything he wanted on earth. Near his house lay a poor man named Lazarus, who had nothing. Lazarus was so poor he ate the garbage the rich man threw out. All the time they lived near each other, the rich man did nothing for the poor man.

In time, both died. The rich man went to hell, where those who do not believe in God or Jesus go when they die. The poor man went to heaven and was comforted by Abraham himself. The rich man cried out to Abraham, "Send Lazarus to me with a drop of water. I am so thirsty here!"

"No one can go from heaven to hell," Abraham said to the rich man.

"Then please send him to my house. I have five brothers. Let Lazarus speak to them so they will not suffer when they die."

"They have Moses and the prophets," Abraham said. "Let them learn from them."

"But they will listen to someone who returns from the dead."

"If they will not listen to Moses and the prophets," Abraham said, "they will not listen to someone who comes back from the dead either."

Jesus was telling the people that they had all been taught how to live properly by Moses and the prophets who came after him. He was also saying that they would not listen to Jesus either, when He would return from the dead, as He had said He would do.

Another story Jesus told was about the Pharisee and the publican, or tax collector. Two men went to the temple to pray. One was a Pharisee who obeyed every law of God but was not kind to people. The other was a tax collector who was disliked because of what he did for a living.

The Pharisee stood in the temple and prayed for himself. "I'm glad I'm not like that publican," he said. "I fast twice a week and give a tenth of all I have to God. I live the way Jews are supposed to live."

The publican would not even lift his eyes toward heaven. He cried tears of sadness and prayed, "God be merciful to me, a sinner."

Jesus told the people that the publican was the one

whose sins were forgiven, not the Pharisee. "Everyone who thinks he is better than others will be brought down. But everyone who is humble [who does not think they are better than others] will be lifted up."

Later Jesus tried to tell His disciples what was going to happen to Him. "We are going to Jerusalem soon," He said. "The Son of man will be taken prisoner. He shall be mocked and treated poorly. He will be beaten, and spit upon, and killed. And then, on the third day, He will rise again."

But they still could not understand what Jesus was saying. They didn't believe Jesus was about to die.

THINK ABOUT IT

✝ *Why weren't the sins of the Pharisee forgiven? Why were the sins of the publican forgiven? Is it hard to be humble?* ✝

STORY 29

Zacchaeus

✝ MATTHEW 20:20-34; MARK 10:35-52;
LUKE 18:35-19:28 ✝

Jesus and His disciples began the trip to Jerusalem and as usual, a crowd of people followed. Many saw Jesus perform miracles along the way and wanted to make Him king of the country. Even His disciples thought that He would be crowned king when they got to Jerusalem. They were so sure of it that they began arguing about which of them would have the most power when Jesus was king. Jesus had tried to teach His disciples this was not going to happen, but they did not understand what He meant. He was talking about the kingdom of God, not a real kingdom here on earth.

As they came near Jericho, people crowded around them. One man wanted to see Jesus very much but he was so short he could not see over the heads of the people in front of him. This man was a tax collector named Zacchaeus. Remember, the Jews thought all tax collectors were sinners.

Zacchaeus climbed up a sycamore tree by the road to catch a glimpse of Jesus as He walked by. But Jesus stopped by the tree, looked up at Zacchaeus, and called out to him. "Come down, Zacchaeus. Today I am coming to your house."

Zacchaeus didn't know how Jesus knew his name, but he was happy to have Him as his guest. Many of the people in the crowd thought Jesus should not be staying with a man they thought was a sinner.

Zacchaeus knew what the people were thinking. As he

stood before the Son of God, Zacchaeus said, "Lord, I give half of what I have to the poor. And if I take too much from anyone for taxes, I will pay him back four times as much as I took."

"I know, Zacchaeus," Jesus said. "And you will be saved. I came to save the lost."

THINK ABOUT IT

✦ *How did Jesus know Zacchaeus was up in a tree? Why would Jesus stay at the home of such a man?* ✦

Palm Sunday

✦ MATTHEW 21:1-11; 26:6-16; MARK 2:1-11;
14:3-11; LUKE 19:29-41; 22:3-6; JOHN 12:1-19 ✦

As they neared Jerusalem, Jesus and the disciples spent the night with their friends Mary, Martha, and Lazarus. Their house was only two miles from Jerusalem. Another friend named Simon gave a dinner for Jesus and Lazarus' family was invited too. Lazarus sat and listened to Jesus speak. Martha worked in the kitchen.

While they were eating Mary came into the room with a container of expensive, sweet-smelling oil. She poured the oil over Jesus' head and feet and wiped His feet with her long hair to honor Him.

One of the disciples named Judas Iscariot thought this was a waste of money. "This oil could have been sold for more than forty-five dollars and given to the poor," he complained. Judas was the man who carried all the money Jesus and the disciples had. He would often take money that belonged to all of them and use it for himself.

"Why are you bothering her?" Jesus asked Judas. "There will always be poor people you can help. But I will only be here for a little while longer. She was perfuming my body for its burial."

Judas was angry with Jesus for correcting him in front of everyone. He went to the priests and asked what they would give him if he arranged for them to capture Jesus.

"We will give you thirty pieces of silver," they said. From then on Judas looked for a way to turn Jesus over to the priests.

The next morning Jesus sent two of the disciples to the next village on the way to Jerusalem. He told them where they would find a donkey tied. "Bring it back here," He said. "The owner will let you take it."

When the men came back with the donkey, Jesus began to ride toward Jerusalem. The people in the crowd put their extra clothing on the road for the donkey to walk on. Others cut down branches from the trees and put them in the road. Others cut palm branches and waved them as they walked toward Jerusalem.

"Hosanna to the Son of David! Blessed is He that comes in the name of the Lord! Blessed be the kingdom of our father David that comes in the name of the Lord! Hosanna in the highest!" the crowd chanted.

They said these words because they believed Jesus was the Christ, the promised Messiah who would set up His throne in Jerusalem. And they were right. Jesus was the Messiah. But He had not come to set up a throne on earth.

Every year Christians celebrate the day Jesus entered Jerusalem riding a donkey. We call that day Palm

Sunday, to remember the Sunday the crowds waved palm branches in honor of a King.

THINK ABOUT IT

✝ *Why did Mary put perfume on Jesus? Do you think she knew He was going to die soon?* ✝

STORY 31

The Last Visits to the Temple

✝ MATTHEW 21:18-23:39; MARK 11:12-12:44;
LUKE 19:45-21:4 ✝

On Monday morning Jesus and the disciples went to the temple in Jerusalem. Remember how Jesus had once chased out the people who were making the temple into a marketplace? That was three years before, and all those people were back again. So Jesus chased them all out again. "My house is a house of prayer, not a den of robbers!" He told them.

There was a Jewish law that said sick people were not allowed in the temple. Only healthy people could go in. But sick people would stay by the temple, hoping to be cured so they could go in and pray. Jesus told all these people to come in, and He made them well again.

The temple was crowded with people who wanted to

hear Jesus speak. They liked the way He told stories they could understand, and He loved everyone, whether they were rich or poor.

The rulers of the temple became angry. Jesus was doing things they thought were illegal and wrong. He was acting as if He were in charge of the temple, instead of them!

At the end of the day Jesus went back to spend the night with His friends Mary, Martha, and Lazarus.

The next morning, on Tuesday, Jesus returned to the temple. This time the Pharisees decided to try and trick Jesus. If Jesus said something wrong, the people would not follow Him and the rulers could arrest Him. The Pharisees pretended to be His followers and asked Him hard questions.

One of them asked if it were right for Jews to pay taxes to the Romans. If Jesus said yes, the crowd would be angry at Him. If He said they should not pay taxes, the Romans might punish Him.

Jesus knew they were trying to trick Him. "Give me a coin," He said. When they did, He asked them, "Whose picture is on this coin?"

"That is Caesar, the Roman emperor," they said.

"Give Caesar what belongs to him. Give God the things

that belong to God," Jesus told them.

The Pharisees saw that Jesus had given the perfect answer. The people were happy, and the Romans would be too. They tried to trick Jesus all day, but nothing worked. At the end of the day Jesus left the temple. He would never speak there again.

THINK ABOUT IT

✢ *Why were the rulers of the temple afraid of Jesus and those who followed Him?* ✢

STORY 32

On the Mount of Olives

✢ MATTHEW 24:1-25:46; MARK 13:1-37;
LUKE 21:5-38 ✢

As Jesus and the disciples were leaving the temple, they looked around them. "What a beautiful building this is," one of them said. "Look at those huge foundation stones!"

"Do you see these great walls?" Jesus asked. "The time is coming when these walls will be destroyed. Not one stone will be left in place. This temple and the city will be in ruins."

This made the disciples sad because they believed what

Jesus said and they loved Jerusalem. Later they climbed to the top of the Mount of Olives and Jesus told them many things that were going to happen in the future. He spoke of wars, earthquakes, diseases, and the destruction of Jerusalem. Then Jesus said He would come again one day as Lord of all. Everyone should be ready for the day He came back. To show what He meant, Jesus told them a story about five young women who were not prepared when they should have been, and how they missed a great feast.

Then Jesus told the disciples what it would be like when He came again. "When the Son of man comes in His glory, all the angels of God will come with Him," He said. "All the people in the world will come before Him. He will put some of them on His right and some on the left. Those on the right will inherit the kingdom of God. Those on the left will be cursed forever."

And how would God choose who was saved and who was not? He would choose those who had cared for others. Those who fed the hungry, visited people in prison, and gave clothes to the needy would be the ones to inherit the kingdom of God. "When you do these things for my brothers, you do them for Me," Jesus said.

THINK ABOUT IT

✛ *Jesus tried very hard to prepare the disciples for His death. Will the disciples be all alone when Jesus is gone?* ✛

The Last Supper

✚ MATTHEW 26:17-35; MARK 14:12-31;
LUKE 22:7-38; JOHN 13:1-17:26 ✚

On Passover Jesus and the disciples went into Jerusalem. Two of them had found a room for them to eat in earlier in the week, and everything was now ready. Remember, the Jews celebrate Passover every year with special food. There was lamb, vegetables, and flat bread to eat.

John, the disciple Jesus loved the most, sat next to Him. When the dinner was ready Jesus took a loaf of bread, broke it into pieces, and blessed it. "Take and eat. This is My body, which is broken for you. Do this and remember Me," He said.

Then He took a cup of wine and passed it around, saying, "This cup is My blood. It is shed for you and for

many so their sins may be taken away. As often as you drink this, remember Me."

Then Jesus took a basin of water and began washing the feet of the disciples, the way a host always did at that time. When He reached Peter, Peter tried to stop Him. "Lord, You should not wash my feet."

"If I don't wash you, you are not My follower," Jesus said.

"In that case, wash my hands and head too!" Peter said.

"No, Peter," Jesus said to him. "Someone who has taken a bath only needs his feet washed. You are clean. But not all the others are." Jesus knew that Judas Iscariot was plotting against Him and would turn Him over to those who hated Him.

Thinking about this made Jesus very sad. "One of you eating here is going to betray Me and turn Me over to those who will kill Me," He said to His friends.

"Is it I?" all the disciples asked. They couldn't imagine who would do such a thing!

"It is one of you," Jesus answered. But He did not say who it was. "It would have been better for that man if he had never been born."

John leaned over and whispered, "Lord, who is it?"

"I will dip a piece of bread into the dish and give it to him," Jesus answered softly. He dipped the bread and handed it to Judas. "Whatever you are going to do, do it quickly," He told Judas. Judas left the room.

Only Jesus and John knew what was going on. The rest of the disciples thought Jesus had sent Judas on an errand of some kind.

Judas realized that Jesus knew what he was going to do, so he went right to the rulers. When Judas told them that Jesus would go by the Mount of Olives on His way back to the house of Mary, Martha, and Lazarus, they laid a trap for Him there.

As soon as Judas had gone, Jesus told His disciples He was only going to be with them for a little while. "You cannot go where I am going right now. But remember this new law: Love one another the way I have loved you."

"Lord," Peter said, "I will lay down my life for You."

"Will you?" Jesus said. "Peter, before the rooster crows early tomorrow morning, you will deny you even know Me three times."

All the disciples promised they would never leave Jesus, but Jesus told them they would. "I will not be alone. My Father will be with Me."

Jesus saw they were all upset by these words. "Don't worry," He said. "You believe in God. Believe in Me too. I am going to make a place ready for you with My Father. When it's ready, I will come back and take you with Me." Jesus talked with the disciples for a long time and prayed for them. At about midnight they left the room and went to the Mount of Olives.

THINK ABOUT IT

✝ *Why didn't Jesus let all the disciples know who the traitor was?* ✝

In the Olive Orchard

✝ MATTHEW 26:36-75; MARK 14:32-72;
LUKE 22:40-62; JOHN 18:1-27 ✝

When Jesus and the disciples reached the garden gate at the Mount of Olives, He left eight of the disciples at the entrance. Peter, James, and John went into the orchard with Him. "Stay here and watch while I pray," He said to the three men as He walked on a little farther.

Jesus knew what was soon going to happen to Him. He prayed, "Father, if it is possible, let this cup pass away from Me. But Your will be done." He returned to Peter, James, and John and found them asleep. The hour was very late. "Couldn't you stay awake one more hour?" He asked Peter.

Two more times Jesus went off alone and prayed to His Father while the three disciples slept. When He was done the disciples awoke to the sound of a crowd coming into the garden. Spears and swords were flashing in the torches the people carried. "The traitor is here," Jesus told His friends.

The people coming with Judas did not know Jesus by sight, so they had worked out a signal. Judas rushed up to Jesus as though he were happy to see Him and greeted Him with a kiss. This told the guards which of the four men was Jesus.

"Who are you looking for?" Jesus asked the men.

"Jesus of Nazareth," they replied.

"I am He. Let the rest of these people go."

As they came to take Jesus, Peter suddenly drew his

sword and hit one of the men with it, cutting off his ear.

"Put your sword away," Jesus told Peter. "This is God's will. Don't you think I could ask My Father for an army of angels if I wanted?" Then He motioned to the guards to wait a minute as He healed the wounded man's ear.

When the disciples saw that Jesus would not let them help Him, they didn't know what to do. They ran from the garden, afraid for their own lives, while the guards tied Jesus up and led Him to one of the high priests, a man named Annas.

Simon Peter and John followed along behind. When the crowd reached the house of Annas, John went in too. But Peter was afraid, and he stayed outside in the courtyard and warmed himself by a campfire.

Inside, Annas asked Jesus about His teaching. "I taught openly in the synagogues and temple," Jesus said. "Ask those who heard me there."

One of the officers hit Jesus on the mouth. "Don't talk that way to the high priest!" he said.

"If I said something wrong, tell Me what it was," Jesus said. "But why hit Me if I told the truth?"

While Jesus was being questioned inside, a servant of the high priest saw Peter by the fire. "You were with Jesus," she said to him.

"No," Peter answered. "I don't even know the man." To get away from her, he walked out to the porch of the house. But a second woman recognized him there. For the second time Peter swore he did not know Jesus. Soon a man came by who knew Peter was a follower of Jesus. "Aren't you one of the disciples?" he asked.

"No!" Peter said. Just then, a rooster crowed to welcome the dawn, and Peter remembered what Jesus had said the night before: "Before the rooster crows, you will deny you know Me three times." Peter raced into the street, crying because he had denied his Lord.

THINK ABOUT IT

✝ *Do you think Jesus wanted to be captured and killed? Why didn't He prevent that from happening?* ✝

STORY 35

The Crown of Thorns

✝ MATTHEW 26:57-27:26; MARK 15:1-15;
LUKE 22:66-23:25; JOHN 18:19-19:16 ✝

From the home of Annas, the rulers took Jesus to Caiaphas, whom the Romans had made the new high priest. All the rulers of the Jews were called together to hear the high priest question Jesus. They tried to find some witnesses who would say Jesus had done something wrong, but they couldn't prove He had broken any laws.

The high priest finally asked Jesus, "Are You the Christ, the Son of God?"

"I am," Jesus said. "And the time will come when you will see the Son of man sitting on the throne of power and coming in the clouds of heaven."

"He says He is the Son of God," the high priest told the crowd. "What do you think of that?"

"He deserves to be killed," the crowd responded.

Then the servants of the high priest and the soldiers who were holding Jesus began hurting Jesus. They spit on Him and covered His face and hit Him. "If you are a prophet, tell us who is hitting You," they said.

The rulers of the Jews and the priests and scribes voted that Jesus should be killed. But only the Roman governor had the power to have a man killed. He might listen to the priests' advice or decide against them. So they brought Jesus to the house of the governor, a man named Pontius Pilate.

Up to this time Judas Iscariot did not believe Jesus would be put to death. Maybe he thought Jesus would perform a miracle and save Himself, the way He had saved others. But now it was clear to him that Jesus was going to be killed.

Judas took back the money he had been given for turning Jesus over to the people. "I sinned. I betrayed a man who did nothing wrong," he told them.

"That's your problem, not ours," the rulers said.

When he saw he could do nothing to save Jesus or take away his own guilt, Judas took the thirty pieces of silver to the temple and threw them on the floor. Then he went out and hanged himself because he had betrayed, or turned in, an innocent man.

The money Judas had thrown down in the temple could not be used for the temple. It was considered "blood money" and unclean. So the rulers took the coins and bought a piece of land to use as a cemetery for people who had no one to bury them. From then on, that land was known as "the field of blood."

Early in the morning the rulers brought Jesus to Pilate. "We caught this man teaching evil and telling men not to pay Caesar's taxes," they said to the governor. "He says He is Christ, a king."

Pilate questioned Jesus. "Your own people brought You to me. Are You the King of the Jews?"

"My kingdom is not of this world," Jesus said. "If it were,

those who follow Me would fight to save Me."

"Are You a king?"

"Yes, I am a king. I came into this world to tell people God's truth."

Pilate went out to the rulers and priests. "I find nothing wrong with this man," he told them. Even Herod, who ruled Galilee, refused to condemn Jesus. When they brought Jesus back to Pilate a second time, Pilate still refused to have Him killed. But the people cried out, "Crucify Him! Let His blood be on us." Still trying to save Jesus, Pilate had Him beaten, hoping that would be enough for the angry crowd. The soldiers made a crown of sharp thorns and put it on Jesus' head, then led Him back out to the people. But nothing Pilate did would make the people stop calling for the death of Jesus. Rather than have all the people rebel against him, Pilate finally gave in. Pilate allowed Jesus to be killed, even though he knew Jesus had done nothing wrong.

THINK ABOUT IT

✝ *Did anyone prove that Jesus deserved to be killed? Did*

STORY 36

The Darkest Day of All the World

✟ MATTHEW 27:31-66; MARK 15:20-47;
LUKE 23:26-56; JOHN 19:16-42 ✟

Jesus was led out of the city to the place where criminals were put to death. This place was called Golgotha in the Jewish language or Calvary in the Roman language. Because Jesus was too weak from the beatings, another man carried the heavy wooden cross to Calvary, the cross on which Jesus would die. When they reached Calvary Jesus was nailed to the cross and the cross was then lifted up and made secure.

Many people had followed Jesus to Calvary. Some were His family and friends. Others were His enemies. His enemies called out to Him on the cross: "Come down from the cross and we will believe in You!"

On either side of Jesus two robbers were being executed that day. One of them said to Jesus, "If You are the Christ, save Yourself and us!"

The second robber told the man to be quiet. "Don't you have any fear of God? We deserve to die, but this man doesn't." Then he turned his head toward Jesus and said, "Lord, remember me when You come into Your kingdom."

"You will be with Me today in heaven," Jesus told the second robber.

Seeing His earthly mother, Mary, standing with John, Jesus asked John to take care of her. From that day on Mary lived in John's home and was treated as if she were his own mother.

At noon darkness fell all over the land. It stayed dark for three hours while Jesus suffered on the cross. Six hours after the cross had been lifted up with Jesus on it, He cried out, "My Lord, my God, why have You forsaken Me? It is finished. Father, I give My spirit to You."

Then Jesus died. At that very moment the huge curtain inside the temple was torn from top to bottom and fell in a heap onto the floor. The Roman officer in charge of the soldiers saw how bravely Jesus died. "Truly this was a good man," he said. "He was the Son of God." After Jesus was dead one of the soldiers ran his spear into the side of His body, to be sure there was no more life in Him. Out of His wounds water and blood both poured out.

Some of the rulers loved Jesus, although they did not dare show how they felt to others. One of them, Joseph of Arimathea, went to Pilate and asked that Jesus' body be given to him for burial. Nicodemus, another good man, saw that Jesus' body was properly prepared for burial before it was placed in the tomb of Joseph of Arimathea. To be sure no one would take the body away, Pilate had the tomb sealed and guards put outside it. Jesus' body stayed in the tomb from that Friday until Sunday morning.

THINK ABOUT IT

✝ *It's never dark at noon. And no human being tore the curtain in the temple in half. What do you think was happening here?* ✝

The Brightest Day of All the World

✝ MATTHEW 28:1-10; MARK 16:1-13;
LUKE 24:1-40; JOHN 20:1-23 ✝

Early Sunday morning Mary Magdalene, another woman named Mary, and a third named Salome went to the tomb. They were bringing more spices for the body of Jesus. They wondered who would roll the huge stone away from the entrance of the tomb. It would be too heavy for them.

But when they came to the tomb, the women saw that the stone was already rolled away and there were no soldiers guarding the tomb.

They didn't know that an angel of the Lord had come down earlier and rolled away the stone. The soldiers on guard had seen the angel and run away, frightened.

Mary Magdalene didn't look in the tomb at all. She ran off to tell the disciples that the tomb was open. If someone had stolen Jesus' body, everyone needed to know about it as soon as possible.

The other two women stayed behind. When they looked in the tomb, they saw that Jesus' body was not there. Instead two angels were there, sitting on each end of the tomb! This frightened the women so much that the angels spoke to them.

"Don't be afraid," the angels said. "You are looking for Jesus of Nazareth. He has risen, as He said He would. Look where He was laid. Then go tell the disciples that Jesus will go to Galilee. You will see Him there."

Mary Magdalene found Peter and John and told them about the open tomb. "They have taken Him away, and we don't know where they have put Him," she told the men.

Peter and John raced to the tomb. All they saw were the burial clothes that had been put on Jesus after His death. John was sure He had risen, as He had told them many times. They left the tomb and went back into town.

Mary Magdalene came back to the tomb. She couldn't run as fast as Peter and John and by the time she got there, they had left. The other two women who had been with her had gone too. Crying, she looked into the tomb.

Peter and John had not seen the angels, but they appeared to Mary Magdalene. "Why are you crying?" they asked her.

Mary Magdalene was so upset she didn't realize she was talking to angels. "They took away my Lord. I don't know where they put Him," she said. As she looked around, she saw another man behind her. Maybe this was the gardener. "Sir," she said, "If you took Him away, please tell me where I can find Him." Only then did she realize she was looking at Jesus.

"Go to My brothers," Jesus told Mary Magdalene. "Tell them I am going to My Father." Mary Magdalene was the first person to see Jesus after He had risen.

Afterward Jesus appeared to the other two women who had gone to the tomb. He told them to have the disciples go to Galilee. He would meet them all there. These women were the second and third people to see Jesus after He had risen from the dead.

The next two to see Jesus were followers of His who were going from Jerusalem to their homes in Emmaus, a town about seven miles from Jerusalem. Jesus talked to them for a long time before they realized they were talking to Jesus, and then He left them.

That night most of the disciples gathered together in a room to talk about the wonders they had seen and heard. The door was locked because the disciples were still afraid they would be killed for following Jesus. Suddenly Jesus was there with them. The men were afraid because they thought Jesus was a ghost. "Touch Me. See My wounds," He said. "A ghost does not have flesh and bones." Then Jesus ate some food before telling His friends that He had great work for them to do.

THINK ABOUT IT

✝ *Why were the disciples afraid when they saw Jesus? Jesus had told them many times He would be raised from the dead.* ✝

The Stranger on the Shore

✢ MATTHEW 28:16-20; MARK 16:14-20;
LUKE 24:50-53; JOHN 20:26-21:25; ACTS 1:1-11;
1 CORINTHIANS 15:3-8 ✢

The night Jesus came to the disciples Thomas was not with them. He would not believe Jesus had risen from the dead when the others told him. Thomas said, "I will not believe unless I can see the marks of the nails [that held Jesus to the cross] on His hands."

Suddenly, Jesus was there again. "Thomas," He said, "come here. Touch My hands and put your hand into My side and believe in Me."

Thomas called out, "My Lord and my God!"

"You believe because you saw Me," Jesus said. "Blessed are those who believe in Me without seeing."

The angels had said that the disciples should go to Galilee, so they all traveled there and waited to see Jesus again. Several days went by without Jesus appearing to them. Finally, Peter decided to go fishing and some of the others went with him. They fished all that night without catching anything, then rowed back toward the shore. They could see a man waiting for them on the shore but they didn't know who it was.

"Did you catch anything?" the man called out to the fishermen.

"No," they called back.

"Throw the net over to the right of the boat. There are fish there."

Only then did John realize the man on the shore was Jesus. "It's the Lord!" he cried out.

Peter saw John was right. He dove into the water and swam to shore to be with Jesus while the others dragged a net full of fish toward the beach. After a breakfast of fish and bread, Jesus talked to Peter, the disciple who had denied Him three times that terrible night. Three times Jesus asked Peter if he loved Him. Three times Peter said yes. Three times Jesus told Peter to take care of others who loved Jesus.

Later the disciples met with Jesus again on a mountain. This time there were 500 people with them and everyone saw Jesus. Jesus told His followers to go out and tell others about God and teach them what He had taught. "I am with you always," Jesus told the people.

Jesus led His disciples to the village of Bethany. He blessed them all, and while He was blessing them, He began to rise into the air. He went higher and higher, until a cloud covered Him and the disciples could not see Him anymore.

Suddenly angels stood with them. "Why are you standing here looking into the sky? Jesus will come again, just as you saw Him go up from here to heaven."

The disciples worshiped their Lord Jesus and went back to Jerusalem to give thanks to God in the temple.

THINK ABOUT IT

✝ *Peter was always jumping in when others waited. Remember the other time he jumped into the lake and walked on water for a while? Why did Jesus ask Peter if he loved Him three times?* ✝

PART 7

Go, and Teach All Nations!

THE BEGINNING OF THE CHURCH

The First Days

✛ ACTS 1:12-2:47 ✛

After Jesus went to heaven those who believed in Him met every day in Jerusalem. The eleven disciples chose another man, Matthias, to take the place of the traitor Judas. Altogether in the world there were about 500 people who believed in Jesus.

Ten days after Jesus went up to heaven, the Day of Pentecost, also called the Fiftieth Day (after the Feast of the Passover), was celebrated by Jesus' followers in Jerusalem. The believers of Christ were all together in an upper room, praying, when suddenly a great wind was heard. Flickering flames seemed to be over the heads of all the people in the room. Then the spirit of God came to them all and that day they were able to talk about Jesus Christ in a new and powerful way.

The sound of the wind could be heard all around Jerusalem! Intrigued by the strange noise, people began moving toward the upper room where Jesus' followers were gathered. Since it was a special day of worship, Jerusalem was filled with people from faraway lands. Many of them knew nothing about Jesus, and they spoke many languages.

They saw the followers of Christ singing and dancing and telling people about God's wonderful works. Not only that, but people from foreign lands could understand what was being said. The disciples, or *apostles* as they would now be called, were given the power to speak languages they did not know, so everyone could hear God's message of love and hope. Some people thought Jesus' followers had

been drinking wine because they were acting so strange.

Peter stood up. "Jesus of Nazareth has been raised from the dead," he told the crowd. "He who died on the cross is now the Lord and the Christ. Turn away from your sins, believe in Jesus, and be baptized in His name. Your sins will be taken away, and you will have the power of the Holy Spirit too."

On that one day 3,000 people were baptized and joined the apostles. All the followers of Jesus acted like one big family. Those who had property or money shared with those who were poor. Everyone was happy, praising God and loving one another. Every day, more and more people joined them in worshiping Jesus as the Christ.

THINK ABOUT IT

✛ *Why were Jesus' followers given the ability to speak in many different languages? What do you think they will do next?* ✛

The Man at the Beautiful Gate

✛ ACTS 3:1-31 ✛

One day Peter and John went to afternoon prayer at the temple. As they walked toward what was called the Beautiful Gate, they passed a man who had never been able to walk. He sat by the gate every day, begging for money.

Peter stopped in front of the man. "I don't have money for you," he said. "But what I do have, I will give. In the name of Jesus Christ of Nazareth, walk!"

Peter took the lame man's hand and helped him get to his feet for the first time in his life. The man was so happy that he followed them into the temple and prayed at their side. When they came out people who knew the man gathered around them, asking who had cured him.

Peter talked to all the people, telling them that the power of Jesus' name had done this miracle. He told them that God wanted to forgive all their sins. All they had to do was believe that Jesus was the Christ, the Savior.

But the priests and rulers heard what Peter was saying and they did not like it at all. They took Peter, John, and the healed man into the guard room and kept them there for the night. Many of those who heard Peter speak believed in Jesus. That day the number of Jesus' believers increased from 3,000 to 5,000 people!

The next day the two high priests joined the other rulers and questioned Peter, John, and the healed man. Peter told them the same thing he had told the crowd. The man had been healed by the power of Jesus' name. Since the healed man was right there to agree that was what happened, the rulers could not say anyone was lying. But they could order the apostles to stop talking about Jesus.

"No," Peter said. "We have to obey God and tell about what we have seen and heard."

The rulers knew the people would be angry if they punished Peter and John, so they let them go. Peter and all the others thanked God for letting them teach the people without fear.

THINK ABOUT IT

✛ *How have the apostles changed? Do they seem like the same men who used to walk and talk with Jesus?* ✛

STORY 3

Ananias and Sapphira

✛ ACTS 4:32-5:42 ✛

Many people who joined the apostles gave everything they had to them. The apostles would then divide the money among the poor people who were with them. No one who followed Christ ever went hungry. This sharing was not a law: A person could keep anything he wanted or give anything he wanted to give. People gave because they wanted to.

But not everyone was honest about their giving. Ananias

and Sapphira were one couple who wanted the honor of giving everything to the poor. But they wanted to keep part for themselves too. This would have been allowed. No one had to give everything they owned. The trouble was this: Ananias and Sapphira lied about what they gave. They sold some land, turned over part of the money, and told everyone they had given *all* the money to the Lord.

Ananias, the husband, gave the money to Peter. But God showed Peter that Ananias was lying. "Ananias," Peter said, "why are you lying to God? You could do what you wanted with your money. But God will judge you for lying to Him."

As soon as he heard that, Ananias fell to the floor, dead. He was taken out and buried by some young men in the room.

Three hours later, Sapphira came into the room. She didn't know what happened to her husband as no one had told her.

"Tell me," Peter said to her, "did you sell that land for so much?" He named the sum that Ananias had given.

"Yes, that was the price of the land," Sapphira said.

"Why did you two decide to bring God's anger down on yourselves? Those who buried your husband are waiting

to bury you."

Just like her husband, Sapphira fell down dead and was buried. From that day on no one lied about what he or she gave to the apostles.

Every day the apostles would go to the porch outside the temple and preach to the people who gathered there. They would heal anyone who was brought to them. As a result, more and more people were added to the early church.

The high priests and rulers had Peter and the other apostles brought to them again. "You must stop talking about Jesus this way," they told them.

"We obey God, not men," Peter said to them.

The rulers were almost ready to kill the apostles, they were so angry with them. But a wise man named Gamaliel told them that would not be a smart thing to do. "If what they are saying is not true, it will pass away; if their words really come from God, there is nothing you can do to stop them. Leave them alone and see what happens." The rulers agreed that Gamaliel was right, and the apostles went back to preaching and teaching outside the temple.

THINK ABOUT IT

✝ *What would have saved Ananias and Sapphira from death? How did Peter discover their greed?* ✝

Stephen with the Shining Face

✝ ACTS 6:1-8:3 ✝

As the church grew, the apostles found they were spending too much time handling the church's money. They were meant to preach, not to be bookkeepers. The members of the early church chose seven men to handle the money and to make sure the poor people had enough. The twelve apostles blessed these men by laying their hands on their heads and dedicated them to their work.

One of these seven was named Stephen. Not only did Stephen help with the church's money, he was also a wonderful preacher. Stephen saw that God's salvation was meant for all men, not just for the Jews, and he shared this message with others.

Stephen was captured and taken in front of the great council of the rulers. When he had a chance to defend himself, Stephen preached to the council. "Your fathers killed the prophets God sent to them, and you have killed Jesus, the Righteous One," he said. All the time he spoke, his face was shining bright, as though he were an angel of the Lord.

What he said angered the rulers so much that they sent Stephen out to be stoned to death. His last words were, "Lord, don't count this sin against them!"

A young man named Saul was there when Stephen was killed. He held the coats of those who were throwing the stones. When Stephen was dead Saul went out to find more followers of Christ. He dragged men and women out of their homes and threw them in prison. He went into the synagogues and took them while they were worshiping and had them beaten.

The twelve apostles were hidden by others in the church, so no harm came to them, but the church was broken up. Its members moved away from Jerusalem to all parts of the country where they would be safer. For a while the church of Christ seemed to have come to an end.

THINK ABOUT IT

✛ *Stephen was the first person to die for the church, or to be a* martyr. *Do you think the twelve apostles will remain in hiding?* ✛

STORY 5

The Man Reading in the Chariot

✛ ACTS 8:4-40 ✛

The Christians who were driven out of Jerusalem by Saul moved to many different cities and towns in the country. Everywhere they went they taught about Jesus and began new churches. Instead of putting an end to the church, Saul had strengthened it.

One of the people who left Jerusalem was named Philip.

He went into the land of the Samaritans. The Lord gave Philip the power to do miracles among the people living here, and many of them joined the church.

When Philip's work in Samaria was done, the spirit of the Lord told him to travel along the road that went south from Jerusalem to Gaza. This was a desert road with no villages or people.

As Philip was walking through the desert, he saw a chariot coming from Jerusalem. In it was an African man reading a scroll as he rode. This man was a nobleman of very high rank who served the queen of Ethiopia. He was not a Jew, but he had made the trip of over a thousand miles to worship in the temple at Jerusalem and learn about God. On the scroll in his hands were writings of the prophet Isaiah.

When Philip saw what the man was reading, he called out to him. "Do you understand what you are reading?"

The man stopped his chariot. "No," he said. "Can you tell me what it means?"

Philip sat in the chariot with the nobleman and read the scroll to him. He explained how Isaiah had said many things about the Savior who was to come, and how Jesus was that Savior. Then he told him all the works Jesus had done, and what it meant to believe in Him.

Soon they came to some water and the nobleman asked Philip if he would baptize him there.

"If you believe with all your heart, I will," Philip answered.

"I believe that Jesus Christ is the Son of God," the man told Philip. Philip took the man into the water and baptized him, and the man went toward his home, happy in the Lord.

THINK ABOUT IT

✝ *Philip was sent into the desert for a special reason. Like Philip, we don't know where we will meet someone who doesn't know about Jesus. What would you share about Jesus if you were asked?* ✝

STORY 6

Saul Sees the Light

✝ ACTS 9:1-31; 22:1-21; GALATIANS 1:11-24 ✝

S aul was still the enemy of the Christians, doing what he could to break up the church. He heard that some people he had chased out of Jerusalem were living and teaching in Damascus. Damascus was in another country far to the north of Judea, a trip of ten days by horse or mule.

At this time most of those who believed in Jesus were Jews. They worshiped God in the temple and lived as Jews.

The only difference between them and other Jews was that they believed Jesus was the Savior, the Messiah the Jews were awaiting.

Saul went to the high priest in Jerusalem and asked for a letter he could show to the Jews in Damascus. With this letter he would have the authority to hunt down and imprison the Jews of Damascus who believed in Jesus. He took a group of men with him and made the long trip.

As they came near Damascus, a light suddenly flashed from heaven. Far brighter than the light of the sun, the brightness blinded Saul and he fell to the ground as if struck by a bolt of lightning. In the middle of the light Saul saw a man whom he had never seen before. Then a strange voice said, "Saul, why are you fighting Me?"

"Who are You, Lord?" Saul asked.

"I am Jesus, whom you are trying to destroy!" the voice answered.

"What do You want me to do?" Saul asked. He was very frightened.

"Go into the city. Someone will tell you what you must do."

The men who were with Saul had seen a light and heard a sound, but they had not seen the Lord or heard the words He spoke to Saul. They helped Saul up and led him into the city, because his sight had not returned. Saul stayed in the house of a man named Judas for three days, waiting to be told what to do next. All that time Saul ate and drank nothing. He just sat in the house and prayed to the Lord. Now he was sure those who believed in Jesus were right. He had seen Him himself.

There was a man named Ananias living in Damascus who believed in Jesus. One day the Lord told him to go to Saul. Ananias knew what Saul had done to the Christians in Jerusalem, but he did as the Lord told him. He put his hands on Saul's head and told him he had been sent to give Saul back his sight and see he was baptized. Saul had great work to do.

The spirit of the Lord came to Saul. He preached in the temple with great power, then went into the desert for a year or so to be alone with God and learn about Jesus.

In time, Saul went back to Jerusalem as a friend of Jesus. But the people there were still afraid of him and thought he was trying to trick them. Barnabas believed Saul was a changed man and took him to see Peter, who welcomed Saul into the church and let him serve as a disciple of Christ.

Saul believed the *gospel*, Jesus' teachings, was meant for all people, not just the Jews. When he preached this message the Jews became angry and planned to kill him. The Lord came to Saul a second time and warned him he was in danger. "Go away from here," He said to Saul. "Go and preach to the Gentiles far away." (Remember, the Jews called anyone who was not a Jew a *Gentile*.)

Saul boarded a ship and made the long journey back to his home, Tarsus, a city in Asia. He stayed there for several years, working as a tentmaker and teaching the people about Jesus.

THINK ABOUT IT

✛ *What did Saul believe about Jesus that not many of His followers believed?* ✛

Peter and Dorcas

✝ ACTS 9:32-11:18 ✝

N ow that there were churches all over Judea, Peter traveled from place to place, preaching and visiting other believers in Jesus. One of these new churches was in Lydda, by the Mediterranean Sea.

A woman loved by many people lived in Joppa, a town near Lydda. Her name was Tabitha in Hebrew or Dorcas in Greek. She loved the poor and helped them in many ways, and everyone in town respected her very much.

While Peter was in Lydda, Dorcas became sick and died. Her body was put in an upstairs room, and men rushed to Peter, asking him to come to Joppa right away. When Peter got to the house he found the upstairs room filled with widows and poor women who had been helped by Dorcas. They were all mourning her death and crying.

Peter sent everyone out of the room where Dorcas's body lay, then he knelt down and prayed. Turning to the body, he called, "Tabitha, arise!" She immediately opened her eyes and stood up, alive and well.

News of Dorcas's healing spread all over Joppa. Many people came to hear Peter speak and were baptized into the church.

The town of Caesarea was about thirty miles north of Joppa. Living in that town was a Roman soldier named Cornelius. Cornelius was a Gentile, but unlike other Gentiles he did not worship idols. He worshiped the God of the Jews, and so did his family.

One afternoon Cornelius was praying in his home when an angel came to him. The angel said Cornelius should send men to Joppa and invite Peter to come and teach in Caesarea. He immediately sent men to Joppa with this message.

Just before the men reached Joppa, Peter went up to the roof of the house he was staying in to pray. Falling asleep, he had what we would call a vision or a dream. In this dream he saw what looked like a great sheet coming down from heaven, as if someone were holding its four corners. In the sheet Peter saw all kinds of animals. Some of them were animals that Jews were allowed to eat, but many were unclean animals, or those that no Jew would ever think of eating.

As Peter watched the sheet in his dream, he heard a voice saying, "Get up, Peter, and eat."

Peter had always followed the Jewish rules about food. He answered, "No, Lord. I have never eaten unclean food."

The voice said, "What God has made clean you cannot call unclean."

Peter heard these words repeated three times, and then the great sheet went back up toward heaven and disappeared. Peter knew this vision must have some meaning for him; as he thought about it, he didn't know what it was.

Just then the men from Cornelius came to the front door

with their message. The next day Peter and some other men from Joppa went to Cornelius's house. There were many Gentiles waiting for him there. Suddenly, Peter knew what the dream was telling him. Jews did not meet with Gentiles in their houses, or eat with them. But God had shown Peter that it was not right for him to call any man unclean because God loves all men. These men needed to hear about Jesus too.

Peter preached to them about Jesus, and the men believed and were filled with the Holy Spirit. Seeing the Spirit had been given to them, Peter baptized them with water and welcomed them into the church.

Peter stayed with Cornelius for several days, eating at his table and teaching the people. Many of the Jewish followers were not happy about this until Peter told them about the message the Lord had sent him in his dream. "God allows the Gentiles to be saved from their sins by Jesus and to have everlasting life too," Peter told the Jewish followers.

THINK ABOUT IT

✝ *What will happen now that the church will let Gentiles as well as Jews become members?* ✝

An Angel Visits Peter

✛ ACTS 12:1-24 ✛

Herod Agrippa was now the king of Judea. A relative of the Herod who killed John the Baptist and the Herod who had killed all the Jewish babies when Jesus was born, Herod Agrippa wanted to please the leaders of the Jews. If he did, they might not cause trouble for the Roman Empire and him.

He captured the apostle James (the brother of John) and had him killed. When he saw how happy this made the chief priests and rulers, he captured Peter and put him in prison. He was planning to kill Peter on the next Passover celebration, as a present for the Jewish rulers.

To be sure he did not escape, Peter was bound in heavy chains. Four guards watched him constantly. No one could go in to see Peter, so the followers of Jesus in Jerusalem prayed for Peter day and night.

The night before Peter was to die, he was asleep in his cell. The four guards were watching him very carefully. Suddenly a bright light shone in Peter's cell and an angel of the Lord stood in front of him. The angel hit Peter on the side and called, "Get up! Quickly!"

Still sleepy, Peter had no idea what was going on. He looked at the angel, thinking he was a man. But when Peter stood up, the chains around him fell to the floor of the prison cell.

"Wrap your robe around you and follow me," the angel said.

Peter thought he was dreaming as he and the angel walked right past all four guards. Not one of them even blinked. When they came to the iron gate by the street, it opened for them all by itself. One street farther, the angel disappeared.

By now Peter was awake. An angel of the Lord set me free! he thought. He had to find a place to hide before the guards saw he was gone. Remembering that a woman named Mary lived nearby, he rushed to her house and banged on the door. He had to get inside!

There were many people in Mary's house praying for Peter. Only one of them, a young woman named Rhoda, heard Peter knocking on the door and went to see who it was. When she heard Peter's voice, she was so happy she didn't even open the door! She ran back to the others and told them Peter was at the door.

"You're crazy," they told her. "He's in prison, with guards watching everything he does."

Poor Peter was still standing outside the door, banging on it as hard as he could. It was dangerous to be outside like that. Finally he was let inside. Everyone gathered around to hear his story. "Make sure you tell this to all the disciples," he said at the end of his story. Then he left Mary's house and hid where Herod Agrippa could not find him.

The next morning Herod heard that Peter had escaped. No one knew how it had happened. The guards watching him had seen nothing, they said. In his anger Herod had the guards killed and a short time later Herod himself died. Peter, however, continued sharing the love and teachings of Jesus for many years.

THINK ABOUT IT

✝ *Peter's friends could not visit him in prison. Why did they pray day and night for him? What does that tell you about the power of prayer?* ✝

The Earliest Missionaries

✛ ACTS 11:19-30; 13:1-14:28 ✛

We know by this time there were believers of Jesus in many other countries. The believers driven out of Jerusalem had taken their faith with them and taught others about Jesus. One of these places was the city of Antioch in the country of Syria. Antioch was 250 miles north of Jerusalem. The little church there grew rapidly, and in it Jews and Gentiles worshiped together.

The main church was still in Jerusalem. The people in Jerusalem were Jews who believed in Jesus. They were not sure that it was right for Jews and Gentiles to worship together as part of the same church. They decided to send someone to Antioch to see how the church was doing there. Barnabas was chosen to go because everyone trusted him. He saw that everyone there—Jew or Gentile—was filled with the Holy Spirit and living the way Jesus had taught people to live. There was nothing wrong with the church of Antioch.

The Antioch church needed teachers and leaders, and the people there asked Barnabas to send them help. The first person Barnabas thought of was Saul, who was still living in Tarsus. Barnabas traveled to Tarsus and brought Saul back with him, and the two men stayed in Antioch for a year, preaching and teaching.

Word came to Antioch that the people in Jerusalem were suffering from a famine, or a lack of food. The people in the

church at Antioch collected all the money they could spare and gave it to Saul and Barnabas. The two men then traveled back to Jerusalem.

When they returned to Antioch, Barnabas and Saul brought along a young man named John Mark as their helper. Soon the Spirit of the Lord told the three men it was time to leave Antioch and travel to other young churches in other countries. John Mark went back to Jerusalem a little later, but Saul—who would now be called Paul—and Barnabas traveled the world with the gospel, the good news of Jesus Christ.

THINK ABOUT IT

✦ *John Mark will later write a famous book of the Bible. Do you know its name?* ✦

The Prison Song

✛ ACTS 15:1-16:40 ✛

So many Gentiles were joining the church that disagreements about them arose: If Gentiles joined, did they have to follow the Jewish laws about food and feasts and offerings? Did they have to become members of the Jewish faith to be followers of Jesus?

Paul and Barnabas, along with other believers, attended a meeting in Jerusalem to talk about these questions. There it was decided that Jewish and Gentile believers were both saved by Jesus and Gentiles did not have to obey the laws God had given to the Jews.

Paul and Barnabas set off on another journey to visit the new churches they had started far away from Jerusalem. This time they split up and took new helpers with them. There were some places neither of them went because they did not think the people were ready for the gospel of Jesus. They only had so much time and effort to spend.

One night while he was in Asia Paul had a dream. In the dream a man from Macedonia (now part of eastern Europe) invited Paul to his country to help the people there. This was one of the countries the missionaries had never been to, but they felt God wanted them to preach there. After a three-day trip by sea, they arrived in Macedonia.

Because few Jews lived in Macedonia, there wasn't a synagogue in which Paul could preach. Besides that, Paul knew no one there, and he had no idea where he would live. One Sabbath in the city of Philippi he met a woman named Lydia who loved God and listened to Paul's message. Soon she was baptized and joined the believers. She invited Paul to stay at her house while he was in the area. He did, and a church began to grow in the city because of his work.

Paul met a young slave girl who was troubled by an evil spirit. The people who owned her made money by letting this evil spirit predict what was going to happen to other people. When Paul healed the girl, her owners were very angry. The evil spirit had gone, and with it, the easy money.

The girl's masters took Paul and his helper Silas to the rulers of the city. "They are teaching the people to do things that are illegal under Roman law," they said to the rulers. Paul and Silas were beaten and thrown into prison.

Around midnight Paul and Silas were praying and singing hymns to God and the other prisoners were listening. Suddenly, there was a great earthquake! Every door in the prison opened, and the chains holding the prisoners fell to the ground.

The jailor awoke with a start and saw that the doors of the prison were open wide. By law, if any of his prisoners had escaped, the jailor would be put in prison in their place. Drawing his sword, he was about to kill himself when Paul called out to him. "Don't hurt yourself! We're all here."

Trembling with fear, the jailor entered the dungeon of Paul and Silas and threw himself at their feet. "What must I do to become a believer?" the jailor cried out.

That night Paul told him all about Jesus, and by morning, he and his family had been baptized.

Roman law was very strict about the rights of a Roman citizen. No citizen could be beaten or put in prison without a fair trial. Any ruler who ignored these rights was in serious trouble. When the rulers who had beaten Paul and Silas found out they were Roman citizens, they came to the prison and asked the men to leave. After meeting with all the believers in Lydia's house and urging them to keep their faith, Paul and Silas left the city of Philippi.

STORY 11

Mars' Hill

✛ ACTS 17:1-34 ✛

Paul and Silas preached in a few more cities of Macedonia. Although Jews joined the church there, most of the new believers were Greeks, or Gentiles who lived in that area. But in each city Paul and Silas had trouble. Those who would not believe stirred up the people and the rulers. They said Paul and

345

Silas were preaching against the Roman Empire when they claimed Jesus was the new king. Macedonia was not a safe place to preach Jesus' gospel.

Paul traveled to Athens, a great city in Greece. The people of that city were well educated. They spent most of their time discussing philosophy and religion, and would listen to all points of view. They also worshiped many different gods. It was said there were more statues of idols in Athens than there were people. There was even a statue to "the unknown god."

Mars' Hill was one of the places the people of Athens gathered to talk about philosophy and religion. They asked Paul to come and talk to them about his new religion and his God. Paul told them about Jesus, and how He had risen from the dead and sent His Spirit to them.

Many of the people there laughed at Paul. Others said they would like to talk with him again. But very few people from Athens became believers.

THINK ABOUT IT

✛ *Why did the people of Athens feel it was necessary to have a statue to "the unknown god?" Why didn't many of that city become believers of Jesus?* ✛

Paul at Corinth

✦ ACTS 18:1-22 ✦

Paul went from Athens to Corinth, another Greek city. While he was there he met a husband and wife, Aquila and Priscilla, who would become his good friends. They were tentmakers like Paul, and he worked with them. On the Sabbath Paul would go to the synagogue and preach to the Jews. But he did not have much success with them and decided to talk to the Gentiles of the city instead.

Slowly a church began to grow in Corinth. Most of its members were people who used to worship idols. While Paul was in Corinth he had another vision. In a dream God told him not to be afraid to speak about Jesus because He had many friends in Corinth.

Paul stayed in that city for a year and a half before going back to Asia. Then he returned to Jerusalem for a visit before going on to Antioch.

THINK ABOUT IT

✦ *How did Paul earn money to live on while he was teaching people about Jesus? Did he need any money?* ✦

Paul at Ephesus

✛ ACTS 18:23-20:1 ✛

From Antioch Paul traveled to the country of Galatia. The people there were happy to hear the gospel of Jesus and treated Paul very well. Many of them became Christians, and by the time Paul left the country, a church had been founded there.

Soon after Paul left, some Jewish teachers came to Galatia and told the people they had to become Jews to follow Christ. The people of Galatia did not know this was false and had already been decided in Jerusalem. They were new Christians and not too sure about what they were supposed to do. Paul wrote them a long letter, telling them they did not have to live by the old Jewish laws. They were free people under Jesus.

Paul's next stop was Ephesus. He had been there before, and this time he stayed for more than two years. God gave Paul great powers to heal. Anything he touched could heal sickness, even a piece of material that he had used to wipe his face.

The city of Ephesus had a great temple that was dedicated to the goddess Diana. People came from all over the world to see this temple. While they were there, many of them bought little gold or silver statues of her made by the people of the town. Many people earned a good living because of this temple.

One of the men who made these statues of Diana was the silversmith Demetrius. He called together other men who did the same work and told them that Paul was preaching against Diana. If he were not stopped, their businesses would be in danger. All the workers rushed into the street

yelling, "Great is Diana of the Ephesians!" Soon more people joined them. Not everyone knew what they were yelling about, but they joined the mob too. Taking two of Paul's missionaries captive, the mob rushed into an outdoor meeting place and rioted there for hours.

A city official finally quieted the mob. "These two men have said nothing against the temple of Diana," he told them. "The city protects the temple. What are you yelling about? If any laws have been broken, we have courts to handle that."

The mob broke up and went back to their homes. Paul gathered all his followers together one last time and then sailed away for Macedonia.

THINK ABOUT IT

✛ *Throughout the Bible various peoples have turned away from the one true God and worshiped idols. Idol worship in Ephesus was a business. If Paul had stayed in Ephesus, what might have happened?* ✛

Paul's Last Journey to Jerusalem

✝ ACTS 20:2-21:16 ✝

Paul was heading back to Jerusalem after his travels. He heard that many of the Jewish believers in Jerusalem were poor and needed help. The Jews who did not believe in Jesus would not help them, so Paul asked the Gentile followers if they would. Leaders of the new churches collected money for Jerusalem and went to meet Paul. They would all go to Jerusalem together.

Paul knew he had to go back to Jerusalem, but he had bad feelings about it too. "The Holy Spirit tells me that chains and troubles will meet me," he told his friends. "But my life is not important to me."

As he traveled toward Jerusalem, Paul met an old man, a prophet, who warned him not to go there. "The Jews who live there will tie you up and turn you over to the Gentiles," he told Paul. All his friends who heard this begged Paul not to go to Jerusalem.

"Why are you so sad?" he asked them. "I'm ready to die in Jerusalem for Jesus, if necessary." He took a boat to Judea and climbed the mountains to Jerusalem for the last time.

THINK ABOUT IT

✝ *Paul sensed what might happen to him when he returned to Jerusalem. Why was he so brave?* ✝

STORY 15

The Roman Citizen

✛ ACTS 21:17-22:29 ✛

About a week after he returned to Jerusalem some Jewish men from Ephesus saw Paul worshiping at the temple. They had heard him speak in Ephesus but had not believed his message. "Men of Israel, come help!" they called out to the others in the temple. "This man teaches against us and against our laws."

Soon a great crowd gathered around Paul and dragged him out of the temple. They yelled and called others to come help them kill him.

The Roman soldiers guarding the temple heard the riot and ran to see what was going on. The guards could not understand the language of the Jews. All they knew was that Paul must be some kind of troublemaker. They took

him away from the crowd and dragged him toward the castle.

Paul quietly spoke to the chief guard. He spoke in Greek, the guard's own language. "May I say something to you?"

"You know Greek?" the guard said.

"Please give me permission to speak to these people," Paul said politely.

The guard thought maybe he could find out what was going on if he let Paul do this, so he gave him permission. But when Paul spoke to the crowd, he spoke in the Hebrew language. The guard couldn't understand a word.

Paul told the crowd what he had done to the Christians when he was named Saul. He had been a good Jew, he said. Then he went on to tell them about the vision he had, and how he now believed that Jesus was the Savior the Jews had been awaiting. This angered the crowd even more so the soldiers took Paul into the castle to be beaten for starting a riot.

"Is it legal for you to beat a Roman citizen without a trial?" Paul asked the guard.

This made all the difference in the world. As a citizen of Rome, Paul could not be put into chains or beaten without a fair trial. Paul was taken into the castle and treated well.

THINK ABOUT IT

✝ *Paul was not only a fearless follower of Jesus, he was also an intelligent man. How do you know God gave Paul a keen mind?* ✝

Two Years in Prison

✛ ACTS 22:30-24:27 ✛

The commander of the Roman guards still was not sure what was going on between Paul and the Jewish leaders. He called a meeting of the chief priests and Jewish rulers. Some of the leaders seemed to be on Paul's side and some were against him. They argued back and forth so much that the guard took Paul away so he would not be harmed.

The next night the Lord spoke to Paul. "Be happy," He said. "You spoke for Me in Jerusalem, and you will speak for Me in Rome." Then Paul knew nothing was going to happen to him in Jerusalem.

Some Jews thought differently. They planned another meeting with Paul and took a vow to kill him as he was being brought to speak with them. Paul heard about the plot and through a messenger warned the chief of the Roman guards. Right away the guard sent Paul to Felix, the Roman governor in Caesarea, with a force of 500 guards to protect him on the way. He also sent along a letter explaining Paul's problem.

Felix kept Paul safely in a castle until the Jewish leaders of Jerusalem could travel to Caesarea to testify at a hearing. Five days later Paul heard them charge him with causing riots and breaking the law. He was also called a leader of the party of the Nazarenes, the name given to what we call Christians.

Paul denied all the charges against him, except for the last. "I serve the God of our fathers, believing all things in the law. I have always tried to keep my heart free from wrong toward God and men," he said.

Felix said he needed to hear what the Roman guard from Jerusalem had to say. Paul was kept at the castle, but his friends were allowed to visit him anytime they wanted.

Many times Paul was called before Felix. But Felix was not looking for information. He wanted Paul to pay him money so Felix would set him free. Paul was kept in the palace for the next two years. Then Felix returned to Rome and a new governor, a man named Festus, came to Judea. To keep the Jews happy, Felix had left Paul in prison.

THINK ABOUT IT

✛ *What kind of man is Felix? Does he remind you of other rulers during Jesus' time? Why or why not?* ✛

STORY 17

Before Rulers and Kings

✛ ACTS 25:1-26:32 ✛

After Festus was named the new governor he went to Jerusalem to see the city. While he was there, the chief priests and rulers asked that Paul be sent to Jerusalem for his trial. Festus told them he was going back to Caesarea soon. They could send some men there to testify against Paul at a hearing if they wanted. This was not what the priests wanted to hear. They had plans to kill Paul as he was being taken to Jerusalem.

At the hearing no one could prove that Paul had broken any Roman laws. "I have done no wrong against the law of the Jews, against the temple, or against Caesar," Paul told Festus.

Festus knew that the Jews wanted Paul tried in Jerusalem. He didn't know they planned to kill him before he got there though. Still, he wanted to keep everyone happy.

"Will you allow us to try you in Jerusalem?" Festus asked Paul.

"I am a Roman," Paul answered. "I should be tried in a Roman court. I ask for a trial before Caesar."

Every Roman citizen had the right to be tried in front of the Roman emperor. If a prisoner knew he couldn't get a fair trial in his own country, he could always ask for a trial before Caesar.

"Very well," Festus told Paul. "I will send you to Rome when the time comes for your trial."

A few days later the king of the land east of the Jordan came to visit Festus. His name was Agrippa and he was traveling with his sister Bernice. Festus told the king about Paul. "They are charging him with disobeying some of their laws of worship. I couldn't understand what they were talking about, so I asked if he wanted to be tried in Jerusalem. He asked to be tried before Caesar."

Agrippa and Bernice asked to speak to Paul. Paul told them everything about his life and work. He gave them the gospel of Jesus and spoke about all the wonders he had seen God do in Jesus' name.

When Paul went back to the palace, Agrippa, Bernice, and Festus talked about him. "This man hasn't done anything wrong. He doesn't deserve prison or death," Agrippa said.

"I know," Festus answered. "If he hadn't asked to be tried before Caesar, I could have let him go."

THINK ABOUT IT

✝ *Why does Paul want his trial in Rome before the ruler of the Roman Empire? What will that prove?* ✝

STORY 18

Shipwrecked

✝ ACTS 27:1-28:1 ✝

Paul and some other prisoners boarded a ship heading toward Rome. A Roman officer and guards went with them, along with some of their friends. A storm blew up as they neared Crete, but the captain decided it was safe to go on to Rome. Soon the ship was driven off its course by the winds into the open sea. The storm was much worse there. Part of the ship's cargo was thrown overboard to make the ship lighter, and men tied ropes around everything else. The storm lasted for days. By now everyone on board was afraid they were doing to die at sea.

Paul told them not to worry. "An angel of the Lord has told me that I will reach Rome safely, along with everyone on this ship. But we have to find an island soon."

For fourteen days the ship bounced around the ocean. Waves smashed over it, threatening to sink it many times. The sailors on the ship tried to escape in a little boat the ship carried, but the Roman officer would not let them go.

No one on the ship had eaten anything for fourteen days and they were getting very weak. "I promise you," Paul told them, "we will all be saved. But you must eat." All 276 people on board ate a meal and began to feel better.

The next dawn they saw land ahead. No one knew where they were but there was a little bay ahead that looked safe. They sailed toward it and grounded in the sand some distance from land.

Now the Roman guards had a problem. If any of their prisoners escaped while swimming to shore, the guards would be put in prison in their place. They asked the Roman officer to kill the captives so this could not happen. But Julius, who had become a friend of Paul's, would not allow his soldiers to kill the prisoners.

When everyone reached the shore they found not one person had drowned or been lost.

THINK ABOUT IT

✛ *Once again God saved Paul from certain death. How do you think Paul will spend his time on the newly found island?* ✛

Paul Comes to Rome

✛ ACTS 28:2-31 ✛

The people from the boat had landed on the island of Melita. The people of the island took good care of them, giving them food, clothing, and places to stay. While Paul was there he stayed in the home of a man named Publicus who treated him very well. When Publicus's father became so sick everyone thought he was going to die, Paul healed him. The people of the island brought all their sick friends to Paul and he was able to heal them all.

They stayed on the island for three months before they found a boat to take them Rome.

The believers who lived in Rome heard Paul was coming and went out to meet him when he reached the city. Paul was allowed to stay in a house instead of in prison,

although there was a guard chained to him all the time. Many people came to talk to Paul while he was a prisoner, and many of his guards became believers while they were chained to him.

Paul was a prisoner in Rome for two years. Then it is thought that he was set free. He preached in many lands for several years, then was captured again. He wrote his last letter from a Roman prison shortly before Emperor Nero had him put to death.

THINK ABOUT IT

✚ *Was Paul's imprisonment in Rome a waste of time?* ✚

STORY 20

The Throne of God

✚ REVELATION 1:9-20; 4:1-5:14 ✚

When the apostle John was an old man he was taken prisoner by the emperor of Rome. He was sent to the tiny island of Patmos and left there.

One Sunday John heard a loud voice behind him. When he turned around, he saw seven candlesticks and among them, Jesus. Jesus looked different from how John remembered Him. He was dressed in a long white robe with a gold shirt. His hair and face shone as white as snow. His eyes flashed like fire.

John fell to the floor and worshiped Jesus. But Jesus touched him and told him not to be afraid. Jesus told John to write seven letters to seven churches. Some of the letters praised the churches for their good work; others told the churches what they were doing wrong and needed to change.

Then John saw a door open in heaven and heard a voice telling him to come. He saw the throne of God and a figure on the throne whom he could hardly see because of the brightness. Around this throne sat twenty-four old men, the elders of the church. They were all dressed in white and wore crowns on their heads. These men took off their crowns and fell down before the throne of God to worship the One sitting there.

Then John saw that the One on the throne was holding a book sealed with seven seals. An angel called out, "Who is good enough to open the book?"

No one in heaven or earth was able to open the book. John felt sad to see this and he began to cry. But one of the twenty-four elders told him not to be sad. "See?" he said. "He who came from David is able to open the book."

Then John saw Jesus standing there, with the wounds of the cross on His hands, feet, and side. He came and took the book and everyone sang, "Worthy is the Lamb who was slain to have the power, and riches, and wisdom, and might, and honor, and glory, and blessing."

THINK ABOUT IT

✦ *Who is the only one good enough to open the book in heaven? Why is Jesus called the Lamb?* ✦

The City of God

✛ REVELATION 7:9-17; 21:1-27; 22:1-17 ✛

Again John saw the throne of God. In front of it and in front of the Lamb, or Jesus, were so many people no one could ever count them. All the people cried, "Salvation unto our God on the throne and unto the Lamb." At that all the angels fell down and worshiped God.

One of the elders said to John, "These people have had great trouble and sorrow. They have washed their robes and made them white in the blood of the Lamb. Because of that they are before the throne of God. They serve Him day and night in His temple."

Then John heard a loud voice saying, "The tabernacle of God is with men. And God will dwell with men, and they will be His people. And He will be their God. And God will wipe away all tears from their eyes. And there shall be no more death. Neither will there be weeping or crying or pain."

Suddenly John seemed to be standing on a high mountain. He saw a glorious city come down out of heaven. Light glowed over the city. Around it was a tall wall, and on each side of the wall were three gates, making twelve gates in all. An angel stood by each gate, and over each gate was the name of one of the tribes of Israel. Each of the walls had twelve foundation stones, and on each stone was written the names of the twelve apostles. Each gate was a huge pearl, and the street of the city was pure gold.

There was no temple in the city because God and Jesus

were the temples. No moon or sun was needed. The glory of God gave all the light that was needed. And the gates of the city were not shut at night because there was no night.

Men from all over the world walked in this city. Nothing evil or unclean ever came into it or any person who sins. Only those whose names were written in God's book were allowed inside.

John saw a river of the water of life coming from the throne of God and the Lamb. The tree of life grew by the river, and the leaves of the tree could heal any sickness. In the city the Lord God and the Lamb reigned as kings.

An angel said to John, "Tell everyone what you have seen and heard. Tell everyone who hears to come. Let anyone who is thirsty come, and whoever wants may have the water of life."

Think About It

✝ *The events described in the book of Revelation, the last book of the Bible, concern the future. These events may sound scary, but if you believe in Jesus Christ, someday you will live forever with Him and all other Christians who have ever lived. Ask your parents or an older Christian to help you understand the book of Revelation. Remember: God loves you and He will* always *be with you.* ✝